Communion with Non-Catholic Christians

Communion with Non-Catholic Christians
Risks, Challenges, and Opportunities

Jeffrey VanderWilt

THE LITURGICAL PRESS
Collegeville, Minnesota

www.litpress.org

Cover design by David Manahan, O.S.B.
Photo by The Crosiers, Gene Plaisted, O.S.C.

1   2   3   4   5   6   7   8

Library of Congress Cataloging-in-Publication Data

VanderWilt, Jeffrey T. (Jeffrey Thomas), 1962–
    Communion with non-Catholic Christians : risks, challenges, and opportunities / by Jeffrey VanderWilt.
       p. cm.
    Includes bibliographical references and index.
    ISBN 0-8146-2895-8 (alk. paper)
      1. Lord's Supper—Catholic Church. 2. Close and open communion. 3. Communicatio in sacris. 4. Catholic Church—Doctrines. I. Title.

BX2236.V36   2003
264'.02036—dc21

2002040582

Contents

Acknowledgments

I thank the following individuals for their assistance. To the members of the Liturgical Theology Seminar of the North American Academy of Liturgy, for many helpful comments as this project took shape over a number of years. To the Department of Theological Studies, Loyola Marymount University, for their patience and prodding. To the faculty of the Bellarmine College of Liberal Arts, Loyola Marymount University, especially Dr. Kenyon Chan, dean of the college, for granting me time to complete this project with support of a College Fellowship during the spring semester 2002. To Theresa Thibodeaux, my student research assistant, for diligent assistance and thoughtful remarks on the earliest drafts of the book. To Barbara Murphy, for marking the final revision of the manuscript and for helping me to recognize the need for careful and sensitive wording. Although my opinions differ from hers, I am indebted to Myriam Wijlens for her groundbreaking study of this issue. Her analysis made my own conclusions much easier to reach and far more accurate. Not least, I thank my parents and Mario Cisneros for their constant support and encouragement.

I dedicate this book to the men and women who hunger and thirst for Christian unity, who seek peace and tolerance among religions, and who work diligently for a more compassionate world. May I, someday, be counted among your number.

To the glory of God, who answers our miserliness with abundance, our poverty with riches, our fears with comfort, our loneliness with community, our sorrows with joy, our warfare with peace, our hatred with love, our mortality with resurrection life.

Jeffrey VanderWilt
May 30, 2002
The Solemnity of the Body and Blood of Christ

Abbreviations

AAS   *Acta Apostolicae Sedis*

CDF   Congregation for the Doctrine of the Faith

DI   *Dominus Iesus*

ESOU   House of Bishops of the Church of England, *The Eucharist: Sacrament of Unity*, London: Church Publishing Company, 2001.

GS   *Gaudium et spes*

LG   *Lumen gentium*

OBOB   Catholic Bishops' Conference of England and Wales; Bishops' Conference of Ireland; Bishops' Conference of Scotland, *One Bread, One Body: A Teaching Document on the Eucharist in the Life of the Church, and the Establishment of General Norms on Sacramental Sharing* (January 27, 1998).

UR   *Unitatis reintegratio*

UUS   *Ut unum sint*

Chapter 1

What Is Eucharistic Sharing?

SOWETO, SOUTH AFRICA (March 29, 1998): U.S. President Bill Clinton, a Southern Baptist, received Holy Communion during Sunday Mass at Regina Mundi Roman Catholic Church in the township of Soweto, outside of Johannesburg, South Africa. As Clinton spoke to township residents, he referred to the building as "this great shrine of freedom" for it had been a center for resistance to apartheid during the previous decades of struggle.[1]

When asked why he permitted Clinton to receive Holy Communion, the parish priest, Fr. Mohlomi Makobane, replied, "You can't quiz the president of the United States before the Mass whether he believes in Catholic doctrine, and you can't send him back to his pew when he comes up to receive communion."[2] In the opinion of some authors, Fr. Makobane's decision to allow Bill Clinton to receive Communion was prudent. It was the right thing to do, they said, given "the customs, the culture, even the guidelines of his own environment [the policies of his own bishops]."[3]

Prior to Vatican intervention, the South African Catholic Bishops supported the priest and his interpretation of the norms for eucharistic sharing. In a public statement following the incident they said that non-Catholics normally would not receive, "but a special circumstance

[1] Ecumenical News International, "Clinton Communion Draws Vatican Inquiry," *The Christian Century* 115, no. 12 (April 15, 1998) 394.

[2] Ibid.

[3] Andrew Greeley, "Clinton-Bashers and the Eucharist," *The Denver Post* (April 11, 1998) B-7.

1

can be said to exist on occasions when Christians from other churches attend a eucharistic celebration for a special feast or event."[4]

Public criticism from some American bishops and the Vatican prompted frequent NPR and ABC political correspondent, Cokie Roberts, and her husband to remark, "You know the world's gone crazy when Bill Clinton gets in trouble for going to Holy Communion."[5]

Bill Clinton is not the first Christian to get in trouble for going to Holy Communion. Clinton's story, however, points up some of the unique difficulties eucharistic sharing poses for Catholics. When, if ever, is it appropriate to share Holy Communion with non-Catholic Christians? What happens if a non-Catholic happens to receive Holy Communion? What measures should Church authorities take to preserve the sacramental and ecclesial character of the Eucharist? This book offers an analysis of the present norms for eucharistic sharing in the Roman Catholic Church.

To Define Eucharistic Sharing

Eucharistic sharing occurs when Christians like Bill Clinton (who is Baptist) receive Holy Communion outside their own Church. Some readers will be familiar with this practice under a variety of different names. They will know it as "intercommunion," "open Communion," "eucharistic hospitality," or even by an old Latin phrase *"communicatio in sacris."*

All these other names will show up later on in this book, but for clarity, I will use the expression "eucharistic sharing." Unlike some of those other terms, "eucharistic sharing" refers only to the practice of receiving Holy Communion by baptized Christians. It is concise and clear, helpfully drawing our attention to the norms and discipline for receiving Holy Communion in the Catholic Church. "Eucharistic sharing" is found in Roman Catholic ecumenical documentation and is the term preferred by the Pontifical Council for the Promotion of Christian

---

[4] "Clinton Communion Gets Mixed Reception," *U.S. Catholic* 63, no. 6 (1998) 9. The South African Bishops revised their guidelines on eucharistic sharing under Vatican orders. In the opinion of Eoin de Bhaldraithe, the wording may have changed, but the disciplinary effect did not. Eoin de Bhaldraith, "Intercommunion," *Heythrop Journal* 43 (2002) 79. Cf. "The New Southern African Guidelines for Eucharistic Sharing," *Interchurch Families* 8, no. 2 (2000) 5–6.

[5] Cokie Roberts and Steven Roberts, "Sacrament Should Serve to Include, Not to Exclude," *The Denver Rocky Mountain News* (Denver) April 12, 1998, Editorial, F-3B.

Unity. Their *Ecumenical Directory* of 1993 says that when the Catholic Church admits non-Catholic Christians to receive a sacrament, this may be called a "sharing in sacramental life."[6] This is especially true of the Eucharist.

Why Is Eucharistic Sharing a Problem?

Some Christians wonder why eucharistic sharing is an issue worth their consideration. Most people they know are entirely happy within their own church. After all, for most North Americans changing churches is so easy to do. They may ask, "Doesn't it all just come down to worshiping in the 'church of your choice?'"

In a nation of shoppers like the United States, our initial impulse is to shop for churches no less than we shop for cars, schools, houses, or banks. There was a time when U.S. banks cashed checks for anyone who approached the teller windows with proper identification. As years passed, check-cashing was permitted for a fee; then only to account holders or when the check was drawn on that particular bank. Many banks will now accept checks for deposit only. "If you want cash," the bank managers say, "use the automated teller machine (and pay our transaction fees)." Modern North Americans do not expect "services" from a bank to which they do not "belong."

There is an analogy here to eucharistic sharing. Why should Christians reasonably expect sacramental services from churches to which they do not belong? If Joe is Presbyterian, why should Joe reasonably expect to receive Holy Communion when he visits a Lutheran, Episcopalian, or any other church? Perhaps Joe should "shop around" for another church, one that better suits his needs and expectations. Some would say that Joe should not expect churches to behave differently from other corporate entities. The problem is that, although churches are "corporate," they are not corporations. Even in the United States where we happily support deregulation of businesses, banks are not entirely free to limit customer and noncustomer access to cash. In a certain sense, we expect this analogy to apply also to churches. It would be absurd to think that churches are entirely free to limit people's access to God's grace.

Many Christians hold that their churches are not free to limit people's access to God's grace, and so they share the Lord's Supper freely and widely. In the United States, Canada, Great Britain, Europe, India,

[6] Secretariat for the Promotion of Christian Unity, 1993 *Ecumenical Directory.* Cf. Miriam Wijlens, *Sharing the Eucharist: A Theological Evaluation of the Post Conciliar Legislation* (Lanham, Md.: University Press of America, 2000) xviii.

Australia, and elsewhere, many Christians share the Lord's Supper together freely and have done so for decades.

Eucharistic sharing is a risk. If so many Christians in so many places around the world have chosen to share the Eucharist with one another, why does the Catholic Church hold a different standard? In chapter 2, I will explore several reasons why Catholics find eucharistic sharing a "risky" business. It is risky because eucharistic sharing touches on very sensitive issues in our understanding of the Church, of ministry, priesthood, and church membership. Non-Catholic readers in particular may find this analysis helpful as they seek to understand the resistance of some Catholic authorities to a more open eucharistic sharing.

Eucharistic sharing is a challenge. Since so many Christians in so many places around the world have chosen to share the Eucharist with one another, there are several reasons to "challenge" Catholic authorities to reconsider the current norms. Catholic authorities can better prepare the Catholic Church for a more open eucharistic sharing. In chapter 3, I challenge some of the theological convictions that underpin the present norms.

Eucharistic sharing is an opportunity. By listening carefully to the many voices of non-Catholic Christians, one hears a strong affirmation of the many positive benefits they have found through a more open eucharistic sharing. For them, eucharistic sharing has led to a deeper sense of communion and a stronger sense of Christian unity. In the Eucharist, these Christians say, they have found solidarity in faith that otherwise would have been unavailable to their communities. In the final chapter of this book, I propose how eucharistic sharing can become an integral part of our search for peace and reconciliation among Christians.

For Whom Is Eucharistic Sharing a Problem?

Some readers will wonder why eucharistic sharing is a problem for Catholics. Of course, problems never exist in a vacuum. A problem is always a problem *for somebody*. In the first place, eucharistic sharing is a problem *for Catholics*. The Catholic Church does not live alone in the Christian world. Because eucharistic sharing is problematic for us—it troubles us, we create policies and procedures to deal with it, it causes us concern—our strategies for coping with the problem set the context for further problems with Catholics and non-Catholics alike. When is eucharistic sharing a problem?

Seven contexts for eucharistic sharing. There exist at least seven contexts when eucharistic sharing can be a problem:

1. When baptized non-Catholics are becoming Catholic.

2. When baptized non-Catholics belong to a family with Catholic members.

3. When baptized non-Catholics attend Catholic worship for family, social, official, or quasi-official reasons (e.g., baptisms, confirmations, weddings, ordinations, funerals, and other occasions).

4. When baptized non-Catholics attend Catholic worship.

5. When baptized non-Catholics are unable to attend their own churches.

6. When baptized non-Catholics are members of a Catholic community (religious communities, universities, hospitals, or ecumenical Christian communities).

7. When Christians from many churches gather in the context of ecumenical worship.

Before we throw up our hands and say, "Eucharistic sharing is a problem for *everyone*," I want to point out that eucharistic sharing is a problem *differently* for different groups of people. The greatest challenge is to balance the many perspectives of Catholics, non-Catholics, clergy, laity, and theologians as they are brought to bear on resolving the problem of eucharistic sharing.

For example, some Catholics perceive eucharistic sharing as a threat to the unity of the Church. Others stress that it undermines our understanding of ministry, since ordained clergy are charged to protect and serve the unity of the Church within their sacramental ministry. A few may believe that admitting non-Catholics to Holy Communion destroys the "purity" or holiness of the sacrament. Others wonder, "How can we live in communion with men and women who choose to receive our sacraments, but do not live within the structures and standards of our common life?" All these concerns pose serious questions. Even if these arguments are faulty, any plan to change Catholic norms would fail unless it speaks effectively to the fears and concerns of these faithful men and women.

On the other hand, there are many Catholics for whom eucharistic sharing is a problem because they desire it. These Catholics sometimes propose eucharistic sharing in order to resolve real-life dilemmas. Consider some fictional examples about an interchurch family.

1. Paul and Betty are getting married. Paul is Lutheran, while Betty is Catholic. May Paul receive Holy Communion along with Betty at their Wedding Mass?

2. Years later, Paul, Betty, and their children attend Sunday Mass together at St. Dymphna's Catholic Church. Paul is still Lutheran

and does not plan to become Roman Catholic at this time. In the interest of family unity, Paul prefers to worship with the remainder of his family at St. Dymphna's. Therefore Paul can rarely attend the Lutheran Church and his access to Holy Communion is extremely limited. May Paul receive Holy Communion together with his wife and children at St. Dymphna's?

3. When Paul dies, his funeral will be held in the Lutheran Church. Paul's funeral includes the liturgy of Holy Communion. The norms of the Evangelical Lutheran Church in America hold that all baptized Christians who believe that Christ is present "in, with, and under" the elements of bread and wine may receive Holy Communion. The Lutheran pastor extends this invitation during Paul's funeral. May Betty, his widow, and the children receive Holy Communion at Paul's funeral?

The Code of Canon Law of the Catholic Church and the implementation of those canons by the National Council of Catholic Bishops in the United States suggest that all these questions should be answered "No." Although the norms allow important exceptions that may be applied by caring pastors to Paul and Betty's case, these exceptions depend on the disposition of the priest or his bishop. The basic stance of the law—presently formulated—is to ban and prohibit eucharistic sharing in most circumstances.

More than a few priests and some bishops would be disposed to relax the guidelines for eucharistic sharing in cases like Paul and Betty's. It could be that some Catholic priests tell people like Paul to receive Holy Communion discreetly, "as though he were Catholic." Like all "don't ask, don't tell" policies, this strategy fails because it encourages Paul to dissemble and to lie. The pastor who encourages Paul to pretend to be Catholic is saying, with a nod and wink, that there is no place for Paul, a baptized and faithful Christian, father and spouse of committed Catholics, *in his own faith* to regularly receive Holy Communion at a Catholic Church along with his family.

Other priests and bishops would point out that Paul and Betty *chose* to marry, Paul *chose* to remain Lutheran. These ministers would bind the couple to the consequences of those choices, however painful and however much Paul and Betty are not responsible for the division of their churches. Any successful plan to limit or to increase access to Holy Communion in the Catholic Church must address pastoral questions such as those faced by Paul and Betty's family. There may be good reasons to limit access to Holy Communion within Paul's family; but these must be very good reasons and they must withstand careful scrutiny.

What Prevents Eucharistic Sharing?

Catholics generally offer several reasons to limit eucharistic sharing. In a 1990 letter to *The Tablet,* an English Catholic periodical, Fr. Michael Simpson, s.j., identified three central problems associated with eucharistic sharing.

1. *The problem of ministry:* Who may minister Communion touches on who may receive it. Catholics premise their discussion of ministry on their understandings of the validity of apostolic succession through ordination of bishops and other clergy.

2. *The problem of the status of Christians from outside of the local church:* The Eucharist signifies belonging to a *particular* community. Catholics premise their discussion of the status of non-Catholics on their understanding of Christian initiation through baptism, confirmation, and profession of faith.

3. *The problem of means and ends of unity:* The Eucharist expresses the unity of the Church even as it provides the means to bring about a deeper Christian unity. Catholics premise their discussion of the Eucharist as the means and the expression of Christian unity on their understandings of sacramental efficacy, the power of sacraments to convey and signify God's grace.[7]

Each one of these problems points to significant theological values at the heart of the question of eucharistic sharing. They will come forward time and again throughout the remainder of the book.

Theological values. The theological values at stake in the question of eucharistic sharing vary among the churches. When Christians share (or fail to share) the Eucharist with one another, they do this because of core convictions about their self-identity, their identity as a Church, and the Eucharist.[8] It is necessary to identify those core convictions, to evaluate them, and to reconsider them in light of the central concerns of Christian faith. For example:

Among Protestants, theological values include hospitality, unity by stages, and a firm conviction that the Eucharist belongs to Christ and not to us. As they see it, while the Church *mediates* the Eucharist (as an instrument) the Church cannot add to its saving value.

Among Catholics, these theological values include unity, apostolic succession in ministry, validity, and pastoral need. As we see it, the

[7] Hugh Cross et al., "Eucharist Experiences Today," *The Ecumenical Review* 44, no. 1 (1992) 52f.
[8] Cardinal Willebrands in the Preface to Wijlens, xviii.

Church *mediates* the Eucharist primarily in and through the ordained priesthood of bishop and presbyter.[9]

Among the Orthodox, these theological values include communion, economy *(oikonomia),* and reconciliation from schism. Orthodox Christians carefully balance the *unity* and the *independence* of each local church within the worldwide body of churches in communion with the Ecumenical Patriarch of Constantinople.

All the churches, however, share a single theological conviction. For all of us, eucharistic sharing is an *ecclesial* issue. That is, it pertains to our understanding of the Church of Christ. To receive and to share the Eucharist is not simply a matter of responding to an invitation extended to isolated individuals.[10] Receiving Holy Communion is not merely receiving spiritual food. It also includes a *profession of faith.* To receive Communion is to pledge one's self to a real community of people and to discern the Body of Christ in their assembly. Comprised of real men and women, this community can be hurt whenever people are unfaithful to their eucharistic pledge. Christians affirm their attachment to one another and to Christ, simultaneously, at every Eucharist, when they say, "Amen," eat the bread, and drink from the cup.

When the Catholic Church speaks of "full communion" in the Church as a prior condition to eucharistic sharing, it is speaking, in the first instance, of that very personal, very real kind of attachment to one another in the Body of Christ. At the outset, it is important to be clear. When Christians practice eucharistic sharing, *relationships*—not rules—are at stake. Eucharistic sharing is more than simply "breaking the rules" for the sake of a "higher value."[11] The "rules" we must understand are intended to preserve real relationships with real men and women.

In the Catholic Church, these real relationships include juridical relationships to bishops and clergy. Eucharistic communion, they say, requires "normally full ecclesial communion," including juridical-institutional union.[12] Therefore, when Catholic authorities speak of "full communion" they also refer to the acceptance of the jurisdiction of the local bishop.

Contemporary North American Christians may become uneasy when they discuss the institutional Church and the idea of the jurisdiction of

---

[9] The Greek and Latin word "presbyter" is often translated as "priest" in English.

[10] David N. Power, "Roman Catholic Theologies of Eucharistic Communion: A Contribution to Ecumenical Conversation," *Theological Studies* 57, no. 4 (1996) 587–611.

[11] Peter C. Bouteneff, "Koinonia and Eucharistic Unity," *The Ecumenical Review* 52, no. 1 (2000) 72–80.

[12] Wijlens, 316.

the local bishop. In the context of our political life, we celebrate freedom, democracy, and egalitarianism. These political values are often hard to square with Christian understandings of discipleship, service, and obedience. The fear of powerful ecclesiastical jurisdictions may motivate some Christians—even many Catholics—to draw away from closer communion with the Catholic Church.[13]

In North America and elsewhere, we have sometimes seen clerical power misused or abused. We have known clergy—Catholic and non-Catholic—to seek power, status, or prestige rather than other, more central Christian convictions. For these men and women, it may be that a more open eucharistic sharing is a threat. A more open eucharistic sharing entails the admission of a large number of Christians who are immune to the influence and control of their rules and authority. A more open Communion may amount, for some clergy, to a loss of influence over their congregations or dioceses. We must be careful to see that norms are based on theology and not anxiety, relying in confidence on the power and promises of God, not the weaknesses and ambitions of human beings.

What Recommends Eucharistic Sharing?

There are several reasons to recommend eucharistic sharing. One of the main reasons given to recommend a more open eucharistic sharing is to heal the wounds of Christian division. However, a more open eucharistic sharing should not be seen as an "ecumenical panacea." The division of the Church is a wound that only an ever more deepening communion can cure. A more open eucharistic sharing, therefore, will be effective only as much as it leads to a deepened communion, a strengthened sense of relationship between and among the now divided churches. As Jean-Jacques von Allmen, the eminent Protestant theologian and ecumenist suggested, *communion itself* is the proper solution to Christian division.[14]

For some theologians, a more open eucharistic sharing cannot help but lead to a deepened reality of communion among Christians. They suggest that sharing the Eucharist applies a *divine remedy* to an ailment (division) from which only God can cure us. Eucharistic sharing, in

---

[13] Michael Welker, *What Happens in Holy Communion?*, trans. John F. Hoffmeyer (Grand Rapids, Mich. / Cambridge: Eerdmans / SPCK, 2000) 158.

[14] Jean-Jacques von Allmen, *The Lord's Supper*, ed. J. G. Davies and A. Raymond George, trans. W. Fletcher Fleet, *Ecumenical Studies in Worship* (London / Richmond, Va.: Lutterworth Press / John Knox Press, 1969) 72.

their view, will "press the churches to get on with what divides them."[15] By promising to share the Eucharist, churches and Church leaders may find themselves helpfully pressed to act toward deeper unity. Simply stated, sometimes you have to force people to "sign the papers" before you can get them to act upon their promises. Eucharistic sharing may be a way of getting people to "sign the papers" on their pledge to work toward Christian unity.

Former Anglican archbishop of Canterbury George Carey states this rather more mildly. In a 1998 statement, he notes the many benefits that have accrued to Anglicans because of a more open eucharistic sharing. He says it has been a "source of great fellowship and joy." Anglicans regard eucharistic sharing with non-Anglican Christians as a visible sign and foretaste of the unity to which they are called. He says that a more open eucharistic sharing is a reminder that the Eucharist does not belong to Anglicans alone. "We do not own it," Carey states. "Rather, it is a gracious gift from God."[16]

Anticipating unity. At best, a more open eucharistic sharing *anticipates* the unity of Christians.[17] Viewed from this perspective, eucharistic sharing is rather like "opening a gift" that is *not yet* set in front of you but you know that God has *already* given it. Another analogy: How many children stumble upon and open a birthday gift that has been stowed away? Yet sympathetic adults—having resolved their chagrin—forgive the child for opening the present early, in the absence of the giver. Remarkably, the gift of Christian unity was never even "stowed away!" It is "hidden in plain sight." Even if we *think* that we are supposed to wait to share a common Eucharist until "the fullness of communion—given only in God's kingdom," do we expect God to be any less sympathetic than the "chagrined, though forgiving" parent of the child in our example?

Why This Book?

This book will challenge some of the theological convictions that presently support Catholic norms for eucharistic sharing. I expect it will especially challenge those who are satisfied with the present norms. These norms presume and maintain the division of the Chris-

[15] Ernest R. Falardeau, "Sharing the Eucharist and Christian Unity," *Ecumenical Trends* 23 (1994) 11.

[16] Teresa Malcolm, "Denial of Eucharist 'Hurts,'" *National Catholic Reporter* (May 15, 1998) 10.

[17] John M. Russell, "Pannenberg on Eucharist and Unity," *Currents in Theology and Mission* 17 (1990) 121.

tian churches. Christians who prefer to maintain the division of the churches must shoulder a burden of proof. When churches decide that it is best for them to maintain their distinctiveness, in each case they ought to be asked to demonstrate how *fidelity* to the *Gospel* requires it.[18] I *do not* endorse a "free-for-all" or "y'all come" approach to the Eucharist. The Lord's Supper should not become a "cattle call." On the other hand, because sacramental life is a product of the exchange of grace and forgiveness between humankind and God who created us, the regulation of access to sacramental life cannot contradict the graciousness of its own source. Therefore, Catholics and Church authorities can more strongly ground future norms for eucharistic sharing on several key convictions about God's generosity, graciousness, and mercy.

Catholics can be challenged to enact a more gracious and hospitable eucharistic sharing without compromising core convictions. This may require some reorganization of our common life. Perhaps it will mean altering some current understandings of church governance. *Risks* and *challenges* will confront us at every turn. Given our core convictions about the abundance of God's grace, *opportunities* will present themselves in equal measure.

The thesis of this book is that the fundamental criteria for reception of Holy Communion at any time and in any place are baptism with confirmation and the recognition (discernment) of the Body of Christ *with all that entails*. Nearly every other criterion is secondary. Most of those other criteria are neither hospitable, pastoral, nor Christian.

Following is a clarification of several important terms and concepts. This will be followed by a brief discussion of the current state of Christian ecumenism with a summary and restatement of the present norms for eucharistic sharing as given in Catholic Church documents.

Some Important Terms and Distinctions

Christian and Non-Christian Men and Women

This book is about Christian understandings of the Eucharist and Catholic norms for eucharistic sharing. For the most part, I will not be referring to non-Christians: Jews, Muslims, Buddhists, and so forth. When I speak about "Christians," I refer to all men and women who consider themselves Christian regardless of their church affiliation. The

---

[18] Jon Nilson, *Nothing Beyond the Necessary: Roman Catholicism and the Ecumenical Future* (New York: Paulist Press, 1995) 43.

community of Christians includes Catholics and non-Catholics, baptized and nonbaptized men and women.

Baptized and Nonbaptized Men and Women

I will sometimes distinguish between "baptized" and "nonbaptized" men and women. In this book, I do not intend to discuss the reception of Holy Communion by nonbaptized men and women. I am aware that this is a live issue in several Protestant churches. In the Catholic Church, that question is a nonstarter. It raises many serious questions about interreligious relationships and about the core convictions of Christian faith. The question of Communion for nonbaptized men and women remains for others to study.

In the estimation of the Catholic Church, some non-Catholic Christians are baptized *validly*, while others are not. For example, Latter-Day Saints, Jehovah's Witnesses, Quakers, and members of the Salvation Army are not usually baptized validly according to Catholic norms. In the past decades, numerous Christian churches have emerged in Africa, South America, and elsewhere. These churches vary considerably in their doctrine of baptism. For instance, among Pentecostals baptism with water is far less important than baptism in the Holy Spirit and the manifestation of spiritual gifts.

In this book, I do not want to touch too heavily upon the question of the validity of baptism. For the sake of argument, I *accept* Catholic norms on the validity of baptism. With this acceptance comes the recognition that not every Christian community *validly* baptizes their members. In writing this, no denigration or diminishment of those communities or their faith is intended. There remain many opportunities for continuing dialogue between Catholics and members of other Christian communities on the validity of baptism.

Catholic and Non-Catholic Christians

Christian men and women will consistently be referred to as "Catholics" or as "non-Catholics." For the purposes of this book, the term "non-Catholic" includes the bulk of Christian churches and Christian men and women. They are Methodist or Anglican, Lutheran, Orthodox, Chaldean, Ethiopian, Baptist, Mennonite, and so forth.

I will not usually speak of "Roman Catholics" because many Catholics (in union with the Church of Rome) are not Roman. The Catholic Church comprises many *rites,* not only the Roman Rite of the Western churches. For example, there are Melkite, Maronite, Coptic, or Ukrainian Rite Catholics. While most Catholics in the United States are of the

"Roman Rite," a significant number are not and they should not be forgotten.

Some non-Catholics say that they are "catholic." They consider themselves part of the "one, holy, catholic, and apostolic Church." Their "catholicity" is not denied when referring to non-Catholic Christians, their churches, or their self-understanding. Rather, the term "Catholic" is meant *only* to distinguish Christians based on their membership in local churches that are in communion with the Church of Rome. "Catholicity" means much more than being a Church in communion with Rome. This admits the possibility that "catholicity" of a sort belongs even to these other churches and Christian communities.

Vatican II spoke of baptized non-Catholics as "separated brethren." This term is insufficient for several reasons. For one thing, many "separated brethren" are actually "sisters." In addition, *Catholic* authorities pronounced the formal acts that "separated" these "brethren" from the Catholic Church. The term "separated brethren" remains in the council decrees. It was revolutionary in its time, but now sounds exclusive, obsolete, and hurtful.

Much more important are the revolutionary changes in the status of baptized non-Catholics because of Vatican II. In the constitution on the Church, *Lumen gentium,* and in the decree on ecumenism, *Unitatis redintegratio,* the bishops of Vatican II brought forward a new insight into the ecclesiological status of baptized non-Catholics. Vatican II would no longer refer to them as "schismatics" or "heretics." The communities and churches of baptized non-Catholics were, in some ways, recognized and affirmed. The baptized non-Catholic was no longer conceived as automatically "unaffiliated," the "man or woman without a Church."[19]

Four themes for post-Vatican II ecumenism. In the council documents four essential themes emerge:

1. Baptism and faith *unite* us more than we could ever be divided.[20]

2. Baptized non-Catholics are not isolated; they live in real communities. Some of them are churches, and all of them are, in some sense, ecclesial.[21]

3. Catholic ecumenism no longer focuses on the conversion of individuals—the ecumenism of return—but on the convergence and communion of Christian communities.[22]

---

[19] Wijlens, xv–xvi.
[20] Ibid., 189.
[21] Ibid., 190.
[22] Ibid.

4. Non-Catholic churches and communities are not impediments to salvation in themselves. They offer real means of salvation.[23]

Lumen gentium says that every baptized Christian is conjoined *(coniunctum)* to the Catholic Church. The idea of a "conjoining" connotes the sacramental and organic character of Christian communion.[24] Since Vatican II, Catholics have tended to avoid the language of "member" and "subject" in official teaching. This represents a significant modification to pre-Vatican II terminology and understandings.

Members and Subjects of the Church

Following the Council of Trent, Cardinal Robert Bellarmine (1542–1621) was concerned to preserve the jurisdiction of the Catholic Church over non-Catholics. This was especially a concern in "Catholic territories" with significant populations of non-Catholics. Bellarmine provided the argument for subjecting baptized non-Catholics to the jurisdiction of canon law. In his argument, Bellarmine distinguished among "subjects" of the Church and "members" of the Church. He thought that baptism incorporates the person into Christ's body and so makes the person a "subject" of Christ. Being a "subject" of the Church is, he thought, a part of the indelible character of baptism. Once it was conferred, it cannot be removed.

Additionally, Bellarmine thought that "membership" in the Church is conferred *after* baptism. He thought membership is impermanent and revocable. It is composed of three bonds *(vincula)*. Bellarmine identified the bonds of faith, sacraments, and authority. Destroy or damage any one of the three bonds, and the Christian has lost his or her membership. If Christians reject the faith, they became a heretic. If they reject the sacraments, they are excommunicated. If they reject authority, they are schismatic.[25]

In 1749, Pope Benedict XIV significantly eased Robert Bellarmine's strict distinction between "subjects" and "members" of the Church. Pope Benedict wrote that those who had been "baptized by a heretic" were to be "excluded from the Church" only if, after reaching the "age

[23] Ibid., 191. *Dominus Iesus* has restricted this understanding of the council to mean that the saving power of a non-Catholic Church *derives* from the Catholic Church. It would be challenging to identify the *means* by which the non-Catholic Church derives this power.

[24] Second Vatican Council, Dogmatic Constitution on the Church, *Lumen gentium* 15. Wijlens, 169.

[25] Wijlens, 41.

of moral awareness" they continued in "the errors of the baptizer."[26] Bellarmine's general principle—that every baptized person is a "subject" of the Church—remains under Benedict's application.

Still, there is a new allowance, a small amount of "wiggle room," in Pope Benedict's modification. Those who were baptized by non-Catholic ministers would suffer no *penalty* until or unless they *explicitly* reject membership in the Catholic Church. In a word, the child is "not at fault" for the heresy, schism, or excommunication of their parents.

Pope Benedict seemed to recognize the weakness in Bellarmine's distinction. The distinction between "subjects" and "members" of the Church—especially with the notion of the "bonds of unity"—may be helpful when we think about men and women who actively undertake to reject or thwart Christian faith. It is much less helpful when we think about men and women of good conscience who have serious concerns about the expression of Christian faith in real communities. Perhaps they cannot concur with the current discipline of the sacraments. Some may even be the innocent subjects of an oppressive abuse of ecclesial authority by powerful members of the clergy.

Distinguishing Catholics from non-Catholic Christians. Ecumenists and theologians often stumble on the historical, but problematic, differentiation of Catholics from non-Catholics on the basis of "degrees of belonging" to the Church of Christ. Simply stated, can you have it both ways with baptized non-Catholics? Can you say non-Catholics are *really* Christian only because they are some kind of "anonymous Catholics" and then say that they are not *sufficiently* Catholic to receive the sacraments in the Catholic Church? This confusing understanding of the status of baptized non-Catholics and their churches in Roman Catholic doctrine and canon law remains a delicate question.

Finally, canon law also distinguishes between non-Catholics who had never been Catholic and non-Catholics who had once been members of the Catholic Church. The Catholic who has left the Catholic Church for a period of time is normally restored to full communion through the sacrament of reconciliation. By contrast, non-Catholics may not receive Holy Communion even if they were to receive the sacrament of reconciliation. The non-Catholic normally does not receive reconciliation from a Catholic minister, except in cases of extreme or grave need.

Christians who leave the Catholic Church for a non-Catholic Church sometimes come under the category of "apostate." This is a regrettable term, but many Catholic authorities would say the expression is

[26] Ibid., 43.

apt. I do not intend to refer to Catholics who may not receive Holy Communion—for whatever reason—until they have observed the sacrament of reconciliation. The discipline for reception of Holy Communion *within* the communion of the Catholic Church is another, though admittedly not unrelated, matter. For present purposes, all things being equal, the arguments presented here will presume the good moral standing of all communicants—Catholic and non-Catholic alike.

Christian Ecumenism

Prior to Vatican II, Catholics thought about "church unity" in terms of helping individual non-Catholics become Roman Catholic. Ecumenists call this attitude an "ecumenism of return." In the pre-Vatican II Catholic Church, "Church unity" was thought to consist of "unity with Rome."[27]

The ecumenism of return remains current among many contemporary Catholic leaders. If Catholic authorities maintain the Council of Trent is the "capstone" or "epitome" of Catholic doctrine, if they hold that Vatican I and II are "interpretive lenses" of Trent, then Catholics may be advised not to hold out hope for Christian unity with Orthodoxy or with Protestantism in the near term. How Church leaders understand the decrees of Trent (and therefore Vatican I and II) is one of the best diagnostic indicators of their readiness to engage in ecumenical dialogue.

Moving away from the ecumenism of return. Since Vatican II, the Catholic Church has moved away from the ecumenism of return. In its decree on ecumenism, *Unitatis redintegratio,* the council officially embraced an ecumenism of convergence, mutual reconciliation, and dialogue. After Vatican II, we must understand unity as the result of ecclesial rapprochement, of changing and converting ourselves, the better to welcome and meet Christ in one another.[28] The council clearly affirmed that there exists a real, though partial, communion among all Chris-

---

[27] The main reason some offer for limiting access to Holy Communion in Catholic Churches is to encourage people to become Catholic. As Bishop Tobin of Youngstown, Ohio, wrote, "I am convinced that a premature invitation to Holy Communion removes one of the most compelling incentives for people to join the Catholic Church . . . The Eucharist is a spiritual magnet that draws people to experience the riches of our Catholic faith. If anyone can receive the Eucharist, why bother joining the Church?" Thomas J. Tobin, "Receiving Holy Communion," *Priest* 54, no. 6 (1998) 29.

[28] Wijlens, 108f.

tians. Ecumenical efforts since the council have been guided by the hope that communion, though partial, would grow into "fullness."[29]

In their deliberation of the status of non-Catholics, the bishops of Vatican II embraced a wider ecumenical vision than had been apparent before their gathering. Underpinning this vision was the realization that Christians are united in baptism and faith. Our unity of faith is stronger than *anything* that could ever divide us. In addition, the council came to understand baptized non-Catholics as members of real ecclesial communities and churches. The bishops understood that all Christians live in communities with varying degrees of access to the means of salvation. The council affirmed that the Holy Spirit works in the separated churches and other ecclesial communities.

Since Vatican II, the best ecumenical efforts, both within the Roman Catholic Church and among non-Catholic churches, have focused on an *ecumenism of convergence.* Through dialogue and patient listening, theologians, Church leaders, and others have focused on church-dividing differences and have sought to establish common ground for statements of faith. In these conversations, Catholic theologians have offered many helpful perspectives. They provided the possibility of eucharistic sharing within the context of pastoral concern. They recognized potential in the concept of a real, though imperfect communion.[30] In many ways, the teaching of Vatican II insists that Catholics rise above polemics and engage in understanding *real* communities of Christian faith. Ecumenism calls Christians to know and to love their neighbors, not necessarily to believe everything they say or do.

Concerns for the Future of Christian Ecumenism

When they talk about "ecumenism," Christian leaders often point to the "agreed statements," and the various national and international organizations of Christian churches and charities. Since the turn of the century for Protestants and Orthodox, and since Vatican II for Roman

[29] Some theologians now wonder if the idea of "partial communion" is not a contradiction in terms. Cf. Johannes Brosseder, "Towards What Unity of the Churches?" in *The Church in Fragments: Towards What Kind of Unity?* ed. Giuseppe Ruggieri and Miklos Tomka (London / Maryknoll, N.Y.: SCM Press / Orbis Books, 1997) 132. Brosseder reminds us that "union" is not a human category and that we have come to embrace a sort of "ecumenical pelagianism" when we suppose that "fullness of communion" can be understood apart from "being filled with the Holy Spirit."

[30] Geoffrey Wainwright, *Doxology: The Praise of God in Worship, Doctrine, and Life* (Oxford: Oxford University Press, 1980) 7.

Catholics, Christians have become expert in assembling delegations, formulating statements, listening to one another, and responding with care and precision to what they have heard.

In the twenty-first century, if ecumenism is not to "wither on the vine," Christians may need to reconfigure their understanding and practice of Christian ecumenism. For example, Cardinal Walter Kasper, current head of the Pontifical Council for Christian Unity, identified three key challenges for Christian ecumenism in the twenty-first century.

1. We must promote ecumenical formation and the reception of the ecumenical results at all levels. That is, we must work hard to inform ministers and faithful Catholics in the results of the bilateral and multilateral dialogues.

2. We must clarify and renew our ecumenical vision. Kasper warns that we are at risk of "losing a generation," if we cannot successfully communicate to them the urgency of the ecumenical mission of the Church.

3. We must harmonize identity and dialogue. Statements from the Roman Catholic magisterium often emphasize the identity and nature of Catholic faith. Occasionally, as was the case with a recent document from the Congregation for the Doctrine of the Faith, *Dominus Iesus,* we have promoted Catholic identity at the expense of dialogue. Our closest dialogue partners have difficulty trusting our ability to grow with them in the expression of faith and the knowledge of truth.[31]

Concern for the present climate. Recent statements from the Vatican have many ecumenists concerned that some Catholic authorities are less than comfortable with the ecumenism of convergence. Substantial agreements between dialogue partners, carefully crafted by earnest and faithful men and women, are questioned for their faithfulness to literal interpretations of Catholic doctrine. Several suggest that what we are witnessing may be called an "ecumenism of lurking suspicions" among some circles of Catholic authorities. Occasionally, these theologians and authorities give the impression that it is not ever possible to state Catholic faith in ways that earnestly respond to Protestant and Orthodox concerns.

In the present climate, it is challenging to maintain reasonable statements of faith that could foster healthy ecumenical relationships with-

---

[31] "The Crisis of Ecumenism, According to Cardinal Kasper: A Delicate Project 'Totally Different from Relativism,'" *Zenit.org* (March 7, 2002), <http://www.zenit.org>.

out receiving opposition from Catholic authorities. For example, an advocate for interchurch families wrote in 1983, "In the case of the interchurch family, the domestic Church is linked with the one Church of Christ as it exists in the two churches of husband and wife." Nothing in this statement is inconsistent with the Vatican II Decree on Ecumenism or the Constitution on the Church. Nonetheless, after the promulgation of *Dominus Iesus* in 2001, it is now risky to say that the "one Church of Christ" may be found *anywhere* outside of the Catholic Church.

Quite apart from official resistance to ecumenical efforts, a vital task for the next century of ecumenism will be for the agreed statements to be discovered and lived on every level. Ecumenical conversation and faith sharing are not the exclusive reserve of scholars, theologians, or clergy. Conversation and faith sharing must happen among Christians within the same neighborhood, town, or city. Catholic authorities can urge us to understand and work with ecumenical partners as they are, as they present themselves to us. In a sense, we need to get down to the business of living together: discerning in each other the Body of Christ. This is called "local ecumenism."

Local ecumenism. While bilateral and multilateral ecumenical dialogues have greatly assisted ecumenical progress during the last thirty years, the bulk of our efforts so far have been "from the top down." The experience of "divided denominations" is quite different than the experience of "divided local churches." Most of the ecumenical movement during the twentieth century has been focused on the reconciliation of "divided denominations." In the twenty-first century, we may need to focus more of our efforts on the reconciliation of local churches.[32] If we are successfully to foster Christian unity, Catholic ecumenist Jon Nilson recommends that ecumenism must focus its energies on work "from the bottom up." Only on the local level can divided Christian communities come to recognize, evaluate, and discern the values and convictions that constitute a genuine "unity in faith."[33]

In the United Kingdom, for instance, ecumenism has gone far where churches, Catholic and non-Catholic, share facilities, worship together on a regular basis, and share outreach and other ministries. In these ecumenical communities, when people hear the word "ecumenism," they have learned to think of their own "living together in faith—week in and week out."[34]

[32] Gerard Kelly, "Intercommunion—Critical for the Future of the Ecumenical Movement and Church Unity," *One in Christ* 34, no. 4 (1998) 527.
[33] Nilson, 5.
[34] Cross, 53.

Ecumenical Worship in the Ecumenical Assembly

Common worship is essential to the search for Christian unity.[35] Ecumenical worship in the ecumenical assembly is one of the principle ways through which Christians are learning to "live together in faith." An ecumenical assembly is any assembly of baptized Christians, both Catholic and non-Catholic together. An ecumenical assembly may be a Catholic liturgy with non-Catholics present, a non-Catholic liturgy with Catholics present, or an assembly of baptized Christians from a variety of churches and ecclesial communities following a mixed form of worship.

Some benefits of ecumenical worship. Ecumenical worship offers numerous advantages to Christian communities. Ecumenists Jane Crawford and Thomas Best enumerate some of these advantages. They note that common worship has become central to ecumenical gatherings. Across the lines of Church divisions, Christian worship shares many basic features. Ecumenical worship successfully combines worship forms from a variety of liturgical traditions. There has been a great increase in the variety of confessional materials, music, ritual, aesthetic, and other expressive elements in Christian worship precisely because of the ecumenical movement. The Lima Liturgy of the World Council of Churches has demonstrated the immense value of "convergence" in forms of worship.[36]

Learning to sing, to worship, and to pray together has been one of the most valuable fruits of the ecumenical movement. In ecumenical worship gatherings, despite any awkwardness we may feel, we are not simply learning *about* one another or learning *from* one another.[37] For that, we could simply attend lectures and classes. Ecumenical progress, however, requires both that we know *about* one another and that we *know* (and grow to love) one another. When we truly pray together, we become far more than superficially "appreciative" of cultural or religious differences. Prayer in common requires that Christian assemblies adapt, adjust, and enter into communion with one another.

Ecumenical worship can provide an impetus for growth in communion. When we worship together, we join fellow Christians in a

---

[35] Jane Crawford and Thomas F. Best, "Praise the Lord with the Lyre . . . And the Gamelan? Towards Koinonia in Worship," *The Ecumenical Review* 46, no. 1 (1994) 78ff.

[36] Ibid.

[37] Emilio Castro, "Ecumenical Worship," in *Christus Spes: Liturgie und Glaube im ökumenischen Kontext*, ed. Paul Berbers and Thaddäus A. Schnitker (Frankfurt am Main: Peter Lang, 1994) 101.

"pilgrimage of obedience" to an authority higher than our own. When ecumenical worship is well conceived, we may be treated to a procession of cultural, theological, and liturgical treasures; the "gifts that differ" among us. For example, I have always been impressed by the solemn and august saging of a worship space by native American Christians. Following the witness and example of other Christians, Catholics have learned again to "speak in tongues," both literally and figuratively. How can we not be thankful to God for these graces received from "outside our gates?"

Some risks in ecumenical worship. For all its benefits, ecumenical worship is not without risk. Ecumenical worship carries the risk of hardening allegiance to the particularities of one's own church. As a student of the liturgy and as a liturgical musician, I am asked often to participate in the worship services of different churches. There is always an element of risk when I worship outside of my tradition. I often find myself wandering in strange liturgical landscapes. At times, I have been "turned off" by the speaking in tongues, the hand waving, or the long and tedious sermons. In general, I find "altar calls"—like the ones at the end of Billy Graham crusades—embarrassing and awkward.

Awkwardness goes both ways. Consider the feelings and experience of non-Catholic friends at worship. Ask them about their experience of "smells and bells," of incense and gospel processions, of not knowing when to stand or kneel. They are describing a similar sense of embarrassment and awkwardness. With these natural and understandable responses to a variety of worship styles, especially troublesome is the possibility that I may have overlooked the profound, sacramental presence of Jesus Christ at their core. There is an exceptional depth in many forms of worship. When I experience worship in the wrong way, I risk trivializing and overlooking the movement of God in that assembly.

I do not suggest that we change our practice of worship to suit the sensibility of others. Instead, I propose that we work hard to avoid the possibility that non-Catholic guests would fail to discern the depth of the movement of God in *our* assembly—even if, at the end of the day, they find our worship is "not their style." It is within our ability always to assist all people—Catholic and non-Catholic alike—in discerning the Holy Spirit at the heart of *our* worship.

Ecumenical worship moves the problem of eucharistic sharing high on the ecumenical agenda. The problem of eucharistic sharing *always* (by definition) occurs within the context of an ecumenical assembly of Christians gathered for worship. As early as 1961, at the New Delhi meeting of the World Council of Churches, council president Dr. Philip Potter put the question to the assembly of delegates. Our unity, he said, "must be sealed." It must extend to the Lord's Table. Potter was quite optimistic in his estimate of the "degree of unity" that ecumenism had achieved to that point. Nonetheless, his concern, to "seal" the unity of the churches, remains vital and valid to the present day.[38]

Historical unity, a myth. Catholics often speak of "Christian unity." We refer to the "early Church" as though there had once been a "golden age" when every Christian agreed peacefully with every other—a lovely story. On the contrary, Christian literature from the beginning is full of polemical—even slanderous—stories about "other Christians." Historians point out that a completely "united" Church has never existed.[39]

Consequently, over the past twenty-five years, Christian theologians have focused on the problem of "communion" in the Church. They understand that unity in the Church is always a "unity in diversity," the definition of "communion." A proper understanding of Christian communion is therefore an essential component of my argument.

Several Types of Communion

The Catholic Church understands that communion with Christ comes to expression in human life through a variety of modes. We receive Holy Communion through the reception of the Body and Blood of Christ in the Eucharist. We receive Holy Communion with one another through participation in the Church, the ecclesial Body of Christ. In addition, Catholic theology understands that local churches receive Holy Communion with the entire Church of Christ through the apostolic succession especially expressed through the primacy of the Church of Rome. Seen as a whole, communion refers to the *manner* in which Christ unites himself to people in the Church, his ecclesial body. Only later did the word communion come to refer to the relation of one church to another.[40] This section will introduce the term "communion" and suggest how it has come to connote so many different—though related—realities.

Institutional and theological communion. In the Vatican II documents, we already identify a tension between two different understandings of communion. First, we understand communion as an indication of *institutional* coherence. Communion is what "organizes" and "structures" the Church, from the local level to the level of the worldwide commun-

---

[38] Crawford and Best, 72.

[39] Brosseder, "Towards What Unity," 133.

[40] Kenneth Hein, *Eucharist and Excommunication: A Study in Early Christian Doctrine and Discipline*, European University Papers (Frankfurt am Main: Peter Lang, 1973) 415.

ion with the Church of Rome and the Bishop of Rome, the Pope. Second, we understand communion as a *theological* reality offered to every Christian, without regard to institutional affiliation, based on his or her faith in and personal relationship to Jesus Christ. We repeatedly affirm how baptism always and everywhere draws the person into the communion of the Body of Christ.[41]

The tension between these different understandings of communion originates in the writings of the apostle Paul. Paul introduced the word "communion" to the Christian glossary in his first letter to the Corinthians (1 Cor 10:14-22). In the letter, Paul was concerned to redefine the standard for common life in the Christian community. He thought the Corinthian Christians were doing an especially bad job of it, and they needed some helpful corrections. In the midst of this argument, Paul introduces the word "communion" *(koinonia).*

Koinonia. Where did Paul find the word? In ancient Greece, the giving and receiving of gifts formed the best model for communion. For Plato, communion expresses itself in the mutual giving and receiving of genuine friendship. Wherever there is friendship, he thought that one had already found a real communion of persons.[42] According to the Greeks, in the tradition of Plato and others, communion was the result of sharing "common life" together. While the word "communion" may sound terribly abstract to us, it is fair to say that it was not an abstraction to the ancient Greeks. Communion simply meant living together in relationship with other beings—in the household, among friends, in a clan, as a citizen, in the city-state—with all the rights, duties, obligations, these relationships entail.[43]

The word *koinonia* does not translate from Greek into English very easily. One of the better ways to translate the original Greek word, *koinonia,* is to speak of "common union."[44] This translation is especially helpful whenever we want to distinguish the social *result* of the Eucharist (Christian community) from the *act* of receiving the Eucharist (as in the phrase "receiving Holy Communion"). The main point: communion always refers to a community of persons, united in relationship

[41] Cf. Susan K. Wood, "Baptism and the Foundations of Communion," in *Baptism and the Unity of the Church,* ed. Michael Root and Risto Saarinen (Grand Rapids, Mich. / Geneva: Eerdmans / WCC Publications, 1998) 45.

[42] Nicholas Sagovsky, *Ecumenism, Christian Origins and the Practice of Communion* (Cambridge: Cambridge University Press, 2000) 11.

[43] Ibid., 17.

[44] Francis J. Moloney, *A Body Broken for a Broken People: Eucharist in the New Testament,* rev. ed. (Peabody, Mass. / Blackburn, Victoria, Australia: Hendrickson Publishers / HarperCollins Religious, 1997) 161.

through a shared focus. When Paul took up this word in his letter to the Corinthians, he meant a "practical participation" in the love of God, expressed through worship and sacraments, and "manifested in a genuine love of neighbor."[45]

Horizontal and vertical communion. Contemporary Catholic theology often understands communion in "geometric" language. We speak of "horizontal" and "vertical" communion. Communion, we say, always involves a "horizontal" and a "vertical" dimension. The "vertical" dimension refers to our communion with God; the "horizontal" to our communion with one another. The "geometric" language helps us to understand how communion always consists of anthropological and theological dimensions. Neither dimension should be ignored or down-played.[46]

Visible and invisible communion. Contemporary Catholic theology also distinguishes among types of communion in "visual" metaphors. The communion of the Church is always visible and invisible.[47] This means there are empirical elements of unity. These elements may be studied for their sociological, cultural, and political qualities. On the one hand, we advance our knowledge of the Church through political, demographic, or cultural studies. On the other hand, there are theological elements of unity. Assisted by reason, faith alone discerns and deduces these "invisible" elements. Informed by Scripture, tradition, and reason, theologians and others attempt to describe the "invisible" relationships between God and the Church.

Active and passive communion. We also distinguish between active and passive communion. In the active sense, communion means "to give a part in" or "to contribute." In the passive sense, communion means "to receive a part in" or "to participate."[48] Either way, we are forced to consider how communion is an *action* and not a *thing*. I remain intrigued by the number of ancient words from Greek that Christians have turned from verbs into nouns during the intervening centuries. Eucharist, theology, baptism, church—in the Greek language, all these terms have significant verb forms. No less than these other words, communion also is a verb and an action. It is something that *God* does to us.

---

[45] Sagovsky, 17.

[46] Congregation for the Doctrine of the Faith, Letter to the Bishops of the Catholic Church on some aspects of the Church understood as communion *(Communionis notio)*, February 25, 1992.

[47] Ibid.

[48] L.-M. Dewailly, "Communio-Communicatio," *Revue des Sciences Philosophiques et Théologiques* 54, no. 1 (1970) 50.

Permanent and less than permanent communion. Communion binds us to one another both permanently and less than permanently. The bond of communion is permanent in the sense that our union to the Body of Christ is intended to last "until he comes." The bond of communion is less than permanent in the sense that, in this lifetime, we remain free to abandon our commitments and to flee from God and one another. Communion is nothing more or less than communion in Christ. Christ grants communion and it is questionable whether any human jurisdiction can deny the reality of communion to another.[49]

Paul expected Christians to maintain deep personal relationships with one another. For example, Philippians 2:2-4 helps us understand the immense depth Paul expected: "Be of the same mind, having the same love, being in full accord and of one mind." We should not read this text as saying that Christian communion is the result of agreement in doctrine alone. Communion in faith is not merely the result of a "shared belief system." It is the result of living together in sympathy, love, humility, and looking to the interests of others ahead of one's own. Beliefs are only a few of the components of that much broader set of relationships that the Church is meant to establish and implant in the world.[50] For Catholics—and many non-Catholics—these relationships are most effectively created by and signified in the sacraments.

Sacramental Communion

Why do we have sacraments at all? Some people think we have them for their effects—they save us, they heal us, they forgive us, and marry us. Others think we have them for their causes—Christ instituted them, the Holy Spirit confers holiness on the recipients. Still others focus on their teachings and doctrines—the sacrament of marriage teaches us how to live in love as Christian families. A truly great twentieth-century liturgical theologian, Odo Casel, points in another, richer direction. Odo Casel held that sacraments are oriented to our "translation from death to resurrection." Sacraments, he said, set us on the way to salvation created by Christ's paschal mystery. In other words, sacraments are our "windows of opportunity." They are "route-markers" for the Church of Christian pilgrims.[51]

[49] Brosseder, "Towards What Unity," 136.
[50] Hein, 117f.
[51] Cf. Edward J. Kilmartin, *The Eucharist in the West: History and Theology*, ed. Robert J. Daly (Collegeville, Minn.: The Liturgical Press, 1998) 272.

According to Catholic faith, we receive communion with Christ and one another through the sacraments of baptism and the Eucharist. We should not think that baptismal and eucharistic communion are two separate realities. They are the same reality expressed through different modalities. Baptism signifies communion in Christ's death and resurrection. Dying with Christ, we receive a share, a *communion*, in his resurrection.

The Eucharist is a continuing act of the Church. It defines what it means to be a "good member" of the Church.[52] Eucharistic Communion is baptismal communion deepened and extended through time. In a certain sense, the Eucharist is baptismal communion, "brought home to rest throughout one's lifetime."[53] The Eucharist becomes, as it were, a *dynamic* continuation of baptism. Therefore, communion in the Church—the Body of Christ—and eucharistic Communion are mutually reinforcing.[54] Both are mutually reinforcing extensions of our baptism into the paschal mystery of the death and resurrection of Christ with the gift of the Holy Spirit.

Communion in the Eucharist is never just a moment alone with Jesus. While the reception of Holy Communion is always intensely personal, it is also corporate. Communion unites us to the whole person of Christ—"my Jesus" and "my Jesus' people."[55] The Eucharist joins Christians less because they share bread and wine. Any meal could do that. Instead, the Eucharist joins Christians because of their common sharing of love for Christ and for one another as members of the Body of Christ. The Eucharist "joins Christians in responsible love for one another."[56]

In proposing and maintaining the discipline of eucharistic sharing, Catholic authorities work very hard to maintain an essential proposition about the Church: We come to eucharistic Communion through communion with the local church. In this life, spiritual communion with Christ always comes to us within a set of visible and real relationships that comprise a local church. Our communion with Christians always and everywhere is *mediated* through our communion with Christians here and now.

Communion by way of relationships. North American Christians very easily lose sight of the relationships that join people in Christian faith.

---

[52] Hein, 421.
[53] Wood, 54.
[54] Dewailly, 62.
[55] Hein, 59f.
[56] Ibid., 62.

There are a number of reasons for this. We live in an individualistic culture. Every area of life—economy, politics, education, and religion—are touched by the values of consumerism. At the same time, we easily forget that Christian faith is communal no less than it is personal. At every turn real men and women, lay and ordained, are relating to one another with respect to each other's faith. They are "forming one another in faith." Through whom, then, does one enter into communion with the Church?

Catholic theologians agree that we enter into communion with the whole Church of Christ by way of communion with the bishop of one's local church. To receive Holy Communion is always to say, "I am in full communion with the Catholic Church, united with the bishop of this local community and with the Pope."[57] In the ancient Church, Christians on journeys or pilgrimage would carry with them "letters of communion" from their bishop as they traveled.[58] Letters from the local bishop functioned like an ancient equivalent to a high school "hall pass"—a token granted by an authority for admission to Holy Communion.[59]

When they received word of ordinations, bishops also would write "letters of communion" to new bishops, sometimes in far-ranging locations.[60] This practice of circulating "apostolic letters" among bishops helped establish communion among the ancient Christian churches.[61] Thus the communion of local churches came to be signified by letters of "admission to Holy Communion" circulated among bishops and other clergy.

Sacraments are for whole communities. The Eucharist is not for the salvation of individuals alone. In the Eucharist, Christ confronts us as whole communities and not just as individuals. Christ saves us by drawing us out of ourselves, out of sinful isolation, and by implanting us into relationship with unlikely people. He heals us as individuals by

---

[57] Catholic Bishops' Conference of England and Wales; Bishops' Conference of Ireland; Bishops' Conference of Scotland, *One Bread, One Body: A Teaching Document on the Eucharist in the Life of the Church, and the Establishment of General Norms on Sacramental Sharing* (January 27, 1998) 62.

[58] Joseph Ratzinger, *Principles of Catholic Theology: Building Stones for a Fundamental Theology*, trans. Mary Frances McCarthy (San Francisco: Ignatius Press, 1987) 244.

[59] OBOB, 63. During the eighteenth and nineteenth centuries, the ministers of some Protestant churches distributed "communion tokens" to men and women who were properly disposed to receive the sacrament, another form of the "apostolic letter."

[60] Dewailly, 60. Dewailly cites Eusebius, *History of the Church* VII.30.17.

[61] OBOB, 63.

restoring our ability to enjoy authentic relationships with others. Communion *is* the enjoyment of authentic relationships with others. It consists of the will to remain in relationship. It consists of the willingness to be healed in relationship. In a word, it consists of the willingness to be *saved*. Communion helps us focus on *relationship* as central to the reality of God, our world, our Church, and the human person.[62] The Eucharist is an efficacious instrument in transposing human relationship along these lines.[63]

Intercommunion

Communion refers also to the relationship that exists between churches and their bishops. Bishops live in communion with one another; therefore, their churches also live in communion. Intercommunion refers to agreements between local churches to share the Eucharist and, in some cases, to share ministers. Bernard Leeming defined intercommunion as two churches agreeing to permit mutual reception of Communion among communicant members and granting freedom to ministers from each church to officiate in the other church.[64] Intercommunion is, in a sense, a more or less permanent arrangement of eucharistic sharing between specific churches. Leeming's definition is much more broad and all-inclusive than eucharistic sharing because it includes the element of shared ministry.

I have tried to limit discussion of eucharistic sharing to the agreement to permit mutual reception of Communion without necessarily granting ministers freedom to officiate in the other churches. According to Leeming's definition, "intercommunion" is allowed in the Catholic Church only between and among local churches in communion with Rome. Only priests ordained in other Catholic jurisdictions may receive faculties (canonical permission) to officiate in a diocese outside their home church. Leeming's definition of "intercommunion" is so broad, therefore, as to come close to a definition of "full communion."

While the word "intercommunion" was once preferred in discussion of eucharistic sharing, the term is now considered a problem. Most

---

[62] Dennis M. Doyle, "Journet, Congar, and the Roots of Communion Ecclesiology," *Theological Studies* 58, no. 3 (1997) 461–79.

[63] Cf. Johann Auer, *A General Doctrine of the Sacraments and the Mystery of the Eucharist*, ed. Johann Auer and Joseph Ratzinger, trans. Erasmo Leiva Merikakis, 9 vols., vol. 6, Dogmatic Theology (Washington, D.C.: The Catholic University of America Press, 1995) 345.

[64] Bernard Leeming, *Heythrop Journal* (1962) 139. Cited in Dewailly, 46.

theologians now agree that the reality once described by the term *inter-communion* is more aptly called simply *communion*. Adding the prefix "inter-" adds nothing to the sense of mutual relationship inherent to the term "communion."

In addition, the term "intercommunion" is a problem because it pre-supposes the division of the Church. It can only speak of a joint col-laboration between two entities that are divided from one another.[65] As Jean-Jacques von Allmen once wrote, "It is not intercommunion that is the solution to resolve the divisions of the Church, it is communion."[66]

Degrees of Communion

A guiding principle for eucharistic sharing in the Catholic Church is the idea of "degrees of communion."[67] According to this principle, Catholics recognize a "real though partial" communion between all the baptized. At the same time, there exist several "degrees of com-munion" between the Catholic Church and Christians of other commu-nities.[68]

Three degrees of communion. The norms suggest that there are at least three distinct "degrees of communion."

1. *Baptismal communion.* There is the baptismal communion of indi-vidual persons. Through baptism, every Christian receives com-munion in the Body of Christ.

2. *Communion of apostolic succession.* There is the communion of churches in apostolic succession, though perhaps also in schism. In the churches founded in apostolic succession, the bishops and other ministers may not live within the full communion of the "college of bishops." Their "collegiality" is impaired and in that sense they may be schismatic. Nonetheless, they have retained the validity of orders and other sacraments as understood by the Catholic Church. Examples of these churches include most of the Oriental and other Orthodox churches.

3. *Full communion.* There is the "full communion" of the Catholic Church, where apostolic succession has remained and the college of bishops is united in communion with Rome. Full communion,

[65] James Arne Nestingen and Wayne Zweck, "Communio, Inter-Communion with Non-Lutheran Churches, and the Lutheran Confessions: A Response," *Lutheran Theological Journal* (Adelaide) 33, no. 1 (1999) 24.

[66] Cited in Dewailly, 63.

[67] Falardeau, 9.

[68] OBOB, 22.

from this perspective, requires both the apostolic succession *and* the primacy of Rome.

This vocabulary of degrees of communion allows churches to recognize and affirm a variety of "degrees" of closeness short of "full union."[69] The advantage to this approach is that it allows Church leaders and ecumenical dialogue partners to emphasize areas of agreement and convergence over areas of disagreement and polemic.

For example, in their teaching document on the Eucharist, *One Bread, One Body,* the Catholic bishops of the United Kingdom and Ireland explain their understanding of the "degrees" of communion. They say that baptism creates a bond among all Christians. This bond, they say, is "real, though partial."[70] Apart from baptismal communion, there exist *deeper* levels of communion that depend on the number of beliefs and practices shared among Christian churches. The more that churches share, the deeper is the level of communion.[71] For this reason, they conclude, the communion of all Christians is "wounded," but not "destroyed."

Differentiation between "full" and "less than full" communion emerged in the ecumenical vocabulary during the years since Vatican II. The distinction affirms the existence of "degrees" or levels of proximity in doctrine and other elements of church life. Seen positively, this distinction assists ecumenism. It has helped many people maintain hope for the possibility of a "full communion" in the imaginable future. By identifying areas of closeness and areas of difference, the conditions for full communion can be named. Eventually, these differences might be overcome.[72]

For all its advantages, the idea of "full" or "partial" communion can be troublesome. For instance, the idea emerges from a contradiction. This contradiction stems from questions about the status of baptized non-Catholics and their communities that were left unresolved by Vatican II. Vatican II maintains that there is a real communion among all the baptized but, at the same time, the "one and only Church [of Christ] remains and continues to remain" in unity with Rome. In a sense, these statements perpetuate the "member" and "subject" distinction of Robert Bellarmine. All the baptized are subjects of the Church, but not all are members. On the level of being "subjects," there is a real communion; but on the level of "membership," there is not. These statements are

[69] Power, 588f.
[70] OBOB, 22.
[71] Ibid.
[72] Wijlens, 137.

difficult to reconcile in a way that does not risk offending our closest ecumenical dialogue partners. Out of their juxtaposition has developed the theme of "full" *(plena)* and "less than full" *(non plena)* communion.[73] *Fullness is a qualitative measure.* When we speak of "full communion," it is important to remember that this is not a quantitative measure. It is a *qualitative* assessment. "Fullness" is not the result of a church having completed a "checklist" of ecclesial "qualities." Instead, fullness of communion refers to the *integrity* of a church's life and being. German Catholic theologian Johannes Brosseder is more blunt. He claims that to speak of "degrees" of being the Church is "nonsense." When we say that a church exhibits the "fullness of communion," we refer to its reception of the Holy Spirit. Brosseder claims, "Either the Spirit is filling you, or you are resisting it." Either you are "in communion" or you are running away from it.[74]

From my perspective, the wisdom in referring to "partial communion" depends on the recognition that Christians are always living "along the way" together. Communion is a gift of God; but like all divine gifts, we have difficulty embracing or comprehending its fullness. Ecumenism, if it is to mean anything, is the willingness to live with one another, even when we are having difficulties embracing or comprehending one another as gifts from God. Simply stated, communion is something we *live* and it is not something we *possess.*[75] It is a gift of God. It is not a product of the Church's attainment.[76]

Types of Eucharistic Sharing

A variety of different words has been used to describe eucharistic sharing. The list of words includes intercommunion, open Communion, *communicatio in sacris,* eucharistic hospitality, eucharistic sharing, Communion, full Communion, and admission to Communion.[77] All refer in some way to the relative access of Christians to the sacraments

---

[73] Ibid.

[74] Brosseder, "Towards What Unity," 132.

[75] Cf. Johannes Brosseder, "Die ökumenische Bedeutung des Bischofsamtes," in *Christus Spes: Liturgie und Glaube im ökumenischen Kontext,* ed. Paul Berbers and Thaddäus A. Schnitker (Frankfurt am Main: Peter Lang, 1994) 87.

[76] David N. Power, "*Koinonia, Oikoumene,* and Eucharist in Ecumenical Conversations," in *Ecumenical Theology in Worship, Doctrine, and Life: Essays Presented to Geoffrey Wainwright on his Sixtieth Birthday,* ed. David S. Cunningham, Ralph del Colle, and Lucas Lamadrid (Oxford: Oxford University Press, 1999) 120.

[77] Wijlens, xvii.

of a church different from their "home church." Catholic theologian Gerard Austin identifies two extremes in our views on eucharistic sharing. On the one side, we can welcome all the baptized to full participation in the Eucharist in an "open Communion." On the other side, we could limit participation only to those who belong to a specific communion descending even to the level of the congregation or parish (closed Communion).[78]

Three types of eucharistic sharing. Although I will mainly refer to "eucharistic sharing," it may be helpful briefly to review these other terms for the sake of completeness and clarity.

1. *Open Communion:* All baptized men and women, when they are properly disposed, are welcome to receive Holy Communion.[79] In a few communities, Holy Communion is open to all men and women whether or not they have been baptized.[80] For some Christians, "open Communion" is seen as a natural expression of baptismal unity. Even when Church jurisdictions live in conflict, they hold that the sacraments belong to Christ and not to any one local church or jurisdictional arrangement of local churches.[81]

2. *Shared Communion:* Churches establish agreements for shared ministry and mutual ordination in shared Communion. The goal of shared Communion is to establish mutually recognized ministry "by stages." These agreements have helped create "full Communion" among "uniting churches" like the Church of North India or the Church of South India, formed from mergers of Presbyterian, Congregational, Methodist, and other churches.

3. *Closed Communion:* Holy Communion is reserved to baptized members in good standing. Various stages of "closed Communion" exist. Communion may be closed on the level of the denomination or worldwide Communion, as it is among the Orthodox or the Catholic Church. Catholic authorities hold that full reconciliation is the normal prerequisite to regular sharing in Holy Communion.[82] Communion may be closed on the level of the local church or parish, as in the case of some Baptist, independent, or nondenominational churches. One of the main reasons proposed for a

[78] Gerard Austin, "Identity of a Eucharistic Church in an Ecumenical Age," *Worship* 72 (1998) 31.

[79] Falardeau, 9.

[80] Wijlens, xvii–xviii.

[81] Wainwright, 8.

[82] OBOB, 93.

"closed Communion" is to limit the possibility of "unworthy eating" of the Eucharist.[83]

A Variety of Perspectives

Orthodox Views

There exists a variety of Orthodox churches, yet they remain united in resistance to eucharistic sharing. As a general rule, Orthodox churches insist on unity before admission to Communion.[84] The Orthodox perspective is that there exists full communion or none at all.[85] Outside the communion of Orthodox churches, there exists no communion. Non-Orthodox Christians are, some Orthodox writers say, either "heretics" or "schismatics."

The statements of Paulos Mar Gregorios in a 1992 issue of *The Ecumenical Review* may help us understand the perspective of the Eastern Orthodox churches. Gregorios defines "eucharistic sharing" slightly differently than I have. He understands "eucharistic sharing" as the result of a "special dispensation during an ecumenical conference or other occasion, and [a church] offering communion to those to whom it normally refuses communion."[86] In any case, Gregorios rejects the propriety of eucharistic sharing as he defines it.

According to Robert G. Stephanopoulos, Orthodox Christians believe that "heretics" are, in no way, "members of the Church," and the "baptism" of the "heretic" is null and void. "Schismatics," in their view, are members of the Church and the Church should rejoice when they return to the Church. Orthodox Christians do not view the "schismatic" as belonging to any kind of a "church" per se. They may have "church-like" groupings, but each schismatic stands on his or her own in relationship to the Church.

In the view of Stephanopoulos, sharing sacraments jeopardizes the continuity of the Church in the apostolic tradition.[87] To receive the

[83] Ernie V. Lassman, "1 Corinthians 11:29—'Discerning the Body' and Its Implications for Closed Communion," *Logia: A Journal of Lutheran Theology* 3 (1994) 15.

[84] Philippe Larere, *The Lord's Supper: Towards an Ecumenical Understanding of the Eucharist*, trans. Patrick Madigan (Collegeville, Minn.: The Liturgical Press, 1993) 65.

[85] Wainwright, 6.

[86] Paulos Mar Gregorios, "Not a Question of Hospitality: A Comment," *The Ecumenical Review* 44, no. 1 (1992) 46.

[87] Robert G. Stephanopoulos, "Implications for the Ecumenical Movement," *The Ecumenical Review* 44, no. 1 (1992) 19.

Eucharist and to be a member of the Church are the same thing according to the Orthodox understanding. Whenever Christians stand to receive Holy Communion, they "manifest" their membership in the one Church of Christ, the local church to which they belong.

On the one hand, the Catholic Church extends the possibility of eucharistic sharing to Orthodox Christians and allows Catholics to receive sacraments from Orthodox clergy. On the other hand, most of these churches do not allow Catholics to receive Holy Communion and would not encourage their members to receive the Eucharist in Catholic Churches.

Protestant Perspectives

There exists a much wider variety of Protestant perspectives. Protestant churches represent the full spectrum of views on eucharistic sharing. From the start it is important to note that, even among Protestants, "open Communion" is not universal. There exist many exceptions among Lutheran, Baptist, and Reformed churches.[88]

Whatever their view on eucharistic sharing, Protestant churches emphasize that Christ himself invites and convokes the Church around the eucharistic table.[89] How we respond to the invitation of Christ is at stake in our decision to admit one another to Holy Communion. The response of many Protestant theologians would be, first, to ask, "To whom does the Supper belong?" It is the Lord's Table, it is the Lord's Supper, they say, and not our own.[90] If they close the table, they conclude, they would be poor disciples of Christ, who was hospitable to many.

In general, Protestant theology emphasizes that Christ calls each man and woman as if "by name." The Church does not "own" the sacraments, and ministers must "get out of the way" of the altar so that Christ can touch and embrace men and women "directly." Therefore, ministry stands "alongside" the relationship between Jesus Christ and each Christian person. Ministers facilitate faith, but do not *mediate* it. For example, in many Calvinist churches, the intent to "get out of the way" was taken literally. Ministers moved away from the front of the altar and began to stand at its side. The minister literally "got out of the way," so that the Lord's Supper could effectively "speak for itself." The practice and policy of "open Communion" is entirely consistent with these points of view.

---

[88] Thomas Ryan, "Eucharistic Sharing: Why the Churches Act Differently," *Ecumenism* 110 (1993) 32.

[89] Larere, 67.

[90] Bernard Thorogood, "Coming to the Lord's Table: A Reformed Viewpoint," *The Ecumenical Review* 44, no. 1 (1992) 10.

Reformed theologian Bernard Thorogood states that focusing on the person who invites us to the Lord's Table is not a Protestant invention. It is a shift in emphasis already apparent in certain medieval assumptions "that the sacraments were in the hands of the hierarchy."[91] The primary location of the debate between some Protestants and the medieval perspective begins here. What *is* the relationship between Jesus Christ and the ministry of the Church?

As a result, for many Protestants, the basis for an "open Communion" extends from their understanding of ministry. First, they say that Christ calls the person into Communion, not the Church. Second, they say that the pastor is not the authority behind the sacrament, but the Church authorizes the pastor to invite men and women into Holy Communion. Third, for most Protestants, their particular church—understood here to mean the "denomination"—is *not* the whole Church. The whole Church, they say, transcends the boundaries of their own denomination to include all the baptized. From this perspective, if a church or communion of churches practices a "closed Communion," it falsely claims to be the "one true Church." "Closed Communion," in this view, connotes an unseemly, self-aggrandizement of one part of the Church at the expense of the whole.

Many Protestants understand their practice of open Communion as a form of obedience to Jesus Christ and his command to "Take, and eat this, *all of you.*" For their part, Catholic authorities have been critical when Protestant ministers invite Catholics to receive the Lord's Supper. For example, archbishop of Dublin, Cardinal Desmond Connell, complained in 2001, "Catholics are being encouraged to break Church rules by receiving Anglican communion."[92] What are these "Church rules" and how shall we understand them?

Norms for Eucharistic Sharing in the Catholic Church

Theologians are charged to examine the principles and sources from which "Church rules" are derived. Theologians serve the Church when they challenge Christians and Church authorities to remain honest with respect to sacramental norms and discipline. Far from seeking to undermine sacramental norms, books like this seek to help churches maintain sacramental norms with integrity.

[91] Ibid.
[92] "Canterbury Objects to Vatican Eucharist Ban," *Christian Century* 118, no. 2 (April 11, 2001) 11.

The Catholic Church presents sacramental norms in a variety of media. Sacramental norms appear within our liturgical books. They appear in the decrees and constitutions of Church councils. They appear in the statements of popes and Vatican departments and commissions. More than this, sacramental norms are implemented by the regional conferences of Catholic bishops. At the end of the day, the local bishop is the ordinary interpreter of liturgical law in his own diocese.

Canon Law in General

Why do we have "canon law" in the Catholic Church? Some readers may wonder why Catholics (and other Christians) should be concerned to follow liturgical norms set forth in canon law. They may recall that the apostle Paul himself said that "we hold that a person is justified by faith apart from works prescribed by the law" (Rom 3:28).

Canon lawyer Myriam Wijlens offers several reasons why canon law is helpful. Canon law provides for "good order" in the Church. It contributes to and serves our common life as we walk the way of salvation. Canon law seeks to help us act out key theological insights and to define and limit ecclesial behaviors accordingly.[93] Canon law exists to serve the Christian community in understanding and following its journey of Christian discipleship. In its own way, canon law helps us along the way to redemption.[94] By the same token, canon law should never be understood as a "law unto itself."

In Catholic theology, canon law is not understood to establish another "way to salvation," and no claim is made that obedience to the law justifies a Christian. Rather, the law understands itself as a code of prudence. The law offers the Church a *prudential path of wisdom* on its pilgrim journey through time. It is established for "good order" and to point the way in a world where "all things are lawful . . . , but not all things are beneficial" (1 Cor 6:12).

Sacramental or liturgical law forms a distinct category of canon law, but aims toward similar ends. John Huels helpfully summarizes, "The primary purpose of liturgical law is to protect the fundamental structures of the sacraments and thereby uphold the unity and catholicity of actual liturgical celebrations in the interest of the good order of the whole celebrations."[95]

---

[93] Wijlens, 5.
[94] Ibid.
[95] John Huels, *One Table, Many Laws: Essays on Catholic Eucharistic Practice* (Collegeville, Minn.: The Liturgical Press, 1986) 31.

Canon law is meant to help, not to hurt. Liturgical law does not exist in order to wound, injure, or embarrass men and women who approach the sacraments in good conscience. When men and women approach the sacraments because they misapprehend Catholic discipline, they should not be punished, embarrassed, or shamed. In seeking to apply canon law in the liturgy, pastors and ministers must be careful always to uphold the dignity of men and women before God and within the Christian community.[96] Liturgical practices that willfully embarrass or shame prospective communicants contradict the intention of the law.

An anecdote points to the high value we should set on the prudent application of liturgical norms. I always require students in my liturgy classes to attend and carefully observe worship in Roman Catholic and other Christian churches. In a recent semester, one of my students returned to class visibly upset following her observation assignment. Marie[97] had attended the Sunday liturgy of a nearby Catholic Church. Like any number of young adults in Southern California, Marie has a pierced tongue. According to Marie, when she approached the priest to receive Communion on the tongue, he visibly drew back, in her words, "with a look of shock on his face." The priest quizzed my student, "Are you Roman Catholic?" She was. He pressed further, "Have you received First Communion?" Now flustered, Marie gave up and lied, "No, I haven't." The priest laid the host back on the paten and dismissed her with a "blessing." Marie said, "He made a quick sign of the cross in front of me and said, 'God bless you, child. You certainly need it.'" Marie was embarrassed and felt ashamed. The priest was within his rights to refuse Communion based on Marie's response; he thought she had not yet received First Communion. But could this awkward situation have been handled more hospitably and charitably? Yes and yes.

In the best sense, sacramental law aims to protect the fundamental structures of the sacraments and to promote communion among Christians by upholding good order of actual liturgical celebrations.[98] The norms seek to prohibit and exclude only those practices that would damage the exchange of grace. They promote and prescribe whatever promotes Christian communion. The best practices in pastoral care, therefore, emphasize how "nurturing" and "permitting" strengthen the vine no less—and far more—than "pruning" and "prohibiting."

Canon 1752, the 1983 Code of Canon Law, states, "The salvation of souls should be the supreme law of the Church." By this, the authors

---

[96] Cf. Ladislas Orsy, "The Interpreter and His Art," *The Jurist* 40 (1980) 27–56.
[97] This is not her real name.
[98] Huels, 31.

understand that, for Christians, no law can be interpreted in isolation from the saving missions of Christ and the Holy Spirit. In every case, the determining factor is not the law, but Christ and the gift of the Spirit.

Current Norms

Vatican II did not forbid eucharistic sharing.[99] When Roman Catholic ministers state that only Roman Catholics may receive Holy Communion, their claim is false.[100] As a general rule, eucharistic sharing exists in the Catholic Church as a form of "pastoral hospitality" offered to *individual* baptized non-Catholics on the basis of serious pastoral need. Only in a limited number of cases does it exist as a form of "eucharistic Communion" offered to local churches independent from communion with Rome.[101]

Code of Canon Law 1917

Prior to Vatican II, the norms for eucharistic sharing were governed by the 1917 Code of Canon Law. The 1917 Code referred to all groups of non-Catholics as sects *(sectae)*. These sects were thought to have no more "saving effect" than any other "fraternal organization."[102] The Code referred to all non-Catholics, whether or not they had been baptized, as non-Catholics *(acatholicae)*.[103]

The 1917 Code placed a blanket prohibition on the administration of sacraments to non-Catholics. Canon 731 §2 says that it is "forbidden to administer the sacraments of the Church to heretics or schismatics, even when they err in good faith and ask for it, unless after having renounced their errors, they have been reconciled with the Church."[104] In addition, canon 1258 §1 prohibited Catholics from taking part in non-Catholic worship "in any way."[105]

The 1917 Code relied on Bellarmine's notion of the bonds of membership. All the bonds of membership are required before the baptized subject may receive the sacraments. In every case, there must be faith in the believing subject, a validly ordained minister, and a valid administration of the rite, for the sacrament to bear any fruit. The three bonds

---

[99] Falardeau, 10.
[100] Austin, 26.
[101] Wainwright, 7.
[102] Wijlens, 49.
[103] Ibid.
[104] Ibid., 53.
[105] Ibid., 65.

(*vincula*) were presented as essential not only for the person in his or her relationship to the Church. The three bonds were seen as essential to the composition of *any* valid and fruitful administration of a sacrament.

Vatican II: *Unitatis redintegratio*, 1964

In sharp contrast, in the decree on ecumenism, *Unitatis redintegratio*, Vatican II said that *communicatio in sacris* is beneficial when it is not used *"all the time"* or *"without discretion" (indiscretim)*.[106] Roughly translated, *communicatio in sacris* means "sharing in sacred things" and refers to "ecumenical worship." Whenever Christians from different churches worship and pray together—even when they do not receive Holy Communion together—they engage in *communicatio in sacris*. While *communicatio in sacris* refers to any liturgical or sacramental rite, it does include the possibility of receiving the Eucharist in Holy Communion.

To say that *communicatio in sacris* is "not to be used indiscriminately" is not the same as saying that it should "not be used at all." The Latin word for "indiscriminate" is *indiscretim*, and perhaps the council did not mean "indiscriminate" in the sense of an action performed unwisely or without prudence. Perhaps the council meant "indiscrete" in the sense of a series of actions performed all the time, without pause.

In the current context, however, it is important to note that saying *communicatio in sacris* is not to be used indiscriminately is not the same as saying that it should not be used at all. In effect, the council held that the Eucharist should not be used "like a tool" or as a "means to an end." Christians must always worship and receive the sacraments with thanksgiving for the grace these actions provide us. In years since the council, the practice of worship with non-Catholic Christians has become widespread, even if a more open eucharistic sharing has not.

The Ecumenical Secretariat 1972

The Secretariat for the Promotion of Christian Unity (now called the Pontifical Council for the Promotion of Christian Unity) has issued several instructions on eucharistic sharing since Vatican II. In 1972, the Secretariat issued its note on eucharistic sharing, *In quibus rerum circumstantiis*. More instructions followed in the 1993 ecumenical directory.

[106] UR 8. Huels, 86. Anne Primavesi and Jennifer Henderson, *Our God Has No Favourites: A Liberation Theology of the Eucharist* (Turnbridge, Wells, England / San Jose, Calif.: Burns & Oates / Resource Publications, 1989) 40.

The 1972 document envisions eucharistic sharing as a response to the *spiritual need* of baptized persons, offered in such a way as not to obscure the emphasis on the Eucharist as the act of the entire Church united in one faith.[107] When baptized non-Catholics cannot receive ministry from their own community because they are dying, in prison, suffering persecution, held hostage, and so forth, they may receive the Eucharist and several other sacraments from the Catholic minister.[108] The 1972 document is important since it provided the basis for the 1983 Code of Canon Law on the question of eucharistic sharing.

One of the key phrases in the 1972 document recommends that eucharistic sharing may occur only when the non-Catholic has no access to his or her own minister "for a prolonged period." Eoin de Bhaldraithe points to the great ingenuity in the design of this particular rule. European bishops, at the time, were eager to provide Communion for Anglicans; but the English bishops did not want to do so. De Bhaldraithe concludes, "Here was the perfect law which allowed both the English and the French to do things their own way."[109] The phrase does not reappear in the 1993 ecumenical directory.

Code of Canon Law 1983

The 1983 Code of Canon Law understands itself as an application and extension of the constitutions and decrees of Vatican II to the life of the Church. As such, the Code interprets and applies Vatican II decrees from documents such as the constitution on the Church, *Lumen gentium,* and the decree on ecumenism, *Unitatis redintegratio*. The norms for eucharistic sharing are laid out in Canon 844. (See Appendix 1.)

Canon 844 begins with a general prohibition of eucharistic sharing. Canon 844 §1 says that "Catholic ministers may lawfully administer the sacraments only to Catholic members of Christ's faithful, who equally may lawfully receive them only from Catholic ministers." In addition, Canon 844 forbids Catholics to receive the Eucharist from non-Catholic ministers—with the exception of Eastern Orthodox and ministers from several other churches that have maintained the apostolic succession.[110]

---

[107] Secretariat for the Promotion of Christian Unity, On admitting other Christians to eucharistic communion in the Catholic Church *(In Quibus Rerum Circumstantiis)* (June 1, 1972).

[108] Ibid.

[109] Bhaldraithe, "Intercommunion," 77.

[110] Thomas Richstatter, "Eucharist: Sign and Source of Christian Unity," *Catholic Update* (May 2000).

Canon 844 accepts a wide variety of exceptions to the general prohibition against eucharistic sharing. These exceptions depend upon "degrees of closeness in communion" to the Roman Catholic Church. It is fair to say that the current law requires "normally full ecclesial communion," but there exists a number of exemptions that should not be overlooked. It is a gross oversimplification to say, "The basic principle is . . . only Catholics may receive Holy Communion."[111] The exceptions to Canon 844 hint at the views of Catholic authorities on non-Catholic Christians and their churches or communities. These views are implied in the exceptions found in § 2, 3, and 4.

1. Orthodox Christians and others "in valid apostolic succession" may receive sacraments from Catholic ministers, in time of need. Catholics may receive sacraments from Orthodox ministers in time of need, but because of Orthodox norms this is not common.

2. Christians from churches "not in valid apostolic succession," "who cannot approach a minister of their own community and who spontaneously ask for them," may receive some sacraments from Catholic ministers in time of need (danger of death or other grave circumstance).

3. Catholics may not receive sacraments from ministers "not in valid apostolic succession" at any time.

The exceptions to Canon 844 assist Catholics who seek to understand and apply the general prohibition with prudence. Viewed optimistically, there has been a *vast* improvement on the issue of eucharistic sharing when it is compared to the 1917 Code of Canon Law and earlier norms.

On the other hand, Myriam Wijlens concludes that the current legislation on eucharistic sharing does not correspond to the doctrine of Vatican II and its decree on ecumenism.[112] Vatican II permitted ecumenical worship and the rule in *Unitatis redintegratio* opens the possibility of eucharistic sharing with due care and consideration. By contrast, Canon 844 limits and prohibits sacramental sharing.

The exceptions to Canon 844 have implications much deeper—and darker—than who may or may not receive Holy Communion from Catholic ministers. They depend on an *implicit negative judgment* on the ecclesial quality of non-Catholic churches and communities. In a word, the 1983 Code establishes the validity (or nonvalidity) of the ordination

---

[111] Cf. Tobin, 29.
[112] Wijlens, 364.

of non-Catholic ministers as the single most decisive factor in the question of eucharistic sharing.

The *Ecumenical Directory* 1993

The *Ecumenical Directory* of 1993 maintains similar norms and exceptions. The directory allows eucharistic sharing with the "Eastern churches," "given suitable circumstances and the approval of church authorities."[113] Before Catholics receive the Eucharist in an Orthodox Church, they must take care to observe the sacramental norms of the Eastern churches "to avoid scandal and suspicion." Catholic ministers may provide sacraments to members of these churches when they ask for them "of their own free will and are properly disposed." Catholic ministers may not proselytize Eastern Christians.

Because all who are baptized are brought into a "real, even if imperfect, communion with the Catholic Church," in certain circumstances, "by way of exception . . . access to these sacraments may be permitted, or even commended, for Christians of other churches and ecclesial Communities." The directory mentions several situations when access to the Eucharist is permitted: in danger of death, in grave and pressing need as established by local authorities. The non-Catholic must not be able to receive the sacrament from a minister of his or her own church. He or she must ask for the sacrament from his or her own initiative. They must manifest Catholic faith in the sacrament and be "properly disposed."

Catholics may only request and receive sacraments from ministers ordained in valid apostolic succession.

Ut unum sint, 1995

Pope John Paul II's encyclical on ecumenism, *Ut unum sint* (UUS), also speaks to the question of eucharistic sharing. The Pope notes, with joy, how helpful it has been that, under certain conditions, Christians may share the Eucharist (UUS 46).

The conditions for eucharistic sharing put forth in *Ut unum sint* differ from those in the 1983 Code of Canon Law and the 1993 *Ecumenical Directory*. They are simpler and closer to recommendations made by Cardinal Willebrands in 1980.[114] For example, the requirement of not

---

[113] Pontifical Council for Promoting Christian Unity, *Directory for the Application of Principles and Norms on Ecumenism* (March 25, 1993).

[114] Bhaldraithe, "Intercommunion," 70. In 1980, Cardinal Willebrands asked that the condition of "no access to one's minister" be removed, since it was less integral

having access to one's own minister has disappeared completely. There is no mention of the local bishop overseeing and defining the process for obtaining permission when certain conditions are met.

In the view of Eoin de Bhaldraithe, *Ut unum sint* "changed the rules." The papal encyclical on ecumenism, he writes, "created a new context under which the whole law is made subject to a new interpretation."[115] He concludes, *when proper conditions are met,* the Catholic minister may not deny sacraments to baptized non-Catholics who request them, even when the guidelines of the local bishops prohibit it.

U.S. Guidelines for the Reception of Communion 1996

Norms for eucharistic sharing are applied by the National Conferences of Catholic Bishops in light of the unique needs of local cultures and communities. In the United States, guidelines for eucharistic sharing were published November 14, 1996, by the Committee on the Liturgy of the National Conference of Catholic Bishops, United States Catholic Conference. (See Appendix 2.)

The 1996 "Guidelines for the Reception of Communion" of the U.S. Catholic Conference helpfully restate the present attitude of American Catholic authorities toward eucharistic sharing: "We welcome our fellow Christians to this celebration of the Eucharist as our brothers and sisters. We pray that our common baptism and the action of the Holy Spirit in this Eucharist will draw us closer to one another and begin to dispel the sad divisions which separate us. We pray that these will lessen and finally disappear."[116]

In the U.S. guidelines, Catholics are reminded of the discipline for receiving Holy Communion. Non-Catholics are welcomed to worship. Members of Orthodox churches, and several other churches, in particular the Polish National Catholic Church, are "urged to respect the discipline of their own Churches." The guidelines note that the Code of Canon Law does not "object" to their receiving the Eucharist. Non-communicants and non-Christians are urged to pray for unity with Christ and one another.

---

to eucharistic faith. The Code of Canon Law was prepared in 1970, but not promulgated until 1983. As a result the current canonical norms are based on the *Ecumenical Directory* of 1967 rather than the instruction of 1972.

[115] Ibid., 78. On complete reordering see P. Beal et al., *New Commentary on the Code of Canon Law* (New York: Paulist Press, 2000) 80–84.

[116] Committee on the Liturgy, National Conference of Catholic Bishops, United States Catholic Conference, "Guidelines for the Reception of Communion," (November 14, 1996).

These norms are specific to the American context. The guidelines attempt to be ecumenically sensitive. The norms apply first to all members of the assembly. Non-Catholics are welcomed to worship. The principles for exclusion from Holy Communion are carefully stated. *Responses to the U.S. guidelines.* Nonetheless, some U.S. Catholics express concern for the bishops' guidelines. In a special article on eucharistic sharing for *U.S. Catholic* magazine, Fr. Richard Szafransky says that he is "embarrassed" by the guidelines for receiving Holy Communion now published on the back page of American missalettes.[117] In 1990, a sample of readers of *U.S. Catholic* were polled on the question of eucharistic sharing. Of those who responded, 87 percent disagreed with the statement that "Eucharistic ministers should refuse Communion to people they believe are in grave sin." In addition, 92 percent agreed that most of the people Jesus ate with would not have met the bishops' guidelines.[118]

There are two principle weaknesses in the present norms. (1) The American norms are less thorough than those given by other conferences of Catholic bishops. (2) They fail to state the many exceptions permitted under the Code of Canon Law.

One Bread, One Body, 1997

Similar norms have been issued by other conferences of Catholic bishops. One of the more substantial documents, *One Bread, One Body* (OBOB), comes from the Bishops' Conferences of England and Wales, Scotland, and Ireland, published in January 1997.

Four conditions for eucharistic sharing. In *One Bread, One Body,* the bishops establish four conditions for eucharistic sharing.

1. The non-Catholic is unable to approach their own minister.[119]

2. There is a great desire to receive and this desire arises from the person's own initiative, not from an invitation.

3. The person manifests a Catholic faith with respect to the Eucharist.

---

[117] Richard T. Szafransky, "Let Everyone Come to Communion," *U.S. Catholic* 55, no. 6 (June 1990) 14.

[118] Ibid., 16.

[119] Ibid., 79. Bhaldraithe claims that ministers may not refuse Communion to non-Catholics when three conditions are present: great desire, they freely request the sacrament, and they manifest a faith that the Catholic Church professes with regard to these sacraments. He cites authority from Pope John Paul II's encyclical on ecumenism, *Ut unum sint.*

4. They are properly disposed to receive the sacrament.[120]

One Bread, One Body is more restrictive than the 1993 *Ecumenical Directory*.[121] The English Catholic bishops deny that the ban on eucharistic sharing is "brought about by sectarian bigotry."[122] They acknowledge the pain that many Christians feel for being unable to share in Holy Communion, but claim that pain is a sign of a deeper "wound."[123] The division of the Church must be healed, they say, but eucharistic sharing is not the proper medicine.

Responses to OBOB. Response to OBOB was highly critical, especially in Ireland. Irish priest, Fr. Gabriel Daly responded, saying, "It is rather like telling sick people they can have their medicine only after they have recovered their health."[124] In another review, reporter for *The London Times*, David Quinn, wrote, "A document like this must unavoidably walk into an ecumenical minefield." He noted how reaction in Ireland was "predictably hostile," especially in *The Irish Times*. Quinn concluded, "The bottom line is that Catholics cannot receive the sacraments of the Reformation churches at all."[125]

The response of the Anglican bishops. The most substantial remarks on *One Bread, One Body* have come from the Anglican bishops. John Hind, Anglican bishop of Europe, said, "In my diocese we welcome all baptized Christians who are in regular standing with their own churches and who are not prevented by their consciences from taking part [in Anglican Eucharist]."[126] In late 2001, the Anglican bishops released a formal response to OBOB. *The Eucharist: Sacrament of Unity* (ESOU) is the formal response of the House of Bishops of the Church of England to *One Bread, One Body*. When he released *The Eucharist: Sacrament of Unity*, George Carey, then Anglican archbishop of Canterbury, said that the Catholic Church is being "hurtful and unhelpful" in its policy regarding sharing the sacraments with members of the Church of England. Responding to the archbishop's statements, the Catholic archbishop of Westminster, Cardinal Cormac Murphy-O'Connor, said, "It is a sign of our maturing friendship that we can reflect on these disagreements

---

[120] OBOB, 114.

[121] Bhaldraithe, "Intercommunion," 79.

[122] OBOB, 97.

[123] Ibid., 6.

[124] Patsy McGarry, "Still 'Sham' if Catholics Take Eucharist Outside Own Church," *The Irish Times* (October 1, 1998) 16.

[125] David Quinn, "Treading Carefully in an Ecumenical Minefield," *Sunday Times* (October 4, 1998).

[126] "Canterbury Objects."

knowing that they are part of the process which will eventually lead to full communion."[127]

In a word, eucharistic doctrine—belief in the Real Presence, belief in eucharistic sacrifice and so forth—are not the decisive issues here. The validity (or invalidity) of Anglican ministry is. Catholic and Anglican authorities have already found near substantial agreement on eucharistic doctrine. The Anglican-Roman Catholic International Commissions have worked on this area for more than three decades. The fundamental disagreement now lies in the area of recognizing Anglican ordinations. Here, Catholic authorities are not likely to budge, given the openness of Anglican churches to the ordination of women.

For this reason, the Anglican bishops believe that OBOB maintains a double standard.[128] Christians from Eastern churches are admitted to Catholic sacraments with relatively few canonical restrictions, even though they are not in "full communion." Christians from Western, non-Catholic churches, however, are admitted to Catholic sacraments with relatively many canonical restrictions. They are put off because they are not in full communion.

Clearly, canon law should strive for consistent norms. Either "full communion" should be the standard for *everyone* or else Catholic authorities should abandon the principle that eucharistic communion is the result of "full communion." The 1983 Code of Canon Law is the source of this confusion. The 1983 Code of Canon Law was the first authoritative document to make "valid ordination" (as opposed to "full communion") the decisive factor in questions of eucharistic sharing.

Reporter for *The Irish Times* Patsy McGarry was highly critical of the document. She wrote that *One Bread, One Body* was a "restatement of the rather legalistic, traditional Vatican position." The bishops, in her view, "barely budge towards a more generous interpretation of the theology of the Eucharist." She noted, with some consternation, the irony of "Churchmen" [sic] telling politicians (Protestant and Catholic) "to get around a table" to resolve the Irish troubles, when they are willing to make, in her words, "comparatively little attempt to advance their own situation."[129]

Following McGarry's comparison to the political troubles of Ireland, could the issue of eucharistic sharing be considered under the category of an "ecclesial disarmament," a "laying down of ecclesial jurisdiction"

---

[127] Victoria Combe, "Carey Calls Catholics Hurtful over Sacraments," *The Daily Telegraph* (March 22, 2001) 9.

[128] House of Bishops of the Church of England, *The Eucharist: Sacrament of Unity* (London: Church House Publishing, 2001) 22.

[129] McGarry, 16.

for the sake of a greater unity? At the risk of pursuing the analogy too far, it would be terribly unhelpful and wrong to compare Catholic and Protestant authorities in Ireland to their militant "counterparts" among the IRA or the "Orange Men." The comparison is not fair, in the first place, because the Protestant and Catholic authorities are not killing people or bombing Irish neighborhoods.

However, is there not something bellicose and territorial in the Irish situation? The Irish situation—and elsewhere—shows that religious loyalties can be *twisted* by thoroughly secular, non-Christian goals and agendas. In Ireland at least, to what extent have the "troubles" been continued and compounded because of the failure of Christians to live in communion with one another? Eucharistic sharing alone will not offer an answer to the Irish troubles. In light of the political difficulties in Ireland—difficulties that could be ameliorated with a stronger commitment to ecumenism—why does *One Bread, One Body* sound so strangely timid?

Evaluating, Interpreting, and Applying the Present Norms

For the most part, when compared to pre-Vatican II understandings, *tremendous progress* has been made in post-Vatican II legislation on eucharistic sharing. Current norms consider the pastoral needs of baptized non-Catholics and seek to provide for those needs. They do not attempt to divorce the baptized non-Catholic from his or her ecclesial community as a prerequisite to eucharistic sharing. The norms recognize that Christians come to the Eucharist with a variety of faith commitments; and the legislation takes those faith commitments quite seriously. Finally, the current norms understand that they are "norms along the way." The norms are not presented as irreformable, unchangeable, or infallible. Instead, we must understand the current legislation for what it is: "the best we can muster for now." The legislation does not rule out the possibility of "communion by stages" at some future date.[130]

At the same time, post-Vatican II legislation on eucharistic sharing *does not correspond* to the decree on ecumenism. The postconciliar norms have been more concerned to limit and prohibit *communicatio in sacris*. The concern of the council, by contrast, was to permit *communicatio in sacris* within the limits of careful discernment.[131]

Broad and strict interpretations of the norms. Even if the current norms are "norms along the way," that does not relieve Catholic ministers and

[130] Wijlens, 364.
[131] Ibid., 364f.

authorities from the duty to apply those norms responsibly and carefully. Canon lawyer John Huels assists us with several important principles for the application of the norms. For example, Huels says that laws extending a "favor" may be interpreted broadly. Likewise, laws that restrict rights or impose burdens must be interpreted strictly. This principle is based on an analogy to God's mercy and justice.[132]

On the basis of these two principles, the portion of the law that permits eucharistic sharing in special cases may be interpreted broadly. Permission to receive the Eucharist, therefore, may be given with a generous amount of flexibility and graciousness, because, in doing so, we seek to reflect the kindness and mercy of God. When ministers decide to prohibit or restrict access to Holy Communion, their decision must be based on narrow grounds. The burdens on the potential communicant may not be excessive or unreasonable.[133]

From a slightly different perspective, Andrew Greeley says that Roman law allows exceptions based on the conscience and discretion of the one who is bound by it. In this important respect, Roman law differs from Anglo-Saxon common law, where discretion is permitted to the one who enforces the law.[134] In our reading of canon law, therefore, we must always understand that the "leniency of discretion" is given to the person who approaches the minister for Communion. Discretion is not the burden of the minister, who should presume the good intention and proper disposition of the recipient.

In the same article, Andrew Greeley claims that the ban on eucharistic sharing is "church law" and not "divine law."[135] Nonetheless, the ban does touch on serious issues in our understanding of the nature of the Church of Christ. In the coming chapters, we will need to examine those serious issues to form a balanced understanding of the problems outlined here.

Review. In this chapter we have reviewed the current norms for eucharistic sharing in the Catholic Church. These norms were presented in the context of a discussion of Christian ecumenism and contemporary Catholic understandings of the nature of "communion." Several important terms were defined and I presented an outline of the main arguments and themes for this book. In chapter 2, I examine several of the main arguments for caution in eucharistic sharing. Why is eucharistic sharing such a "risky business"?

---

[132] Canon 18. Huels, 92.
[133] Ibid.
[134] Greeley.
[135] Ibid.

The Current Norms: A Schematic Diagram

Baptism	baptized	baptized	baptized	nonbaptized
Membership	confirmed 1st communion	non-Catholic	non-Catholic	men and women
Type of Church	Catholic	from a Church *in* apostolic succession	from a Church *not* in apostolic succession	Christian or non-Christian
May or may not receive the Eucharist	Yes	Occasionally	In grave circumstance	Never

Questions for Reflection and Dialogue

Each chapter includes a section of "Questions for meditation and dialogue." These questions are offered as a way for readers to explore the ideas and themes of each chapter in light of their own experience and knowledge. The questions are also intended to assist readers who engage in small, informal dialogue groups.

1. What are the norms for eucharistic sharing in your own parish, congregation, or diocese? How do you experience eucharistic sharing in your own parish, congregation, or diocese?

2. Do you believe a more open eucharistic sharing would assist Christian ecumenism? Do you believe it would set back Christian ecumenism? Why or why not?

3. As noted above, in 1990 the editors of *U.S. Catholic* asked their readers about eucharistic sharing. Do you agree or disagree with the following two sentences? Why or why not?

   a. "Eucharistic ministers should refuse Communion to people they believe are in grave sin."

   b. "Most of the people who ate with Jesus would not have met the U.S. bishops' guidelines."

For Further Reading

Falardeau, Ernest. *A Holy and Living Sacrifice: The Eucharist in Christian Perspective.* Collegeville, Minn.: The Liturgical Press, 1996.

Larere, Philippe. *The Lord's Supper: Towards an Ecumenical Understanding of the Eucharist.* Trans. Patrick Madigan. Collegeville, Minn.: The Liturgical Press, 1993.

McPartlan, Paul. *Sacrament of Salvation: An Introduction to Eucharistic Ecclesiology.* Edinburgh: T&T Clark, 1995.

VanderWilt, Jeffrey. *A Church without Borders: The Eucharist and the Church in Ecumenical Perspective.* Collegeville, Minn.: The Liturgical Press, 1998.

Wijlens, Myriam. *Sharing the Eucharist: A Theological Evaluation of the Post Conciliar Legislation.* Lanham, Md.: University Press of America, 2000.

Chapter 2

Risks or Some Reasons for
Caution in Eucharistic Sharing

DUBLIN (December 7, 1997): The President of Ireland, Mrs. Mary McAleese, a Roman Catholic, received Holy Communion with her family during an Anglican liturgy in Dublin, Ireland.[1] In a public opinion poll taken following the media coverage, 78 percent of the Irish population approved of the President's action.

Normally, Roman Catholics are not permitted to receive sacraments from non-Catholic ministers. Among those who noted their disapproval was Catholic archbishop of Dublin, Cardinal Desmond Connell. Connell said that Catholics who receive Communion in a Protestant Church are engaging in a "sham" and a "deception."[2] The Prime Minister, Mr. Bertie Ahern, strongly defended the President and called it ironic that "the Church was condemning an act of reconciliation and bridge-building between the denominations." Another commentator, journalist Patsy McGarry, wryly observed, "These same politicians have been urged for years to get around a table and work out an agreement by the very churchmen who themselves have made comparatively little attempt to advance their own situation."[3]

Cardinal Connell's language leaves us wondering, what exactly was "shammy" and "deceptive" in McAleese's receiving Holy Communion at the Anglican worship service? A deceiver is someone who acts contrary to the trust of another person, that trust having been gained by the erection of a "sham" or a "false front." English speakers sometimes

---

[1] Martin Pulbrook, "Wresting Authority from the Hardliners," *The Irish Times* (December 30, 1997) 12.

[2] "The Bread of Strife?" *U.S. Catholic* (March 1998) 8.

[3] Patsy McGarry, "Still 'Sham' if Catholics Take Eucharist Outside Own Church," *The Irish Times* (Dublin) October 1, 1998, Opinion, 6.

call the deceit and the sham a "wolf in sheep's clothing." The wolf is the deceiver only when he pretends to be a sheep; his sheepish countenance, the sham.

Once President McAleese *returns* to the Roman Catholic Church, we begin to see problematic consequences from her actions. For when she returns after having received the Anglican Eucharist, her "irregular state" will become apparent. In her home church, McAleese could then be a deceiver if she disavowed or denied the earlier act. If she pretended as if the Catholic Church did not believe receiving the Anglican Communion was "irregular," that might be somewhat "shammy." Strictly speaking, the sham and the deception was not her reception of Communion in the non-Catholic context. The sham or deception could only take place if one had ever done so, *but later denied it.*

President McAleese's Communion did not erect a false front since she never expressed an intent to leave the Roman Catholic Church. She received Communion in full knowledge that it was "against the norms." If anything, her act takes on the appearance of an "act of civil disobedience," an action comparable to Rosa Parks refusing to sit at the back of a Birmingham bus. For its part, the Church of Ireland (Anglican) never thought that McAleese was deceptive. She came to their service of worship a Roman Catholic. She received Communion as a fellow baptized Christian according to their norms. She left, to their understanding, no less Roman Catholic than when she arrived. From the perspective of Anglican Church authorities, there was nothing deceptive or "shammy" in sharing the Eucharist with McAleese.

As reported in the media, in calling McAleese's Communion a "sham and a deception," Archbishop Connell referred to the act of receiving Communion itself. He did not mean to foreclose the later possibility of reconciliation between her and the Catholic Church. In the context, it is difficult to avoid the impression that, in condemning McAleese's *reception* of Communion, Connell was also criticizing the *Eucharist* of the Anglican Church as such. Let us give the cardinal the benefit of the doubt. I do not want to believe he meant to say that the Anglican *Eucharist* is "shammy" or deceptive.

When Church authorities say that an act is a "sham" or a "deception," we must note two things. First, the words "sham" and "deception" are not standard canonical or theological terms. Clear definitions for these terms do not exist in the standard vocabulary for discussion of the sacraments. Had Connell said that McAleese's Communion was "invalid" or "illicit," we would be much more certain as to his meaning. Second, to call something a "sham" or a "deception" is just another way to call it fraudulent and the work of a "con artist." The rhetoric is inflammatory. There is always an element of risk when Church authorities use noncanonical language to incite public condemnation of Catholics who worship with non-Catholic Christians according to their conscience.

Reasons for caution. Even if McAleese's reception of Communion was not a sham, it remains possible that other people do receive the Eucharist for less than honorable reasons on occasion. For this reason alone, caution in eucharistic sharing is a good idea. It is a good idea that Christians not receive the sacraments indiscriminately. For example, some people wonder, if people are mainly "of good will" and if the Eucharist is so "helpful to us," why is the Catholic Church so restrictive? Bishop Thomas J. Tobin, of Youngstown, Ohio, writes that the problem is twofold. First, some people are not "of good will." Second, the Eucharist is far more than merely "helpful."[4] From another perspective, a respondent to the 1990 *U.S. Catholic* magazine poll compared open Communion to building another tower of Babel. "It makes no more sense for everyone, regardless of religion, to receive Communion than for everyone regardless of language to build a tower. The result in each case is chaos and dilution . . ."[5]

In the best case, a more open eucharistic sharing should not foster more "chaos and dilution." On at least one point I *agree* with Bishop Tobin: Not all people are "of good will" and the Eucharist is much more than merely "helpful." The "hard sayings" of Jesus challenge us and sometimes shock us. Catholics and other Christians must listen to them with care. Nonetheless, one of the main reasons for this book is to present some arguments for a relaxation of the Catholic norms. In suggesting that access to Holy Communion should become more open, I accept the responsibility first to examine why access to Holy Communion should remain more closed. Consequently, this chapter explores some reasons for placing limits on the reception of Holy Communion. What really makes a more open eucharistic sharing such risky business?

Risks

In this chapter, I examine five "risks" inherent to eucharistic sharing. These risks include:

1. *Failing to agree in eucharistic doctrine.* Eucharistic sharing presumes that communicants hold a number of shared beliefs regarding the

---

[4] Thomas J. Tobin, "Receiving Holy Communion," *Priest* (June 1998) 29.
[5] Richard T. Szafransky, "Let Everyone Come to Communion," *U.S. Catholic* (June 1990) 19.

meaning, nature, and purpose of the Eucharist. May Catholics risk sharing Holy Communion with Christians who do not agree with us fully in their theology of the Eucharist?

2. *Failing to unite in the Church of Christ.* The Eucharist is a public event combined with interior moments. It is a tangible sign of the visible and invisible reality of the Church. Since the Eucharist manifests the Church of Christ, the question who is (and who is not) a member of the Church of Christ bears on who may receive Holy Communion.

3. *Failing to maintain the apostolic succession.* Catholic authorities are concerned to maintain and certify the validity of sacramental worship. Among other things, for a celebration of the Eucharist to be valid the minister must be a priest or bishop, validly ordained by a bishop in apostolic succession. In addition, the minister must be himself a bishop or a priest authorized by a bishop. He must have "faculties"—permission—to offer the liturgy in the local church.

4. *Expressing a "nonexistent" unity.* Some say that we risk celebrating a "nonexistent" unity if we share the Eucharist with baptized non-Catholics. In a word, the argument goes, we must "have unity" before we can "express it" in the sacrament of unity. Catholic theology understands that the Eucharist is both a means toward unity and a visible expression of unity insofar as it already exists here among us.

5. *Indiscriminate reception of Holy Communion.* Finally, there is the risk of "indiscriminate communion." St. Paul wrote that those who receive the Lord's Supper unworthily eat and drink to their own destruction. Church authorities understand they hold a solemn duty to protect men and women from receiving Holy Communion unworthily. Christian ministers therefore "fence the table." They provide policies and procedures to limit admission to Holy Communion. These measures range from simple forms of "gate-keeping" to excommunication.

Risk 1:
Failing to Agree in Eucharistic Doctrine

Eucharistic sharing presumes that communicants hold a number of shared beliefs regarding the meaning, nature, and purpose of the Eucharist. Should Catholics risk sharing Holy Communion with Christians who do not agree fully in the theology of the Eucharist? How much must Catholics agree in eucharistic doctrine in order to share Holy Communion?

In the late 1960s, during the earliest discussions of "intercommunion," some theologians—notably French theologians from the Group of Les Dombe—proposed that a shared belief in the Eucharist was sufficient to permit eucharistic sharing.[6] In the years that followed, Catholic theologians have moved away from these early and optimistic proposals. Now Catholic authorities appear to require that Christians must share belief in everything a Church professes in order to share the Eucharist.[7] From this view, only *full* agreement in faith and doctrine makes possible the sharing of Holy Communion. Agreement in doctrine, they say, is the premise of life in communion; communion is an "all or nothing" proposition.

Manifesting Catholic faith in the Eucharist. For a more moderate example of this dynamic, consider the first premise of *One Bread, One Body.* There, the English Catholic bishops maintain that it is right to expect anyone who receives Communion in the Catholic Church "to manifest Catholic faith in the Eucharist."[8] In their view, manifesting Catholic faith in the Eucharist not only encompasses agreement to doctrine about the Eucharist. It also includes several key elements of Catholic faith in the Church—beliefs about the ordination of clergy and about their communion with the Bishop of Rome.

The bishops especially note three characteristic elements of Catholic faith in the Eucharist:

1. *Real presence*: The belief in the real presence of Jesus in the Eucharist.

2. *Sacrifice*: An understanding of the Eucharist as a sacramental participation in the sacrificial death and resurrection of Jesus.

3. *Ecclesial ministry*: The understanding that the Eucharist is an act of the whole Church as it offers itself to God and receives itself from God *through the mediation of the clergy.*

---

[6] Jeffrey VanderWilt, *A Church without Borders: The Eucharist and the Church in Ecumenical Perspective* (Collegeville, Minn.: The Liturgical Press, 1998) 76f.

[7] Cf. Congregation for the Doctrine of the Faith and the Pontifical Commission for the Promotion of Christian Unity, "The Official Response of the Roman Catholic Church to ARCIC-I," December 1991; and Idem, "Official Response of the Roman Catholic Church to *Baptism, Eucharist, and Ministry*" in *Churches Respond to BEM: Official Response to the "Baptism, Eucharist, and Ministry" Text*, Vol. VI, Faith and Order Paper 144, ed. Max Thurian (Geneva: World Council of Churches, 1988) 20–25.

[8] OBOB, 9.

Ecumenical agreement. Quite importantly, on all three points, the official ecumenical dialogue groups of the Catholic Church have shown significant agreement among Catholic, Orthodox, and many Protestant churches. In summary form, the dialogue groups agree that the Eucharist is the highest expression of the unity of the Church. It is, they say, the summit and source of Christian life. They agree that the Eucharist offers the basis and the criterion for the renewal of Christian life. They agree that communion with Christ is offered and renewed with faithful men and women by way of baptism and the Lord's Supper. Most agree that the presence of Christ is given and received in Holy Communion, though admittedly few would agree to a doctrine of transubstantiation. Many also agree that the Eucharist is the ordinary means of participating in the once-and-for-all sacrifice of Christ from the cross. In the Eucharist, they agree, the Holy Spirit is the principle actor in the Church as a whole and in each member of the Church.[9] This, the fruit of over three decades of ecumenical dialogue, demonstrates that differences among Christians in their faith in the Eucharist have become less distinctive and less divisive.

The significance of these theological agreements should not be understated. In the last thirty years, Protestant and Catholic theologies of the Eucharist have surmounted tremendous differences. They have largely lost their post-Reformation polemical edge and significant and substantial areas of agreement have emerged. If, on the level of theology, significant and substantial convergence has occurred, on the level of popular faith—the "eucharistic folklore" that animates beliefs about the Eucharist in the typical Church—significant and substantial differences remain. Ecumenical progress in the coming decades will depend on a renewed commitment to convergence on the level of popular faith.

The "Modern Average Catholic Theology" of the Eucharist

Western Christians first manifested significant division on doctrine of the Eucharist centuries before the Reformation, during the eleventh and twelfth centuries. In particular, some medieval theologians had difficulty formulating a doctrine of the Real Presence. Scholars have shown how, in many respects, the views of Martin Luther and other reformers are related to these medieval controversies. Even the views of Thomas Aquinas were controversial in his day and were condemned

[9] Michael Welker, *What Happens in Holy Communion?*, trans. John F. Hoffmeyer (Grand Rapids, Mich. and Cambridge, England: Eerdmans Publishing Co. and SPCK, 2000) 4. See also VanderWilt, 70–108.

for a time after his death. In a word, disagreement on doctrine of the Eucharist hardened because of Reformation and post-Reformation arguments, not because the Reformers were introducing "new ideas."[10] As much as the Reformers were seen to attack belief in Real Presence, eucharistic sacrifice, or priestly ministry, so much more would the bishops at the Council of Trent rise to defend them. Just as the twentieth-century bishops of Great Britain and Ireland chose to focus on Real Presence, sacrifice, and priestly ministry in their teaching document—OBOB—so too did the sixteenth-century bishops at the Council of Trent focus on similar areas in their doctrine of the Eucharist.

Interpreting the Council of Trent. For this reason, eminent Catholic theologians like Edward J. Kilmartin and David N. Power have been concerned to offer careful and cautious interpretations of the decrees of Trent.[11] When theologians read the decrees of the Council of Trent, they recognize some essential rules for interpreting the acts of that council. First, it is impossible to treat the decrees of Trent as the "capstone" or "epitome" of Catholic doctrine. Second, the bishops at Trent under-stood that they were responding to a crisis. Third, the aim of the council was to rule out several problematic perspectives found in the writings of the Reformers or in the exaggerations of their more zealous followers.

Cardinal Joseph Ratzinger endorses the value of reading Trent with care from within its historical context. The decrees, he says, are partial and they are polemical. They do not presume to give a "treatise on the Eucharist" or a "summative statement" of Catholic doctrine. They speak only to the limits beyond which the Catholic should not proceed and they do not explore the "permissible center." At the end of the day, Ratzinger states, the bishops at Trent worked hard to protect the priestly quality of Christian ministry, its inherent relationship to the priestly and intercessory ministry of Jesus Christ. They rejected the view that ministry is a function of the "preaching office." They did not agree with

[10] See Gary Macy, *Treasures from the Storeroom: Medieval Religion and the Eucharist* (Collegeville, Minn.: The Liturgical Press, 1999).

[11] Cf. Edward J. Kilmartin, *Church, Eucharist, and Priesthood: A Theological Commentary on "The Mystery and Worship of the Most Holy Eucharist"* (New York & Ramsey, N.J.: Paulist Press, 1981); Idem, *The Eucharist in the West: History and Theology,* ed. Robert J. Daly (Collegeville, Minn.: The Liturgical Press, 1998); David N. Power, "*Koinonia, Oikoumene,* and Eucharist in Ecumenical Conversations," 116–26, in *Ecumenical Theology in Worship, Doctrine, and Life: Essays Presented to Geoffrey Wainwright on His Sixtieth Birthday,* ed. David S. Cunningham, Ralph del Colle, and Lucas Lamadrid (Oxford: Oxford University Press, 1999); and Idem, "Roman Catholic Theologies of Eucharistic Communion: A Contribution to Ecumenical Conversation," *Theological Studies* 57, no. 4 (1996) 587–611.

the Reformers that Christian ministry is principally a "ministry of the Word."[12] On many other important questions, the council was silent.

Before Vatican II, many seminaries and schools of theology tended to treat the decrees of Trent as "summative statements." They failed to teach the "permissible center" in eucharistic doctrine. This theological climate has formed the views of many in the present leadership of the Catholic Church. Kilmartin refers to these views as the "modern average Catholic theology of the Eucharist."

The "modern average Catholic theology of the Eucharist" is a simple handle for a very complex reality. The "reality" is that Catholic authorities do not agree 100 percent on the nature and reality of the Eucharist, but something closer to 90 or 95 percent. Within this range, there exist several central elements, the "normative views" of most Catholic authorities. Perhaps the modern average theology would emerge if one assigned a five-page essay on the Eucharist to a number of Catholics, then summarized and "averaged" their views. My guess: the results would read like Kilmartin's "modern average Catholic theology of the Eucharist."

Emphasis on the consecrating power of the priest. For example, Kilmartin demonstrated that the modern average theology combines the late medieval emphasis on the *consecrating power* of the priest to a *minimized* understanding of the communion of the faithful. The result is a short-circuited understanding of the relationship between Christ and the Church. The modern average view inserts the power and person of the priest between Christ and the Church. Kilmartin concludes, the conceptualization creates the "erroneous impression that the relation Christ-priest-Eucharist is normative . . . ." The Church enters into the transaction only because of its relation to the priest.[13]

Kilmartin finds this dynamic in some of the writings of Pope John Paul II. In his encyclical letter on the Eucharist, *Dominicae coenae*, the Pope conceives of the Eucharist as derived from the liturgy of the Last Supper. It is, he says, a continuation of the Last Supper in the Church. Consequently, the Pope does not appear to see the Eucharist as an act of the whole Church. Rather, the Pope presents it as an act of Christ, performed in and through the ministerial priesthood, on behalf of and for the sake of the Church.[14]

---

[12] Joseph Ratzinger, *Principles of Catholic Theology: Building Stones for a Fundamental Theology,* trans. Mary Frances McCarthy (San Francisco: Ignatius Press, 1987) 249.

[13] Kilmartin, *Eucharist in the West,* 365. See also Robert J. Daly, "Robert Bellarmine and Post-Tridentine Eucharistic Theology," *Theological Studies* 61, no. 2 (2000) 239–61.

[14] Kilmartin, *Eucharist in the West,* 366.

In many ways, the average theology looks much less like theology than it looks like "folklore." Certainly, these views are theological and they are based on Church teaching. In this "theological folklore," we usually do not find dangerous, false, or heretical ideas. Still, the folklore departs from the fullness of Catholic faith because it overemphasizes one or two elements of Christian faith at the expense of other, more central elements. This folklore is noteworthy more for what it fails to state than for what it says, less for what it emphasizes than for what it omits.

Eucharistic Consecration and the Real Presence of Christ

One of the central elements of Catholic faith is the doctrine of the real presence of Christ in the Eucharist. This doctrine provides a solid, central core to our liturgical life, to our theology, to our catechesis, to our cultural heritage, and to our folklore. On the other hand, Catholics have also acquired the erroneous impression that other Christians do not believe in the Real Presence. No less than the doctrine of the Real Presence, this negative impression of non-Catholic Christians adds an additional element of complexity to our theological folklore, to our sense of Catholic identity. It creates in us a "polemical edge," a concept within a group's self-definition that sharply distinguishes insiders from outsiders. In this case the polemical edge works something like this: Because we believe in Real Presence, they must not. Belief in Real Presence makes us distinctively Catholic. This is a highly problematic foundation for faith, for once it is discovered that belief in the Real Presence is not distinctively Catholic, what remains to distinguish us from them?

The doctrine of the Real Presence is not the problem. Many Catholics speak as though non-Catholic Christians do not believe in the real presence of Christ in the Eucharist.[15] In part, they believe this because their non-Catholic friends have told them so. At least in the United States, many non-Catholics think they are not supposed to believe in the Real Presence. "That's only for Catholics to believe," some of my Protestant students say. Thus Protestant faith is wounded by these polemical dynamics no less than Catholic faith. In addition, the media perpetuate these misunderstandings of eucharistic doctrine. For example, through

---

[15] Harry McSorley, "Eucharistic Sharing: A New State of the Question for Roman Catholics," *The Ecumenical Review* 22 (1970) 113. Whenever I offer the undergraduate course in liturgy, I poll my students on their understanding of the doctrine of Real Presence. Many students dismiss the Eucharist as merely a symbol because they have the mistaken impression that symbols are not real and cannot offer real relationships to another person.

my research for this book, I found some journalists holding forth that the real presence of Christ in the eucharistic elements remains the sole, decisive issue for eucharistic sharing.[16] Therefore, many Christians believe that the main obstacle to a more open eucharistic sharing is the doctrine of the Real Presence. This belief is mistaken. It is long overdue for correction. In point of fact, eucharistic sharing does not hinge on the doctrine of Real Presence in most cases.[17]

For instance, many Protestants do believe in the real presence of Christ in the Lord's Supper. Martin Luther was an adamant defender of faith in Christ's promise to be present "in, with, and under" the forms of bread and wine. Second-generation Reformer John Calvin was no less insistent than Luther. He understood that Christ is present to us through the Lord's Supper because the Holy Spirit draws us into a nearly ecstatic union with the Lord. The Spirit, he said, carries us "on high to the place where Christ dwells."

How Christ becomes present. Catholics and non-Catholics differ on the doctrine of real presence in their understanding of how Christ becomes present, of how best to describe the reality of presence. Like most Eastern Christians, Protestants generally reject the terminology of "transubstantiation." They maintain we should not presume to know how Christ becomes present to us in the Eucharist. They say our principal duty is to believe in Christ's promise to be present to us in the breaking of the bread. We should trust in the power of the Holy Spirit to establish Christ's presence among us.

The purpose for Real Presence. Similarly, Catholics and other Christians differ in their beliefs on what Christ wants us to do with his presence in the Eucharist. In general, Catholics emphasize the act of consecration. Catholic authorities continue to stress the high value and appropriateness of worshiping the Lord who comes among us in the Eucharist. In contrast, other Christians emphasize the act of communion. They stress the purpose for the presence of Christ. He comes among us in order to be received and shared in Holy Communion. Protestant dialogue partners have asked Catholics to consider the risk of idolatry in popular eucharistic devotions. In these contrasts, room remains for dialogue and convergence.

Unlike modern Christians, some ancient Christian authorities did not distinguish consecration and Communion so sharply. For example,

---

[16] Paul Johnson, "Why Tony Blair is Right to Take Communion in Our Churches," *The Spectator* London (October 10, 1998) 27. Billy FitzGerald, "Tentative Advance in the Sharing of Communion," *The Irish Times* (April 21, 1998) 14.

[17] Thomas Ryan, "Eucharistic Sharing: Why the Churches Act Differently," *Ecumenism* 110 (1993) 29.

in all the scriptural accounts of the Last Supper, the words of the Lord
—the consecration—take place after the eating and the drinking, not
before it (Mark 14, Matt 26, Luke 22, and 1 Cor 11). In each text, Jesus
provides a new interpretation for the Passover meal and the special
foods of the meal only after the disciples had eaten them. As with so
many other signs of Jesus' ministry and message, Jesus interpreted his
actions for his followers only after he had performed the deed. Simply
put, until the disciples had eaten the meal with Jesus, they could not
have understood its new meaning.[18] This is all the more ironic when we
expect Christians today, unlike Jesus' own disciples, to comprehend
the meaning of the Eucharist before they receive it.

In comparison to the more ancient understandings, the modern average theology downplays the reception of the Eucharist in Holy Communion. Kilmartin points out that the modern average Catholic
theology limits the participation of the Christian assembly in the sacrifice of Christ to the moment of consecration. The ritual of Holy Communion, he notes, is not considered an essential part of the eucharistic
sacrifice. It is "integral," but not "essential."[19] "The unity of the Church
as a gathered body," as one theologian remarks, "seems diminished"
when the reception of Holy Communion in the midst of Christian
community is made nonessential to the Eucharist because the decisive
event was thought to be the consecration.[20]

A more balanced approach. A more balanced appreciation for the purpose of the consecration, its aims and ends, has gone missing in the
modern average view. Why does Christ become present? Christ becomes present not merely to be here, not only to assist our participation
in the Cross. Christ becomes present to share communion with us and
to establish communion among us.

The mystery of presence. In the Eucharist and in the Church, Jesus offers
himself to us as a gift with an "enduring presence."[21] Faithful Christians are impelled to receive this gift in faith. They do not simply adore
the gift from a distance. They also seek to enter into it, to receive it with
gratitude, and to be transformed by it. Real Presence, we should recall,
is not a theological problem. It is a *mystery.*[22] *Real* Presence is something
that will always evade the grasp of theological and intellectual reflections

---

[18] Welker, 52.
[19] Kilmartin, *Eucharist in the West,* 365.
[20] Welker, 31.
[21] Walter Kasper, "Unity and Multiplicity of Aspects in the Eucharist," *Communio*
12 (1985) 138.
[22] Norman Young, "Sacrament, Sign, and Unity: An Australian Reflection," in
Ecumenical Theology in Worship, ed. Cunningham et al., 103.

upon it. After all, if we could figure it all out, solve the problem, it would barely amount to the presence of a person, the presence of Christ. It would simply amount to a "mental datum," a mere "fact." Data do not change our hearts; but relationships do.

Eucharistic Sacrifice as the Self-Offering of the Church

The second key focus in the modern average theology of the Eucharist is on the doctrine of the eucharistic sacrifice. Catholics often refer to this doctrine as the sacrifice of the Mass. On this point, there has also been a tremendous ecumenical convergence. The problem, as traditionally formulated, results from the need to connect the paschal sacrifice of Jesus Christ from the cross to the eucharistic sacrifice of the Church from the altar. In other words, how does the Eucharist enable Christians from every time and place to participate in the paschal sacrifice of Jesus Christ? How are the altar and the cross intrinsically linked?

For their part, Protestants stress the sole sufficiency of the paschal sacrifice of Jesus Christ from the cross. Protestant theologians point to the New Testament phrase, "once and for all" *(ephapax)* when they say that Christ put an end to all sacrifice. For our part, Catholics stress the possibility of receiving a share in Christ's paschal sacrifice by way of the Eucharist. The Eucharist, we say, is an action of the whole Church— Christ and his entire Mystical Body. Therefore, when we say that the Eucharist is a sacrifice, we are not saying that it is another sacrifice. We are saying that it is continuous with the sacrifice from the cross. In a word, the sacrifice from the cross and the sacrifice of the Mass are the same sacrifice offered to God by the same person (Christ) for the same reason but beneath different appearances.

Kilmartin helpfully summarizes a Catholic doctrine of eucharistic sacrifice. The Eucharist, he says, is a communication of the sacrifice of Christ to the Christian community. It has as its goal to draw us into Christ's total gift of self to the Father. It has as its consummation the Father's loving acceptance of that gift.[23] In the Eucharist, Christ and the Church perform the gift of self-offering in concert. The Church does not add to the self-offering of Christ. Rather, because of the gift of the Holy Spirit, the Church is added in to Christ's self-offering.[24] In other words, as much as later human actions are added in to Christ's self-offering during each eucharistic liturgy, these later acts of worship are not intrinsically efficacious. Their power to save derives entirely from the sacrificial and saving work of Christ.

[23] Kilmartin, *Eucharist and Priesthood*, 11.
[24] Ibid., 10.

Admitting What We Cannot Know:
Negative Theology (Apophaticism) and the Eucharist

One of the more troubling characteristics of the modern average Catholic theology on the Eucharist is its swaggering self-confidence. Certainly, we think, the doctrine on the Eucharist has no room for development. Surely, all that is essential to say about the Eucharist has already been written in Church documents and catechisms. Our sense of certitude allows less leeway for convergence in ecumenical dialogue. The very richness of our eucharistic doctrine ironically becomes an ecumenical liability. Several contemporary theologians have pointed out ways to say less about the Eucharist. They urge us to be more cautious and less swaggeringly self-confident in speaking about the sacraments.

Theologians commonly distinguish between positive and negative theologies. Positive *(catabatic)* theologies establish positive comparisons and analogies between earthly and heavenly realities. Statements like "God is Father; God is Son; God is Holy Spirit" both describe and conceal the complex relationship between what it means to be "God" and what it means to be a "father," a "son," or a "spirit." When theologians need to recall and explore the disconnect between the earthly and the heavenly realities they use negative *(apophatic)* theologies. They distinguish sharply between who God is from what we can know about God. From the view of apophatic theology, to say that "God is not a father; God is not a son; and God is not a spirit" is not heretical. The words focus our attention on the fact that, though God is Father, God is not any kind of earthly father and God's fatherliness is quite distinct from that of a biological father.

Theologies of the Eucharist also benefit from the tension between the positive *(catabatic)* and the negative *(apophatic)* poles of theology. When they focus on the negative *(apophatic)* dimension of the Eucharist, theologians do not mean to be disrespectful to the reality of the Eucharist. They do not mean to deny fundamental realities about the Eucharist. *Apophatic* theology seeks rather to explore the areas of unlikeness. They think of all the ways that our words about the sacrament are broken, because they do not adequately convey the divine reality in its fullness. When theologians speak *apophatically,* they are seeking to protect and serve the transcendence and awesomeness of God.

For example, in a quite profound statement, eminent Catholic theologian Eamon Duffy reminds us that even within the "full communion" of the Catholic Church there are limitations. "Every true Eucharistic rite," he writes, "must enact within itself both the simultaneous possibility and impossibility of access to the heart of God . . ." In Duffy's view, Holy Communion is a symbol of both distance and closeness to the divine realities it signifies.[25] If we were truly close to those realities, we would not need the Eucharist, for we could literally embrace the Lord with corporeal arms, instead of "arms of faith." If we were too distant from those realities, all the ages of human prayer and sacrifice would not be sufficient, for our rites would only be little towers of Babel, reaching up to a far-off divinity.

In other words, the Eucharist is always a "failed communication."[26] Jesus' communion with us is always a partial communion. We cannot plumb the depths of the reality of eucharistic Communion. In the Eucharist, if Christ is present to us as an act of radical self-communication, then the Eucharist is also a painful reminder of Christ's absence. It reminds us of our distance from the one who has risen and ascended into God's glory. As one author put it, "For until we too are raised . . . communication with Jesus can only fail of ultimacy."[27]

This idea of a failure of ultimacy is particularly instructive in the ecumenical context. The failure of ultimacy in the Eucharist is a result of human limitations; it is not a limitation on God. God is always truly present to us through the Eucharist. The problem is that we are not always truly present to God. There are no barriers between the Lord and his desire to embrace us in Holy Communion. Rather, our own inability to embrace the Lord in full communion is the premise for Christ's opening his arms to receive us. Christ embraces us so that we may embrace God and one another.

Why Failing to Agree on the Doctrine of the Eucharist Is a Risk

Failing to agree in full on the doctrine of the Eucharist should not be seen as a particularly significant barrier to eucharistic sharing. Human beings have a remarkable ability to form community in the context of significant disagreements. If that were not true, we could not have institutions like the United Nations, labor unions, political parties, charitable organizations, and so forth. The ability to get along, to agree to disagree, is a significant gift that God has given the human species.

In the context of the Eucharist, it is possible to share the Lord's Table with many men and women from many times and places. The Church has always comprised a variety of perspectives on the meaning and

---

[25] Eamon Duffy, "Afterword," in *Catholicism and Catholicity: Eucharistic Communities in Historical and Contemporary Perspectives*, ed. Sarah Beckwith (Oxford: Blackwell Publishers, 1999) 153.

[26] Denys Turner, "The Darkness of God and the Light of Christ: Negative Theology and Eucharistic Presence," in *Catholicism and Catholicity*, 41.

[27] Ibid., 45.

purpose for the Eucharist. Within the Catholic Church, we already live in communion with men and women from different times and places and some of them held strangely different ideas about the Eucharist. The significant risk is not that Christians would hold different ideas about Real Presence or sacrifice. Our ideas about the Eucharist are beneficial mainly because they signify a commitment to behave according to our words. The greater risk is that Christians would fail to be present to Christ and to one another in the Eucharist. The greater risk is that Christians would fail to enter into the act of Christ's self-giving.

The doctrine of presence is not the issue; living in the presence of Christ is the issue. The Christian community is hurt when Christians fail to discern the presence of Christ. The Church is wounded when Christians act as if Christ were nowhere near, as if Christ were not present in their neighbor. The doctrine of sacrifice is not the issue; living in the sacrifice of Christ is the issue. The Church is wounded when Christians refuse to carry the Cross for others, when they fail to be Good Samaritans, when they fail to be Christ for one another.

As one of my teachers, Fr. Robert Taft of the Oriental Pontifical Institute, is fond of saying, "Words are words; and things are things." Christians will always work hard to find words more adequate to the reality of the Eucharist. The risk is not that our words would disagree. The risk is that the consequences of our words would cause us to miss the presence of Christ among us. The risk is that communicants would fail to enter Christ's sacrificial love. We would have failed to carry the cross.

Risk 2:
Failing to Unite in the Church of Christ

One of the great theological advancements of the past century was to recover the ancient Christian understanding of the relationship between the Church and the Eucharist. In seeking to understand the Eucharist, we come also to understand the Church; and vice versa. The Eucharist is the preeminent "sacrament of the Church."[28] The Body of Christ is the foundation of the Church and of the Eucharist.[29] When we discuss the problem of admission to Holy Communion, we are not only describing a problem of whom to invite up to the altar. We are really

[28] Philippe Larere, *The Lord's Supper: Towards an Ecumenical Understanding of the Eucharist*, trans. Patrick Madigan (Collegeville, Minn.: The Liturgical Press, 1993) 76.

[29] Secretariat for the Promotion of Christian Unity, On Admitting Other Christians to Eucharistic Communion in the Catholic Church *(In Quibus Rerum Circumstantiis)*, sec. 2, *Acta Apostolicae Sedis* 64 (1972) 518–25.

addressing the question of who belongs to us—whom have Christ and the Holy Spirit given us to love as sisters and brothers? Therefore, the doctrine of the Church—what theologians call ecclesiology—bears weightily on the question of eucharistic sharing.[30]

The "Modern Average Catholic Ecclesiology"

Just as we identified and moved beyond the modern average Catholic theology of the Eucharist, in this section, I will identify and move beyond the modern average Catholic theology of the Church. The modern average ecclesiology derives, again, from reading the decrees of Trent as though they represented the fullness of Catholic doctrine. It strongly emphasizes the characteristics of the Catholic Church that set it apart from other Christian churches. For the most part, the modern average view fails to explore the permissible center of Catholic ecclesiology.

The Church is sociological and theological. Jesuit priest and theologian Cardinal Avery Dulles reminds us that the Church has inward and outward features. Outwardly, the Church is sociological. Sociologists, demographers, economists, historians, or political scientists may study it empirically. Inwardly, the Church is theological. Theologians study the Church by way of analogies, metaphors, and images drawn from revelation, Scripture, mystical experience, liturgy, and sacraments.[31] Theologically, we name the Church "bride of Christ," "heavenly City," the "new Jerusalem," "people of God," "communion of saints," or "Body of Christ." Sociologically, we name the Church a "community," a "culture of cultures," an "institution," or a "hierarchy." Together, the sociological and the theological terms help us understand the Church.

As I see it, the "modern average ecclesiology" has great difficulty maintaining and balancing the tension between the Church as a sociological institution and as a theological reality. For example, Protestants tend to view the Church as something that is invisible and known to God alone. They stress that the Church consists of the elect, all whom God has chosen for salvation.[32] Since none can be entirely certain that they number among the elect, they can only hope—or doubt—that they number among the saints of God. By contrast, Catholics tend to stress the Church as something that is visible and knowable. We focus on the Church that can be touched, witnessed, seen, and heard. As Cardinal Robert Bellarmine once wrote, "The Church is as palpable as the Republic of Venice."

---

[30] Ryan, 29.
[31] Avery Dulles, "The Ecclesial Dimension of Faith," *Communio* 22 (1995) 423.
[32] Larere, 76.

As a result, Catholic ecclesiology emphasizes some of the visible marks of the Church: communion with Rome, apostolic succession in ministry, and observing valid forms of sacramental worship. Protestant ecclesiology emphasizes some of the invisible marks of the Church: sanctity of life, evangelical ministry, and radical dependence on God's grace. Protestants, therefore, tend to stress invisible membership. Genuine membership in the Church of Christ remains hidden, even from the members. God reveals one's status in the Church only at the last judgment. Catholics, on the other hand, have stressed visible membership. Recall Bellarmine's bonds of membership; faith, ministry, and obedience, each of the three bonds can be seen. You can look at people and know whether or not they are members. While Bellarmine knew that membership can be lost and regained during the course of one's life, an aura of confidence and certainty surrounds his system that is much less evident in the Protestant ethos.

Apophatic ecclesiology. The challenge for Catholics, as for Protestants, is to reappraise our use of metaphors to describe the Church. We all use political metaphors, like "kingdom of God." We all use organic or biological metaphors like "the Body of Christ." We all draw sociocultural analogies when we speak of the "people of God."[33] Metaphors help Christians focus on important characteristics of our Church as a worldwide and centuries-long community of faith. They give us concrete means to explore fundamental ideas about what it means to live together in faith.

However, metaphors for the Church become problematic when we use them too narrowly, too broadly, or when we forget their limitations. When we confuse the characteristics of earthly kings and kingdoms with God's dominion, we start getting into trouble. Imagine the "people of God" as a group of wandering vagabonds, and we forget how to live cohesively and in peace. Stress too much that the "Body of Christ" is mystical and we forget that the Church is institutional and palpable. In ecclesiology, just as in eucharistic theology, there remains a need for *apophatic* theology.

A Church of Human and Institutional Limitations

The Church of Christ is institutional and human and suffers from all the inherent limitations of our humanity. The churches must maintain a social structure. Without a sense of self-definition, they would dissolve into social chaos. Openness to every type of belief is not an option for a

---

[33] Carl E. Braaten, *Mother Church: Ecclesiology and Ecumenism* (Minneapolis: Fortress Press, 1998) 28.

viable human community.[34] Limitations in the expression of faith are both helpful and necessary for the survival of Christian community.

Until recently, however, a strong contrasting theme in Protestant theology has been to restrain the sociopolitical dimensions of the Church. For example, German evangelical Emil Brunner saw "institutionalism" as, at best, a "stifling necessity" in the life of the Church. He preferred to see the Church as a graced community living together in intensely personal, "I–Thou" relationships.[35] What accounts for the Protestant instinct to limit the institutional life of their churches?

Understanding the Reformation. The leaders of the Protestant Reformation saw the government of the Catholic Church as the subject of a "hostile takeover" by men who were hardly interested in the faithful preaching of the Gospel of Christ. It is a sad fact of history that many popes and bishops of the late Middle Ages and Renaissance were captivated by their pursuit of political power, wealth, and prestige. The Reformers thought they were setting up church governments in exile. They thought their churches would be provisional and interim bodies until such time as the entire Church could be reformed.

In the view of Lutheran theologian, Carl Braaten, the Reformation should be seen as a call to catholicity. The Reformers resisted the intensifying Romanization of the Western Church.[36] In the centuries since the Protestant Reformation, he says, many Protestants have become acclimatized to the status quo. The division of Western Christianity has hardened. The governments in exile were content to go their own way. They had come to expect reunion with other Christians (Protestant, Roman, or Orthodox) no more than North Americans expect to reunite with England, France, or Spain.[37]

Long before Vatican II, the eminent French Dominican, Cardinal Yves Congar, helpfully reframed Catholic conceptions of the Protestant Reformation. In Congar's view, Martin Luther addressed questions that the Church of his day was ill-prepared to answer. Luther's excommunication was not a judicious or prudent response to his questions and concerns. The Council of Trent did not answer Luther's objections directly. Rather, the council responded only to the most extreme views of a handful of Protestant theologians. Some of them, Congar states, were purely "straw men." Since the Council of Trent, Fr. Congar concludes,

[34] James M. Gustafson, *Treasure in Earthen Vessels: The Church as a Human Community* (Chicago: University of Chicago Press, 1961) 62f.

[35] Ibid., 29.

[36] Braaten, 12.

[37] Ibid., 26.

anti-Protestant polemic diminishes the Catholic Church. We continue to misunderstand Protestant concerns.[38]

If one challenge for Catholics is to listen and respond to Protestant concerns, a challenge for Protestants may be to recover the sense of provisionality in their churches. In consumer marketing, manufacturers occasionally build flaws into the design of their products. They call this planned obsolescence. Parts of the automobile are designed to break down after a certain number of miles. In Braaten's view, Protestantism has its own kind of planned obsolescence. As an institutionalized protest movement, he says, Protestantism exists to become obsolete. It should regard itself primarily as an institutionalized call to reform issued to other members of the Christian community.[39]

The concern for Catholics should be to recognize how our present situation, hardened since the Council of Trent, is also provisional and incomplete. If, as Cardinal Ratzinger states, the division of Christianity wounds the Catholic Church, then we should not be overly patient with our woundedness. Our incompleteness needs, also, to be healed. We must come to recognize our need for non-Catholic Christians and to rejoice in how they complete us.

Recognizing an abundance of gifts. The modern average Catholic ecclesiology has great difficulty recognizing the abundance of gifts that exist outside of the Catholic Church. For example, the 1917 Code of Canon Law and the ecumenism of return exhibited an all-or-nothing ecclesiology. Either a Church is visibly one or it has no part in the Church of Christ. Either you are a member of the Catholic Church or you have no part in the Church of Christ. Outside of the visible boundaries of the Catholic Church, one should find only error and confusion.

During the last twenty years, some statements on eucharistic sharing from Catholic authorities still derive from that all-or-nothing perspective. Parties to these statements speak about baptized non-Catholics as though they were members of other religions. They disproportionately emphasize juridical union over serious pastoral need. These authorities lament ambiguity. They claim that baptized non-Catholics contradict their faith when they seek to receive Holy Communion from Catholic ministers.

In contrast, Vatican II offers a more balanced perspective. The council recognized many of the precious gifts that God has given non-Catholic Christians and their churches. *Unitatis redintegratio* names some of these "saving elements" in the non-Catholic churches: the Word of

---

[38] Cf. Ibid., 15.
[39] Ibid., 25.

God, genuine holiness, sanctity of life, heroic witness to faith, and so forth.[40] The observation of the English Catholic bishops: the holiness, love, and zeal of non-Catholics often put the Catholic Christian "to shame."[41] Therefore, when Vatican II claims that the Catholic Church is uniquely gifted with the fullness of the means of salvation, this does not mean that Catholics and their ministers are the only perfect Christians. It means that Catholics may not refuse to recognize and rejoice in the gifts of non-Catholics or their communities.[42]

Unitatis redintegratio does not say why these saving elements of the Church exist outside the unity of the Catholic Church. If we were holding on to a pessimistic view, we might see it as a tragic scattering of the Body of Christ, an unfortunate "scattering of pearls." From a more optimistic view, however, Catholics may see it as part of the ecstatic outpouring of God's grace. God and the gifts of God overflow the limits of our institutional structures.

But are they churches? Even if the non-Catholic communities have saving elements, may we call them churches? A recent document from the Congregation for the Doctrine of the Faith, *Dominus Iesus*, claims that Vatican II does not allow Catholics to call non-Catholic communities of baptized Christians "churches." In the absence of a valid apostolic succession, these communities are not really churches. They are more or less impaired or defective "ecclesial communities."[43] While the Eastern churches maintain the apostolic succession, as a whole they do not form a "Church" apart from or alongside the Catholic Church, because they are not in union with Rome. *Dominus Iesus* claims that the non-Catholic communities derive their efficacy from the "very fullness of grace and truth entrusted to . . . the Catholic Church."[44]

These new claims are unusually troublesome. Vatican II often spoke of "churches or ecclesial communities." In each reference, however, the word "or" may not be read as the exclusive or—one or the other, but not both. The word "or" must be read inclusively. *Unitatis redintegratio* did not declare that ecclesial communities may not be called churches. When the council chose to speak of "ecclesial communities," the bishops did not decide the ecclesial status of any one particular church.[45]

---

[40] Myriam Wijlens, *Sharing the Eucharist: A Theological Evaluation of the Post Conciliar Legislation* (Lanham, Md.: University Press of America, 2000) 137.
[41] OBOB, 21.
[42] Ibid.
[43] Congregation for the Doctrine of the Faith, On the Unicity and Salvific Universality of Jesus Christ and the Church *(Dominus Iesus)* (June 16, 2000) 17.
[44] DI 16, cf. UR 3.
[45] UR 3.

The council used this nomenclature to indicate their openness to the possibility that these other communities are genuine parts of the Church of Christ. The council's forbearance indicates doubt, not certainty; openness, not conclusion.

Even if Vatican II allows Catholics to understand that some ecclesial communities are not churches in the strict sense, it does not allow us to deny their genuine ecclesial character. Instead, *Dominus Iesus* attempts to change the plain meaning of the conciliar texts. The new document now understands the term "ecclesial community" as a judgment against the possibility that these other communities are churches. The bishops of the Congregation have redefined what was once a term of inclusion into a term of division.

The Church of Christ subsists in the Catholic Church. With a key phrase in the Constitution on the Church, *Lumen gentium*, Vatican II concluded that the Church of Christ is found in the Catholic Church (it *subsists* there), but that the Catholic Church is not the exclusive manifestation of the Church.[46] Earlier drafts of *Lumen gentium* stated that the Church of Christ exists in the Catholic Church, but the council held that was too restrictive a definition. In changing to "subsists in" the council affirms that elements of the Church do, in fact, exist in other Christian communities.[47] The decree on ecumenism, *Unitatis redintegratio*, repeats the doctrine of the subsistence of the Church of Christ in the Catholic Church. In his encyclical on Christian unity, *Ut unum sint*, Pope John Paul II also reaffirms the doctrine when he states,

> It is not that beyond the boundaries of the Catholic community there is an ecclesial vacuum. Many elements of great value *(eximia)*, which in the Catholic Church are part of the fullness of the means of salvation and of the gifts of grace which make up the Church, are also found in the other Christian Communities.[48]

When *Lumen gentium* says that the Church of Christ subsists in the Catholic Church, the council understood that the Church of Christ is present (subsisting) in the Catholic Church. Subsistence refers to a transcendent reality existing or expressing itself in the form of a finite thing. The council did not say that the Catholic Church is the exclusive, finite expression of the Church of Christ.[49]

[46] LG 15. Wijlens, 191, 202f.
[47] Ernest R. Falardeau, "Sharing the Eucharist and Christian Unity," *Ecumenical Trends* 23 (1994) 10.
[48] UR 3 and UUS 13.
[49] Wijlens, 202f.

The 1993 directory on ecumenism also offers an affirmative, but not exclusionary definition of *Lumen gentium*'s "subsists in." The definition offered by the Pontifical Council for the Promotion of Christian Unity affirms Catholic self-understanding as the place within which the Church of Christ subsists, but does not preclude the self-definition of other Christian communities. When we say that the Church of Christ subsists in the Catholic Church, we are saying that "the entirety of revealed truth, of sacraments, and of ministry that Christ gave for the building up of his Church and the carrying out of its mission is found" within and among us.[50]

One Bread, One Body offers a helpful and moderate understanding of the doctrine of subsistence. In the view of the bishops of the UK and Ireland, to say the Church of Christ "subsists in" the Catholic Church means four things. One, the fullness of the means of salvation is found in the Catholic Church. Two, the "entirety of revealed truth" is found there. Three, the sacraments of Christ are found there. Four, so also one finds the hierarchical and apostolic ministry of the Church of Christ in the Catholic Church.[51]

In *The Eucharist: Sacrament of Unity* (2001), the Anglican bishops of England point to the Roman Catholic discussion of the phrase "subsist in." With alarm they express concern for the effort of some Vatican authorities to narrow the Catholic understanding of this important phrase from *Lumen gentium*.[52]

Dominus Iesus thus stands nearly alone in interpreting the doctrine of subsistence so narrowly. The Congregation for the Doctrine of the Faith (CDF) says that *Lumen gentium* meant to say that the Church of Christ "subsists only in" *(solummodo)* the Catholic Church.[53] The CDF began this narrowing trend with its 1998 *Notification on Church: Charism and Power* by Leonardo Boff.[54] Despite its limitations and novelty, *Dominus Iesus* does offer some helpful new perspectives on this doctrine.

Dominus Iesus rightly claims that the Vatican II teaching on subsistence balances two truths. On the one hand, Catholics believe that the Church of Christ fully exists—without defect—in the worldwide body of local churches in communion with Rome. On the other hand, Catholics acknowledge that "elements of sanctification and truth" exist—

---

[50] Pontifical Council for Promoting Christian Unity, *Directory for the Application of Principles and Norms on Ecumenism* (March 25, 1993) 17.

[51] OBOB, 20.

[52] House of Bishops of the Church of England, *The Eucharist: Sacrament of Unity* (London: Church House Publishing, 2001) 7.

[53] DI 16. They use the word "solummodo."

[54] DI n. 56. Cf. AAS 77 (1998) 756–62.

abundantly—outside the Catholic Church. In a sense, the Church of Christ has such a surplus of being that the worldwide communion of churches with Rome cannot fully contain it, even when they are as comprehensive as they seek to be. The grace with which God is saving the world always overflows the boundaries of any one Church. It is this same overflow that allows the local churches to form the communion of a universal Church. It is this same overflow that allows for any meaningful discussion of ecumenism and Christian unity.

A simple metaphor can help us think about the abundance and overflow of the Church of Christ. Sometimes at weddings, the wine steward will build a huge pyramid of champagne flutes. Once the champagne is uncorked, servers will pour whole bottles of champagne into the topmost glass. The champagne bubbles up and pours down the sides of the pyramid. Every glass is filled and overflowing into more glasses beneath it. The lowest tier of champagne glasses stand up to their hips in champagne.

This metaphor helps me envision the subsistence of the Church of God. The pyramid of champagne flutes is like the communion of local churches that comprise the Catholic Church. The champagne represents the infinite grace and mercy of God. Just as no single champagne glass can hold all the champagne, no single Church can contain all the grace and mercy of God. Just as the entire pyramid of champagne glasses cannot hold all the champagne, no one communion of local churches on earth—even the Catholic Church—can contain all that grace.

What should we think about the glasses that were not an original part of the pyramid? Do they contain any of the precious champagne? Would a gracious host deny a toast to anyone at the wedding banquet because his or her glass was not filled during the original, festive, flourish of pouring? Like the champagne in our analogy, God's grace flows in, through, and out of us. God graciously extends grace into areas of life that are far beyond our sphere of influence. This is simply to acknowledge the intrinsic character of grace. It may never be contained.

An incarnational Church. One of the main theological problems with the doctrine of subsistence is that the term "subsistence" refers primarily to God. When we say that the Church of Christ subsists among us, we are referring to God incarnate in human community. Since the nineteenth century, many eminent Catholic theologians have said the Church is a "continuation of Christ."[55] They say it is the sacramental

[55] Johann Auer, *A General Doctrine of the Sacraments and the Mystery of the Eucharist,* ed. Johann Auer and Joseph Ratzinger, trans. Erasmo Leiva-Merikakis, 9 vols., vol. 6, *Dogmatic Theology* (Washington, D.C.: The Catholic University of America Press, 1995) 344.

prolongation of the Incarnation.[56] Saying this they mean that the Church of Christ represents the faithful subsistence of God among us from the Pentecost to the end of time. Because there is only one God, there should be only one subsistence. However, since human community is finite, it could never comprise the fullness of God's universality. Stress too strongly the idea that there is only one subsistence of God among us, and the human community is doomed to live in a permanent state of warfare (those who live with God against those who do not). Stress too weakly the doctrine of one subsistence, and the Christian community is doomed to live in a state of impotent dissolution.[57]

God Transcends Institutional Limitations: The Church Is a Communion

The Church is first and foremost a sacramental reality. It is the communion of Christ's body within the world. In a secondary sense, the Church is an institutional reality. The Church exists as a counter-cultural communion in a world of division, enmity, and strife.[58] On both the sacramental and the institutional level, the Church is a communion. On the sacramental level, it is a communion in Christ. On the institutional level, it is a communion of men and women in faith. On the worldwide level, the Church takes on the appearance of a "communion of communions."[59]

A communion of communions. The particular genius of seeing the Church as a "communion of communions" is that it both acknowledges the place of distinctiveness and openness. The churches are distinctive on the local level, with respect to culture, language, place, and time, yet God unites them in a communion that is both catholic and universal. The communion of communions does not exclude diversity, but comprises it within a coherent and viable social structure. Many Catholic, Orthodox, and Protestant theologians now accept and build a "com-

---

[56] Larere, 76. Dennis M. Doyle, *Communion Ecclesiology: Vision and Versions* (Maryknoll: Orbis Books, 2000) 36.

[57] Because the "subsistence" of the Church of Christ refers first and foremost to God as such, the addition of the word *"solummodo"* by the CDF amounts to an unjustifiable restriction on the sovereignty of God. To say the Church of Christ subsists only in one communion of churches and in no other requires that God cannot subsist anywhere else or that God has chosen not to subsist anywhere else.

[58] Doyle, 15.

[59] Cf. J.M.R. Tillard, *Church of Churches: The Ecclesiology of Communion*, trans. R. C. DePeaux (Collegeville, Minn.: The Liturgical Press, 1992).

munion ecclesiology" from this fundamental affirmation of the Church as a communion.

Eminent Catholic theologian Joseph Komanchak identifies two potential extremes in communion ecclesiology. On the one side, the idea of communion is nebulous and insubstantial. Mutual good feelings cover up profound disagreements. The idea of "communion" becomes little more than an agreement to disagree and the parties to the disagreement remain fundamentally unchanged by the encounter. On the other side, the word "communion" conceals a notion of the Church "otherwise untouched by Vatican II." The meaning of "communion" collapses into the concepts of collegiality of bishops and papal primacy. On this extreme, there is less appreciation for the integrity of the local church. Under the rubric of "communion," local bishops are made to cede their apostolic authority to bureaucrats and central authorities.[60]

Recent discussions among Catholics have focused on the terms "local" and "universal" Church. The term "local church" refers to the diocesan church. A local church is the communion of Christians in a locality organized under the ministry of a bishop in apostolic succession. The term "universal Church" commonly denotes several concepts. Sometimes the "universal Church" means the Church of Rome. Other times, it means the Roman Curia. More often, it denotes the Pope, as though he were a "universal pastor" with a direct pastoral relationship to every baptized Christian. Frequently, in their public statements, Vatican authorities use the phrase "universal Church" in a way that excludes non-Catholic Christians.

A local church. For Roman Catholic ecclesiology the basic ecclesiological unit is the local church, or diocese. Within each diocese, there may be any number of parishes, chapels, or oratories, but none of these smaller units are independent of the diocese. Only the diocese, as a whole, its bishop, other clergy, and laity together, stands alone to form an independent, local church, established in apostolic succession.

When we consider other Christian churches, the term "local church" takes on a different complexion. In some churches, the local church more properly refers to the local congregation. Nevertheless, in most non-Catholic denominations there exist higher levels of authority to which the local congregation is accountable: the synod, the annual conference, or the classis.

According to Vatican II, each local church is a whole Church. No one local church can go it alone. According to Catholic ecclesiology, independent groups cannot constitute themselves as a church. A local community becomes a local church only by being constituted and received

[60] Cf. Doyle, 5.

by the universal Church.[61] The union or assembly (*ecclesia* means "coming together") of the local church is fully ecclesial only to the extent that it is "in union with the whole Church of Christ" (it is Catholic) and it is "in union with all the other comings together" (local churches).[62]

A universal Church. In the Catholic Church, the universal Church comprises a "communion of local churches."[63] The universal Church arises in and out of the local churches and their communion with one another.[64] It is the "worldwide community of the disciples of the Lord."[65] This universal communion is what makes eucharistic sharing possible among Catholics around the world. The CDF asserts that the universal Church is "ontologically and temporally prior" to any one local church or group of local churches. By this they mean to exclude the idea that the universal Church is a confederation of local churches. It is not the sum of all local churches.

Protestant theologians understand the term "universal Church" in a much more inclusive fashion. For instance, the Anglican Communion and its member churches regard themselves as part of the whole Church. Just as local and particular churches in the Catholic Church regard themselves as both whole churches, but not independent churches, the Anglican Communion understands itself entirely in this fashion. Anglicans also regard other Christian churches as no less parts of the whole.

Catholicity and the Eucharist

Most Christian churches, especially our closest ecumenical dialogue partners, affirm that the Church of Christ is catholic as stated in the Nicene Creed. The word "catholic" is from the Greek expression "*kataholos*," and means "according to the whole." The word means that every instance of a thing forms part of a cohesive whole; yet each part of the whole is no less the whole than any one part. It is "turned toward a center which assures its unity."[66] Because it is catholic, every fragment of the Church "shines with its own light."[67]

---

[61] Ratzinger, *Principle of Catholic Theology*, 293.

[62] Ibid., 252.

[63] Congregation for the Doctrine of the Faith, Letter to the Bishops of the Catholic Church on Some Aspects of the Church Understood as Communion *(Communionis notio)* (1992) 7–8.

[64] LG 23. Doyle, 133.

[65] *Communionis notio* 7.

[66] William T. Cavanaugh, "The World in a Wafer: A Geography of the Eucharist as Resistance to Globalization," in *Catholicism and Catholicity*, 77.

[67] Giuseppe Ruggieri, "The Unity of the Church through the Unity of Humankind," in *The Church in Fragments: Towards What Kind of Unity?*, ed. Giuseppe Ruggieri and

The word "catholic" does not mean "universal." For a thing to be universal, it would have to be a single solitary thing. It would be spread out and everywhere. The universal thing is ubiquitous.[68] In our world, universalization (sometimes called globalization) allows others to be different but only at a very high cost. Universalization requires that others be "merely different." They may not be genuinely different and their difference must remain on the surface.[69]

Authentic catholicity is antithetical to globalization and universalization. Neither catholicity nor ecumenism should be seen as ecclesial counterparts to globalization or other forms of imperialism. Instead, the Eucharist is the "means by which God implants divine life among us. The life of Christ and God's Holy Spirit are enfolded, by way of the Eucharist, in every culture, time and place."[70] In the Eucharist, the world is given the possibility of new and better sorts of global relationships. Christ substitutes a "looking out for myself alone" with a "being for other men and women without exception."[71]

The Eucharist is catholic. There are many eucharistic liturgies. They occur here and now, there or then, in one place or another. Every eucharistic liturgy is different. Not one Mass is the same in every respect as any other Mass. Nevertheless, in each of the many liturgies only *one* Eucharist ever happens. It is therefore worth considering why Christians speak of the Eucharist in the singular rather than in the plural form: "Eucharists." Certainly, we have the "one Lord, one faith, one Baptism," of Paul and the "one bishop, one Eucharist, and so forth" recommended by Ignatius of Antioch. Our insistence in referring to the Eucharist in the singular is premised on its catholicity.

The contemporary Eucharist is the result of countless adaptations to our spaces and times, to our cultures and frames of mind. The multiplicity is an adaptation to our finitude. Neither you, nor I, nor even the Pope, can be at every eucharistic liturgy on any given day. However, God joins our liturgies in communion and that requires that the Eucharist be catholic. In this sense, "catholic" means that every Mass is a whole Eucharist. There are not many "Eucharists" but only one Eucharist, and every Mass participates in that one.

In a speech from May 4, 1979, Pope John Paul II said that "in every Eucharistic celebration it is the whole faith of the Church that comes

---

Miklos Tomka, *Concilium* (London & Maryknoll, N.Y.: SCM Press & Orbis Books, 1997) 148.

[68] Cavanaugh, "World in a Wafer," 70.

[69] Ibid., 75.

[70] Auer, 359f.

[71] Ruggieri, 150f.

into play; it is ecclesial in all its dimensions that is manifested and realized."[72] A reason for caution in eucharistic sharing is that we would limit the ecclesial dimensions of the Eucharist too narrowly, that we would emphasize the universal at the expense of the catholic.

God Transcends Human Expectations: Salvation and the Church

The Church is a "saving mystery" because Christ joins a human communion (the disciples) to his saving mission. *Dominus Iesus* says that this saving mystery belongs or pertains *(pertinet)* to the Church.[73] English readers should not read the verb "belongs" as though we were talking about material possessions. The saving mystery is not something that belongs to the Church because we own it. The saving mystery belongs to the Church only so much as the Church is a faithful instrument of Christ's saving deeds. In ordinary English, the Church is a means of salvation; but Christ is its cause.

The Church is a communion of saints elected by God. By this, we mean to say the Church is a dimension of the salvation revealed by Christ and the Spirit.[74] How we configure our churches conforms to our thoughts about salvation. Churches and theologians, however, as often as not conform their thoughts about salvation to the configuration of their churches. We define salvation primarily in terms of those with whom we would like to receive communion. Theology serves sociology rather than the other way around. We make our ideas about God serve our need for institutional coherence and risk turning faith into idolatry.

Scholar of comparative religion Martin Jaffee says that Judaism, Christianity, and Islam are not merely monotheistic religions. They are elective monotheists. The central characteristic of elective monotheism, Jaffee states, is not the oneness of God. The key characteristic of elective monotheism is God's desire to summon one portion of the human community to serve God in love and obedience. The elective monotheist asserts a chasm between God's will and the behavior of most human beings. The elective monotheist believes that only one human community can know and obey the true will of God.[75]

---

[72] *L'Osservatore Romano* (May 14, 1979). Cited in Carl Maxcey, "Roman Catholics and Intercommunion: Unity or Union," *Ecumenical Trends* 16 (1987) 90.

[73] DI 16.

[74] Doyle, 15.

[75] Martin S. Jaffee, "One God, One Revelation, One People: On the Symbolic Structure of Elective Monotheism," *Journal of the American Academy of Religion* 69, no. 4 (2001) 760.

Jaffee's analysis of elective monotheism challenges Christian theology. To the extent that Christians practice an elective monotheism, they assume that God—who is love—"does not do so indiscriminately."[76] Jaffee points out that our social and political advantage is to say that the love of God is scarce and the mercy of God is scarcer still. He concludes, the tragic irony of elective monotheism is that the "capacity of God to love intensely and exclusively is translated, as often as not, into the human capacity to hate intensely."[77] In the ecumenical context, Jaffee's analysis provides a valuable, cautionary note.

A pilgrim Church. At its best, the Christian tradition resists the risks identified by Martin Jaffee. For theologians and Church authorities like St. Augustine, it did not matter whether you were in the worst level of humankind or numbered among the best and most respectable. It mattered only in what direction you were moving. Are you moving toward God and God's will or are you moving toward your own (inherently distorted) will? The Church, Augustine and others remind us, is always on the way. The pilgrim Church is always in change for it exists in the movement of time. It is always finding itself in new situations, for it always finds itself drawn into new relationships with others.[78] One's ecclesial identity is not a fixed category. Who we are, as a Church, is constantly being constructed and reconfigured. This is simply a result of being in time. The bonds of history have not yet released the Church.[79]

Both the Church and the Eucharist are "for the time being." They are given to us for the time of pilgrimage, our period of wandering from the time of the Resurrection to the time of the Second Coming of Christ.[80] Therefore, we must always include within our theologies the interim and provisional character of the Eucharist and the Church. Too frequently, Church documents imply that the Church (because it is perfect) cannot change and cannot grow in holiness.

The Eucharist is a pledge of God's eternal promise to us; but we live on the way, on a pilgrimage journey. The Eucharist and its promises, therefore, are something we cannot entirely grasp or own. God is too powerful and too holy. Real holiness, like a hot coal in the mouth of Isaiah, changes the pilgrim into the prophet; the disciple into an apostle.[81]

[76] Ibid., 774.
[77] Ibid.
[78] Doyle, 15.
[79] Theresa Berger, "'Separated Brethren' and 'Separated Sisters': Feminist and / as Ecumenical Visions of the Church," in *Ecumenical Theology in Worship, Doctrine, and Life*, 228.
[80] Auer, 350.
[81] Isa 6:6-8. Cf. Duffy, 156f.

The prophet does not exist because God elects her. The prophet exists because God elects through her to speak. One risk in maintaining a more closed eucharistic sharing is that we would have lost sight of the prophetic dimension of the Eucharist. We would think that Holy Communion was given primarily for our own sakes and not for the sake of others.

Why Failing to Unite in the Church of Christ Is a Risk

The risk in eucharistic sharing is not that we would fail to unite as a human community. We unite in human community on our own, by ourselves, through a variety of means. Human community is relatively easy to accomplish; and the more exclusive the community, the easier it is to establish. The greater risk in eucharistic sharing is that we would unite in entirely the wrong way. We risk uniting in a hegemonic, totalitarian, or authoritarian sense. We risk uniting in a way that asks other people to sell out their souls to conform to our desires. The risk in a premature eucharistic sharing is that we would unite in an insubstantial or ephemeral way. We might unite for self-serving reasons that insulate us from the transforming dimensions of God's grace. We would have unity but not communion.

Focused or bounded. Human communities appear in two basic types: focused or bounded. Focused communities find their coherence by defining a focus or organizing principle. Those who are on the way toward the focus are members of the community; those who reject or have turned away from the focus are not. Bounded communities find their coherence by defining a circle around the group. Those within the circle are members of the community; those outside the circle are not.

At Pentecost, the Church transcended its boundaries and engaged a new focus. Fears had focused the pre-Pentecostal community; doubts and anxiety had bound them. After the arrival of the Holy Spirit, the disciples had to open the doors and windows of the Upper Room. The Spirit impelled them to speak in a way that would draw many people into the mystery of Christ's death and resurrection. The divine energies refused to be contained within that small dining chamber. This was now a church for the nations, speaking with great boldness about the hypocrisies of the state (Rome) and the religion (the Temple establishment). This was a Church on the way, a Church freed from the fear of slavery to sin and death.

In our day, the Church that was opened in Vatican II now also seeks to be that timorous and anxious Church of the closed Upper Room. The risk in eucharistic sharing is not that Catholics would limit Holy Communion to members of our own, worldwide communion of local churches. The risk is that Christians would use the Eucharist to establish unity instead of communion. The risk is that Christians would use the Eucharist to foster globalization instead of catholicity. The risk is that Christians would use the Eucharist to claim God's election for themselves instead of proclaiming salvation through Christ for all.

Risk 3:
Failing to Maintain the Apostolic Succession

One of the main difficulties in ecumenical conversation about the Eucharist is the failure of Christians to share a common understanding of ministry and ordination.[82] Eminent German Protestant theologian, Eberhard Jüngel, claims that the main hindrance to eucharistic sharing lies in disagreement over the understanding of ministry.[83]

Catholic authorities are concerned to maintain and certify the validity of sacramental worship. Among other things, for a celebration of the Eucharist to be valid, the minister must be a priest or bishop, validly ordained by a bishop in apostolic succession. In addition, the minister must be a bishop himself or a priest authorized by a bishop. He must have faculties—canonical permission—to offer the liturgy in the local church.

Cardinal Ratzinger has identified two central elements of post-Vatican II ecclesiology. First, we have turned to the episcopate as the "fundamental form of the sacrament of orders." Second, from this follows a link to the concepts of apostolic succession and tradition.[84] Each of these two characteristics touch on the question of eucharistic sharing. In a slogan, for real Eucharist, you need real priesthood. This helps, in part, to explain why Catholics may not ordinarily receive the Eucharist from non-Catholic ministers. It does not illumine why non-Catholics may not normally receive the Eucharist from Catholic ministers, for a significant number of non-Catholics do accept and maintain apostolic succession.[85]

---

[82] Meinrad Scherer-Edmunds, "Let's Stop Posting Bouncers at the Table of the Lord," *U.S. Catholic* (June 2000) 24.

[83] "Theologieprofessor Jüngel: Gemeinsames Abendmahl Nicht Zu Verhindern," *Deutsche Press-Agentur—Europadienst* (June 16, 2001).

[84] Ratzinger, *Principles,* 242.

[85] Thomas Richstatter, "Eucharist: Sign and Source of Christian Unity," *Catholic Update* (May 2000).

The Modern Average Catholic Theology of Ministry

Like the modern average theology of the Eucharist and of the Church, the modern average Catholic theology of ministry emphasizes a direct relationship between Christ and the priest at the expense of the relationship between Christ and the Church. For example, Edward Kilmartin notes the failure of both *Lumen gentium* and John Paul II's *Dominicae Coenae* to develop the ecclesiological foundation of the hierarchical ministry of the Eucharist.[86] In his encyclical on the Eucharist, Pope John Paul II sustains the teaching of the Council of Trent about the simultaneous institution of Eucharist and holy orders at the Last Supper, despite biblical scholarship that suggests ministry and Eucharist cannot both be developed entirely within the framework of the Last Supper narratives.[87] The Pope maintains that Christ is the author and principal priest of the Eucharist.[88] Instead, Kilmartin objected, the foundation of all ministry is the Church. The only liturgical actor, he said, is the whole Christ, head and members, acting in communion with one another.[89]

Historical considerations on priesthood. Eucharistic theology from the late Middle Ages concluded that the priest is given power to act as a minister of the Eucharist by ordination. Through ordination, the priest receives this power from Christ.[90] Since the Middle Ages, Catholic theologians have viewed the sacrament of ordination as the occasion for a transmission of power. They came to understand apostolic succession narrowly, as though it were a conduit of apostolic and divine energy.

Theologians from the eleventh to twelfth centuries offered three principle reasons why priests outside the Church are unable to celebrate the true Eucharist. They simply asserted there is no sacrifice outside the Church.[91] These sources do not provide extensive theological arguments because they followed an allegorical method for interpreting the sacraments. Another school of thought was that "the angels" would not be present at the liturgy of a priest outside of the communion of the Church.[92] Since the early Roman eucharistic prayer—the

---

[86] Kilmartin, *Church, Eucharist, and Priesthood,* 5.

[87] Ibid., 7.

[88] Daly, 17.

[89] Kilmartin, *Church, Eucharist, and Priesthood,* 8.

[90] Kilmartin, *Eucharist in the West,* 131f.

[91] These were Odo of Cambrai (ca. 1050–1113), Rupert of Deutz (1075–1129), Honorius Augustodunensis (ca. fl. 1198–1130s), and Stephen of Autun (d. 1139–40). Cf. Kilmartin, *Eucharist in the West,* 137, 42.

[92] The view of Bede (d. 735) and Peter Lombard. Cf. Kilmartin, *Eucharist in the West,* 136f., 43.

Roman Canon—includes reference to the angels "taking this sacrifice to the heavenly altar," in the absence of the angels, the heavenly church of saints would also be absent. There could be no communion. Finally, the Victorine theologians, in particular Hugh of St. Victor and Alger of Liège, repeated the opinion of St. Augustine. They believed that the sacrament of a priest outside the Church was valid, but not fruitful.[93]

A stronger foreshadowing of the modern average perspective on priesthood appears in late thirteenth-century theologies on the final cause of the Eucharist. The theology of Thomas Aquinas epitomizes the new theology of the thirteenth century. For Thomas, the final cause of the Eucharist—its end or goal—is the Church. He claimed the ultimate reality of the sacrament (the *res sacramenti*) is the unity of the Church. For Thomas, Church unity is not a precondition for the Eucharist; it is the result of it.[94]

The problem remains in that, for an effective Eucharist, you have to have an effective priest. Effective priesthood becomes the precondition for the unity of the Church. As a result, the modern average theology of ministry holds that priests have power to establish the Eucharist and the Church by way of the Eucharist. Consequently, our understanding of the Church is torn in two. On one side we have powerful clergy; on the other side, powerless laity. For clergy, the Church is understood in jurisdictional terms. It is a juridical institution that authorizes and transmits their power to convene the Body of Christ. For laity, the Church is understood in spiritualized terms. Their communion in Christ's Mystical Body through the reception of Holy Communion was made to depend on obedience to the jurisdictional and sacramental power of the clergy.

The power of the priesthood, the faithfulness of God. These conceptions cause us to wonder about the power of the priest. How much does the constitution of a local church depend on the sacramental power of its ministers? Instead of relying on more biblical models of service and discipleship, some Catholics today express their understanding of ordination in metaphors lifted from the electric company. The power company analogy sees no source for priestly authority apart from the original, first-century ordination of the apostles by Jesus. By all means, to understand Jesus Christ as the first-century source of all ministry is an essential theological datum; but alone it is insufficient. To see the historical Jesus as the source of all priestly power presupposes that human relationships by themselves can maintain the Church in apostolic vigor.

---

[93] Kilmartin, *Eucharist in the West*, 137f.
[94] Ibid., 152f.

The power company analogy amounts to imagining that, after the Ascension and the first gift of the Holy Spirit, God has pretty much left the Church to its own devices, to maintain the circuits and transistors. Missing from the analogy, however, is the important role of new direct input from God, by the power of the Holy Spirit. What theologians call the pneumatological dimension is missing.

The modern average Catholic theology of ministry easily overlooks the role of the Holy Spirit (the pneumatological dimension) because we have, historically, stressed the *ex opere operato* character of sacramental ministry. According to the *ex opere operato* doctrine, the moral character of the bishop or priest does not affect the validity of the sacraments he administers. To reassure ourselves that our sacraments continue to access the grace of Jesus Christ, we rely on the validity of ordination, more than the moral character of our ministers.

Theologians today are reconsidering the limitations of the *ex opere operato* doctrine. In these reconsiderations, we have come to see that this sacramental guarantee says far less about our priests and bishops. Seen positively, the *ex opere operato* character of the sacraments assures us that God is faithful even when our validly ordained ministers are not. The *ex opere operato* principle does not confer a right upon the minister except to do and to serve the will of Christ. The Eucharist is not the work of the (potentially sinful) presider; it is the work of the (absolutely sinless) Christ.[95] When we read statements about the importance of valid ordination for the sacraments we must remember that the faith of the Church, in the end, still depends on God, and not the faith of the priest or bishop.

Just as God has built the Church from stones "rejected by the builders," God nourishes the living building of the Church by way of blunt instruments, through the sacramental ministry of lisping prophets, fearful disciples, timid apostles, and a crucified Savior. The student of Scripture understands this, for God has been spending time with less than the best exemplars of humankind since before the days of Noah. Our ministers are not, by nature, essentially different or more sacred than the remainder of the baptized. Even though we recognize a host of saints among the clergy, ordained hands are not intrinsically more sacred than any others.[96]

We should take care not to reduce ministry to the power to consecrate the sacraments. Ministry must always be related to the source of

---

[95] von Allmen, 83.

[96] Anne Primavesi and Jennifer Henderson, *Our God Has No Favourites: A Liberation Theology of the Eucharist* (Turnbridge & San Jose: Burns & Oates & Resource Publications, 1989) 96.

its power. While Christian ministry is conveyed by means of the sacraments, ministers do also receive an essential authority directly from the Word of God and from the Holy Spirit. For this reason, Catholics should bring a more balanced attention to the qualitative dimensions of ministry. As much as these concerns point to a reorganized conception of priesthood, they also point to a reorganized conception of the episcopate, the role and ministry of bishops.

The Historic Episcopate

Among the ancient Christian authorities, Ignatius of Antioch represents some of the most decisive influence on Catholic conceptions of the episcopate. In the view of Ignatius, where the bishop is, there is the Church.[97] For him, unity with the local bishop was the only requirement for membership in the Church. Without the bishop's consent, no matter how much a meal might "look like the Lord's Supper" it was, he said, "served by the devil."[98]

For Ignatius, unity with the bishop was the only empirical validation he could imagine for unity with Christ and the Church. Whoever does not stand in unity with the bishop, he thought, is a schismatic, has already judged himself, and is unclean. Ignatius' ecclesiology of unity with the bishop results in an ironclad logic of inclusion and exclusion. For him, the schismatic is always self-excluding. In the present, ecumenical context, however, many Christians are excluded by decree, but not in conscience. These Christians do not easily fit Ignatius' all-or-nothing approach.[99]

Historic evidence must be read very carefully. Some theologians read ancient Christian writers, like Ignatius of Antioch, for confirmation of what ought to be. When we read Ignatius in this preferential fashion, it is clear that he wanted only one bishop to preside in each Church (*Smyrnaeans* 7.1-2). However, we can read Ignatius still more carefully, with an eye to discerning what was. With the more careful reading, we can see that, despite what Ignatius wanted, in some churches people "beside the bishop [or his delegate] could lead the Church at Eucharist."[100]

---

[97] Kenneth Hein, *Eucharist and Excommunication: A Study in Early Christian Doctrine and Discipline, European University Papers* (Frankfurt am Main: Peter Lang, 1973) 211.

[98] *Smyrnaeans* 9.1. Ibid., 213.

[99] Ibid., 216.

[100] Nathan Mitchell, *Mission and Ministry: History and Theology in the Sacrament of Order,* ed. Monika Hellwig, *Message of the Sacraments* (Collegeville, Minn.: Michael Glazier/The Liturgical Press, 1982) 170.

Ignatius argued against this practice because he thought others were doing things the wrong way. Ignatius' protestations offer better historical evidence of what he was arguing against than of what he was arguing for.

The ancient Church did not immediately accept Ignatius' argument or the practice of appointing a single bishop for every local church. Other ancient sources—including the New Testament—exemplify a variety of alternative ministerial arrangements including apostles, bishops, elders, deacons, widows, prophets, miracle-workers, preachers, and teachers (cf. Acts 14:23, 15:6, 21:10; 1 Cor 12:10-29, 14:37; Eph 2:20, 4:11; 1 Tim 3:1-2, 8-13, 5:17; 1 Pet 5:1-5). For a variety of reasons, Christians forgot the existence of alternate models. Ancient Christians received Ignatius' arguments for one bishop for each local church.[101] In the contemporary Church, it may be necessary to restore a broader, more biblical understanding of ministry. To wed the earlier charismatic–servant understanding of ministry to later institutional–juridical models will be exceptionally challenging.

The jurisdictional episcopate. Influential medieval writers, such as Thomas Aquinas, thought the bishop was just a priest with a larger jurisdiction added on. They did not recognize the episcopate as a distinct level of ordination. The jurisdictional understanding of the bishop caused many to see the ministry of bishop as qualitatively indistinct from the priest.

Some of the earliest reformers adopted this view in rejecting the ministry of the bishop. For example, Wycliffe claimed that the bishops were "arrogant usurpers" of the "rights of the priest." Luther, Calvin, and others, collapsed all ministries into the ministry of the Word (preaching) and assembled jurisdictional powers under the secular ruler (prince or city council) or under independent church boards (presbyteries or consistories).[102]

The restoration of the historic episcopate has been a primary agenda item for modern ecumenical discussions among Protestant churches. For example, the *Porvoo Statement* and the *North American Concordat* mark significant milestones in the relationship between Anglican and Lutheran Churches. Lutherans usually regard episcopacy as a matter of indifference with respect to Scripture *(adiaphora).* One bishop in the local church, they believe, is not the only valid expression of apostolic succession. In seeking agreed statements with Anglicans, Lutherans

---

[101] Frances A. Sullivan, *From Apostles to Bishops: The Development of the Episcopacy in the Early Church* (Mahwah, N.J.: Newman Press, 2001) 229.

[102] Cf. Aidan Nichols, *Holy Order: The Apostolic Ministry from the New Testament to the Second Vatican Council* (Dublin: Veritas Publications, 1990) 57.

have insisted that no negative evaluation of existing and prior ordinations is stated or implied. From the perspective of Anglicans, the concern has been to assure the apostolic succession among Lutheran bishops. For Anglicans, restoration of episcopal orders among Lutherans—along with a mutual laying on of hands by Episcopal and Lutheran ministers at new ordinations—is a sufficient remedy for any lack of validity that may or may not have once existed.[103]

Relational episcopate. As these non-Catholic churches work hard to restore and invigorate the historic episcopate, their conversations may be particularly instructive for Catholics. The challenge in discussions of the episcopate is to balance the jurisdictional role of the bishop—which could as easily take place in councils, synods, and commissions—with the sacramental significance of having one bishop within each local church. The relational character of the episcopate needs, again, to be rediscovered and enacted. For the Catholic Church, this may demand we revisit the question of the overwhelming size of our local churches.

In the realm of jurisdiction, we need to consider how centralizing forces may use the historic episcopate to impose narrow uniformity in the Church. We should rather go to the formulation of the eminent nineteenth-century Catholic theologian Johann Möhler, who held that the Church "contains within itself all legitimate antitheses." In Möhler's view, the episcopate exists to preserve the tension between these legitimate antitheses, not to resolve them.[104] The episcopate exists to establish the foundations needed for expansiveness of thought and the inclusion of all within the Church. This does not mean that Church authorities must allow anything to happen. It means that no one may stay in the Church and remain unchanged from the person he or she was before baptism. Authentic relationship in community requires that we live in peace with men and women with whom we disagree.

As a sacramental sign and cause of unity, the office of the bishop (and its occupant) must be committed not only to the unity of a denomination. The bishop must work toward the unity and concord of all the men and women in the diocese (Christian, non-Christian, Catholic, and non-Catholic).[105] As Johannes Brosseder recommends, the episcopacy takes on a more effective and apostolic character when what he calls "purely denominational" matters are carried out in the full light of

---

[103] Günther Gassmann, "Anglican-Lutheran Convergence and the Anticipation of Full Communion," *Journal of Ecumenical Studies* 34 (1997) 1–12.

[104] Doyle, 34.

[105] Cf. Johannes Brosseder, "Die ökumenische Bedeutung des Bischofsamtes," in *Christus Spes: Liturgie und Glaube im ökumenischen Kontext,* ed. Paul Berbers and Thaddäus A. Schnitker (Frankfurt am Main: Peter Lang, 1994) 91.

day.[106] Catholics could go far in this direction. On the local level, bishops could adopt the example of Vatican II with its significant group of non-Catholic visitors. Diocesan synods and councils could include representation from non-Catholics in the local region. On the national and international levels, conferences and synods of Catholic bishops could invite and encourage the participation of a significant number of non-Catholic consulters. Where they are not already doing so, Catholic bishops should work actively to acquire firsthand knowledge of the faith and concerns of non-Catholics in their own dioceses.

For Catholics, our relationship to the local bishop is the primary means of our relationship to the whole Church of Christ. We enter into communion with the universal Church of Christ in and through our local bishop. The pastoral and sacramental relationship between Catholics and their bishop is best signified in the sacrament of confirmation.

A special case of episcopacy: The "universal pastor." In the Catholic Church, the ministry of the papacy is a special form of the relational episcopate. Just as each Christian unites to the whole Church by way of relationship to the local bishop, so each local bishop unites to the whole Church, and to the entire college of bishops, by way of relationship to the Bishop of Rome. The primacy of the Church of Rome is a special form of regional organization of local churches. When bishops of local churches come together, they express their unity in public through the creation of primacies. Among their number, they appoint regional metropolitans and patriarchs.[107]

For some Catholics, the primacy of the Church of Rome should be the main thrust of Catholic ecclesiology. They value the collegiality and regional groupings of local churches less than the central authority of Roman jurisdiction. In some cases, they seek to assert a direct, pastoral relationship between the pope and every Catholic. In a new term, a novelty really, they say he is a "universal pastor." Unwittingly, Roman centralism devalues the relationship between the bishop and his local church. By subordinating the pastoral role of the local bishop to the Pope, the catholicity of the local church is equally diminished, for the local church is made to function as merely a part of the whole and not as an integral, sacramental expression of Christ's body on earth.[108]

Two brief comments on this centralizing trend: First, subordination to the jurisdiction of the Roman primacy is not the same as the unity of

---

[106] Ibid.

[107] Ratzinger, *Principles of Catholic Theology,* 253f.

[108] Johannes Brosseder, "Towards What Unity of the Churches?," in *The Church in Fragments,* ed. Ruggieri and Tomka, 134.

the Church.[109] The unity of the Church derives from the unity of God and not from the jurisdiction of a single minister. The jurisdiction of the papacy is to be the "first among equals" *(primus inter pares)*, and papal primacy is best expressed through relationships with other bishops within the context of collegiality.[110] Second, alongside the primacy of Rome, one may also speak of a "primacy of the Whole." By this, I mean that there exists also a primacy in the gathering of the worldwide episcopate in ecumenical council. The primacy of an ecumenical council must always be seen to balance and support the primacy of the Bishop of Rome.

Validity

In our considerations of eucharistic sharing, we nearly always run up against the problem of mutually recognized ministries. For Catholics, Anglicans, and Orthodox Christians, apostolic succession is an essential quality of valid ordination. Members of these churches ask their ecumenical dialogue partners, without valid ordination, how can there be a valid Eucharist?

Validity is a key issue for Roman Catholic authorities. In order to be valid, the Eucharist must be celebrated by a priest or bishop ordained in apostolic succession.[111] To say a sacrament is not valid is not the same as saying it is not real. No one denies that an invalid marriage is real. It is no less a legal marriage and requires a civil divorce. Likewise, even if a Eucharist is invalid, that does not mean it is not real, but it may mean that something is missing or it is in some way deficient.

Historical considerations. The distinction between validity and liceity or fruitfulness was the invention of St. Augustine. The distinction formed an essential component to his critique of the Donatists.[112] The followers of Donatus (fourth century, North African) believed that Christians who had renounced their faith under persecution required rebaptism if they were later to rejoin the Church. Similarly, they thought priests and bishops who renounced their faith should be reordained and that anyone baptized by them must be rebaptized. Augustine argued, against the Donatists, that the sacraments received by these backsliders remain valid. The ordinary means of rejoining the Church is penance.

---

[109] Ibid., 132.

[110] Cf. Thomas P. Rausch, "Archbishop Quinn's Challenge: A Not Impossible Task," 71–88, in *The Exercise of the Primacy: Continuing the Dialogue,* ed. Phyllis Zagano and Terrence W. Tilley (New York: Crossroad Publishing Co., 1998).

[111] John M. Huels, *One Table, Many Laws: Essays on Catholic Eucharistic Practice* (Collegeville, Minn.: The Liturgical Press, 1986) 96.

[112] Nichols, *Holy Order,* 56f.

The sacraments of heretical Christians, Augustine thought, were valid but not fruitful.

Validity is the result of a strict application of minimal legal norms to satisfy the reasonable doubts of a prospective communicant. To say that the eucharistic rites of non-Catholic Christians are not valid is not the same as saying that they cannot give grace or that they have no saving power. What Catholic authorities are saying, however, is that, in the absence of an apostolic succession, they cannot be certain that the reasonable expectations of faithful Christians can be satisfied with respect to these rites.

Liceity is also a key issue for Roman Catholic authorities. Some sacramental celebrations, though valid, are not licit. For a valid sacrament also to be licit, the presiding minister must have faculties—permission from the bishop—to perform the sacrament, the recipient must be properly disposed, and the sacrament must follow the proper form.[113]

A defect in orders does not imply an absence of orders. The current, official perspective of the Catholic Church holds that most non-Catholic ministers are not true priests. I acknowledge that this may sound hurtful to many non-Catholic readers. From this perspective, if the minister is not a true priest, the ritual blessing and breaking of bread and wine is also not a true Eucharist. In part, this explains why Catholics are prohibited from receiving bread and wine at the Communion service presided over by a non-Catholic minister. It does not explain why canon law normally prohibits the non-Catholic from receiving Holy Communion from Catholic ministers, where the minister is a true priest, and the ritual is a true Eucharist.[114]

Nevertheless, even within the official perspective, room for growth is possible. This speaking of a lack of orders is a relatively late development and it is not present in the Vatican II documents. *Ut unum sint* marks the first appearance of this view since the council.[115] Thus, *Unitatis redintegratio* spoke of a defect and not an absence of orders in the non-Catholic churches. It is contrary to the decree of the council to say that there is no order among non-Catholic churches.[116] A defect in order does not imply an absence of order. In fact, there cannot be a defect unless the defective thing is already present. Unfortunately, the *Ecumenical Directory* of 1967 did not take these distinctions into account.[117]

[113] Huels, 96.

[114] McSorley, 114.

[115] UUS 67. Richstatter.

[116] Eoin de Bhaldraithe, "Forum: May Catholics Receive the Protestant Eucharist?," *Worship* 76, no. 1 (2002) 81.

[117] Eoin de Bhaldraithe, "Intercommunion," *Heythrop Journal* 43 (2002) 77.

In addition, because of the essential positive features of the Protestant Eucharist, the Vatican II decree on ecumenism does not explicitly forbid the Catholic to receive Communion from a non-Catholic minister, even if the 1983 Code of Canon Law does.[118] The council understood the Protestant Eucharist as a fulfillment of Christ's promise to be present. Even if it is not a sacrament according to every single legal norm, it is still sacramental in the sense that it "effects grace . . . and strengthens their [the Protestants'] bond with Christ."[119]

The council thus celebrated the substance that is evident in non-Catholic churches. They chose, at that time, not to criticize weaknesses in the non-Catholic expressions of faith. By and large, later documents like the Code of Canon Law and *Dominus Iesus* have overlooked the positive dimensions of the Vatican II decrees.

Apostolic Succession

Defining apostolic succession. Roman Catholics prohibit eucharistic sharing with Protestants since "those churches have broken with apostolic succession." The ecumenist asks, "Who is the final arbiter of apostolic succession?"

In his personal, theological writings, Cardinal Ratzinger offers a considerable narrowing in the concept of apostolic succession. In his view, apostolic succession must always be linked to the communion of churches. There is no apostolicity outside of full communion. From this principle, he will also strongly link apostolic succession to communion with Rome and the Bishop of Rome.[120] It is very important to point out that this remains Cardinal Ratzinger's opinion as an eminent Catholic theologian. This view is not mandated by Catholic doctrine. Ratzinger, therefore, disputes the self-understanding of many Protestant bishops. He calls their claim to apostolic succession "apocryphal," the result of "liturgical romanticism." Present Protestant understandings of episcopate, he writes, are the result of a "sentimental search for origins played out in a nostalgia for liturgical ceremony."[121]

More recently, the CDF has responded to the question of apostolic succession with similar, negative outcomes. *Dominus Iesus* states that Catholics are required to believe in the apostolic succession and in the historical continuity of the Church founded by Christ with the Catholic

[118] Bhaldraithe, "Forum," 82.
[119] Ibid.
[120] Ratzinger, *Principles of Catholic Theology*, 246.
[121] Ibid., 245f.

Church.[122] This has proven especially hurtful for relations between the Catholic Church and the Anglican communion.[123]

[122] DI 16. The CDF now also requires Catholic theologians to distinguish "sister churches" from "other Christian communities." The designation "sister church" may only refer to ecclesial communities with a valid episcopate and Eucharist. (Note on the Expression "Sister Churches," June 30, 2000.) Christian churches without a valid apostolic succession are supposed to be called "ecclesial communities." Whenever the term "church" is plural, it can only refer to local or particular churches (the diocese or the patriarchate).
Read in a positive light, the CDF letter is more about preserving the Catholic understanding of the term "mother Church." The letter understands the mother Church as the worldwide communion of local churches in union with Rome. It must be pointed out, however, that this understanding bypasses the historical origin of the term. In the ancient Church, one's mother Church was the local church where one was baptized. It referred especially to the "mother font" from which one was re-born in Christ.
[123] In their response to *One Bread, One Body*, the Anglican bishops remark upon the disrespect they felt when the English Catholic bishops wrote that they could not affirm the validity of Anglican orders (OBOB, 41). The Anglican bishops saw that *One Bread, One Body* understands non-Catholic Christians not to be members of the "One, Holy, Catholic, and Apostolic Church" (ESOU, 19).
The Anglican bishops claim that the Catholic bishops made a number of erroneous assumptions about the Church of England in *One Bread, One Body*. In effect, the Anglican bishops are saying, "When you speak about us, we want you to consult with us and acknowledge our self-understanding." Dialogue, they suggest, presumes that both parties are equally speaking partners as they are listening partners.
Catholic authorities should not expect Anglican bishops to allow questions about the validity of their ordinations to go unanswered. The Anglican bishops state that Catholic authorities have defined the term "validity" too narrowly. They strongly urge that Catholic authorities reconsider the arguments regarding the nonvalidity of Anglican orders once put forward in Pope Leo XIII's encyclical on the nullity of Anglican orders, *Apostolicae curae*, "in light of developments during the past century" (ESOU, 15). If Catholic authorities require Anglicans to accept the findings of *Apostolicae curae* as a condition to full communion, this amounts to a vicious "Catch-22." "Deny your own ecclesial integrity or we will deny it to you ourselves."
Anglicans could continue asserting that they hold valid orders in apostolic succession. If the historical evidence that historians and theologians have brought forward were objectively reevaluated and if *Apostolicae curae* were set aside, then the ban on eucharistic sharing between Anglicans and Roman Catholics would be moot in a moment. *Apostolicae curae* ruled on the basis of historical facts as they were then understood. In light of new historical evidence or a more careful examination of that evidence, the decision could be reversed without abrogating any of the *divine iuro* norms upon which the earlier decision was made and from which the earlier determination was constructed. Thus, even if it were falsely said that *Apostolicae*

It would be helpful, at this point, to note that many other non-Catholic Christians believe in the apostolic succession. They also believe in the historical continuity of the Catholic Church with the Church founded by Christ. For their part, Protestant Christians have preferred to err on the side of recognizing the Church of Christ outside of their own denominations. For example, Anglicans believe that the "Catholic Church" consists of all the baptized, arranged in local churches, and organized according to principles stated in the Chicago-Lambeth Quadrilateral: the ecumenical creeds, Scripture, sacraments, and the historic episcopate.[124] For them, a positive evaluation of their own ecclesial status does not necessarily entail a negative evaluation of any other Christian Church.

Dominus Iesus raises, but does not answer, two serious questions. Are Catholics allowed to agree with non-Catholics who believe that their non-Catholic Church is part of the "One, Holy, Catholic, and Apostolic Church"? Are Catholics allowed to agree with non-Catholics who believe that their non-Catholic Church is continuous with the Church founded by Christ? Because *Dominus Iesus* is silent on these two questions, I conclude that it is not inappropriate to say, as a matter of personal opinion, that some non-Catholic churches are no less part of the

---

curae is infallible—a status that Pope Leo XIII did not assert for this document—that does not mean the judgment as to validity may not be changed. However, this reevaluation depends upon the will of Catholic authorities to undertake it. We may ask, why do Catholic authorities prefer not to perceive the validity of Anglican orders?

There are several possible reasons for this preference. The ordination of women as priests and bishops among Anglicans ranks high on the list of possible reasons. There was also a history of bad relations between Anglicans and Catholics on the British Isles that, to some extent, exists to this day. The second-class status of eighteenth- and nineteenth-century Catholics in the United Kingdom remained a painful memory and reality for English Catholics. In that context, *Apostolicae curae* appears less as a judgment against the Anglican Church. It more takes on the complexion of group self-esteem or *esprit de corps* by an oppressed minority. Today, Roman Catholics and non-Anglicans outnumber Anglicans in the United Kingdom. To the extent that Roman Catholics sustain the judgments of *Apostolicae curae,* they no longer need to do so for purposes of group maintenance.

In light of the refusal to reevaluate *Apostolicae curae,* it looks as though Catholic authorities do not desire assent to the teachings of the Catholic Church from communicants as much as they desire an assent to the authority of the ministers of the Catholic Church. Refusing to acknowledge the reality of ministry in other Christian churches is not a particularly effective reason for caution in eucharistic sharing (Cf. Power, "Roman Catholic Theologies of Eucharistic Communion").

[124] ESOU, 18.

"One, Holy, Catholic, and Apostolic Church," and are continuous with the Church founded by Christ.

Vatican II does not require Catholics to profess that there is no historical continuity between the Church founded by Christ and every other non-Catholic, non-Roman Church. Just because a Church may or may not stand in apostolic succession does not entail there is no continuity between that Church and Christ. There may be an impaired continuity, but Vatican II prohibits us from saying there are no elements of the Church outside of the Catholic Church.

Qualitative dimensions of apostolicity. For many non-Catholics, apostolic succession is less a characteristic of any one person's ordination. For them, it describes the quality of a Church's faithful life in Christ. Members of these churches helpfully remind us that apostolic succession, by itself, is no guarantee that a Church has been faithful to the Gospel. As Braaten points out, "The claim of the succession theory to be the exclusive guarantor of valid ministries and sacraments is not found in the New Testament. It is . . . a result of the later struggles between orthodoxy and heresy . . ."[125] As Catholic theologian Aidan Nichols concedes, many of the Reformers wanted to enhance the quality of ministry. In protecting the *ex opere operato* character of priesthood, Trent may have done too little to insist on qualitative reforms.[126]

Therefore many non-Catholics would ask us, what have you done to safeguard the evangelical character of your ministries? If a community does not "walk its talk" and actually live the Gospel of Jesus Christ, how can there be a valid Eucharist? Apostolic succession of the bishop, they would say, is no guarantee that the bishop's local church remains in the apostolic fold. Certainty with respect to the one does not promise certainty with respect to the other.[127] For authentic apostolic succession, we must look to a third element. In Protestantism, this has been an evangelical criterion: the Church is apostolic insofar as the Gospel is preached rightly. In Catholicism, the guarantee of faithfulness has been measured according to the communion of bishops with the Pope.

Yet communion with Rome is also no guarantee of fidelity to the fullness of the apostolic faith. When we then search the history books and find bishops—even popes!—acting in poor faith and failing to transmit the fullness of the Gospel message, all our claims to infallibility and magisterium sound a bit anxious.[128] If nothing else, apostolic succession should not be a sign of anxiety in the midst of human failings. It should

---

[125] Braaten, 35.
[126] Nichols, *Holy Order*, 90.
[127] Brosseder, "Ökumenische Bedeutung," 89.
[128] Ibid., 90.

signify confidence in the paschal mystery of Christ and commitment to live within the mystery of Resurrection faith.

Validity does not excuse poor quality in ministry. The doctrine of the faithfulness of God expressed in the phrase "*ex opere operato*" is not an excuse for poor ministry from morally deficient members of the clergy. Upholding the *ex opere operato* character of the sacraments because of God's faithfulness should not distract us from attending to the essential *qualitative* dimensions of Christian ministry.

Ecclesial dimension of apostolicity. Apostolic succession is much more than an "unbroken chain of hands on heads." The ritual means of validating ministry has varied considerably over the centuries.[129] It must be more than simply retaining a "valid ordination." Ordination, by itself, does not guarantee that the recipient will remain "apostolic" and "faithful." Apostolicity cannot be transmitted unless it is somehow lived out in real, ordered communities. It needs to be realized in the life of a community by means of efficacious, sacramental signs. Otherwise, we find ourselves in touch with a "lovely tradition of human wisdom" and not an authentic encounter with the living God.

The monarchical episcopate is the norm since the ancient Church. In its historical context, the apostolic character of the one bishop did not *constitute* the apostolic succession of his Church, it *expressed* it.[130] Apostolic succession is, therefore, a quality of both the bishop and the bishop's local church. In the present ecumenical context, we may ask, therefore, whether some churches have maintained an apostolic succession in their ecclesial life, although they *express* apostolicity outside of the succession of a single, local bishop.

Transmission of apostolicity, an analogy. In the arts, students sometimes seek out teachers according to their pedigree. From my youth, I recall my fascination with the musical lineage of my organ teacher. I wanted to know who her teachers were, and who their teachers were. Somehow, I managed to figure out that I was directly linked to J. S. Bach through my organ teacher, and her teachers, and their teachers before that. Thousands of organists—more and less skilled than I—claim a similar lineage. Lineage does not substitute for musicality. Moreover, lineage does not guarantee authentic performance practice. As much as my teacher taught me to play and to hear with her techniques and with her musical ear, she could never transmit the fullness of her sense of musicality to me. I had to acquire musicality for myself, under her guidance.

---

[129] Mitchell, 175.
[130] Brosseder, "Ökumenische Bedeutung," 88.

Apostolic succession, I suggest, is very similar to the transmission of musicality. Bishops do not learn their "apostolicity" the way computers can; they are not theological and pastoral clones of the men who ordained them. Just as lineage did not guarantee that I would be "musical," it does not guarantee apostolicity for ministers. Rather, apostolicity requires active participation in the community of apostles; the college of bishops. This is no different from saying that "musicianship" requires active participation in the community of musicians.

The community of musicians forms a community of active interpretation. Musicians are always listening, evaluating, imitating, and modifying the performance of other musicians. Likewise, the college of bishops forms a community of active interpretation. The best bishops are always listening, evaluating, imitating, and modifying their ministry in dialogue with other bishops, their local clergy, and the men and women of their local communities. The entire college of bishops ensures the apostolicity of the Church in a way that a single bishop, acting alone, cannot.

Why Failing to Maintain the Apostolic Succession Is a Risk

Throughout this section, I have repeatedly pointed to the qualitative dimension of ecclesial life and ministry. The value in maintaining the principle of apostolic succession is not so much in the pedigree of an unbroken chain of hands on heads. Rather, it is seen in the apostolic and evangelical character of the ministerial relationships we seek to maintain in all of our churches. Ministers must be accountable to Christ, to their communities, and to one another.

One risk in a more open eucharistic sharing is that we would send members of our communities to ministers who are not accountable. Another risk in a more open eucharistic sharing is that we would welcome Christians to the table who have no intent to live in relationship with the local church—its members and its authorities. Catholics signify membership in the local church through authentic relationships with the local bishop.

Accountability in apostolic ministry. Holding men and women accountable to one another is an essential component of authentic Christian relationships. Catholic ecumenists like Jon Nilson urge Catholic authorities to heed the call for stronger structures of accountability within the Catholic Church. Ecumenical progress, Nilson warns, will depend on Catholics establishing canonical norms that afford Christian communities authentic accountability from their bishops and other clergy.[131] To

[131] Nilson, 78f.

the extent that Catholic authorities insulate themselves from account-ability for their decisions, Nilson says that their ministry will be ques-tioned, however much it may be apostolic and valid.

Ministry with authority. The Latin word for authority is *auctoritas.* This word comes from the Latin verb *augere,* and means "to augment" or "to increase in growth."[132] An authority, in the Christian context, is someone who nurtures others and calls them to an increase in faith. Authority thus describes a particular sort of leadership and absolutely excludes several modern takes on the word.

Therefore, an authority is not someone who dominates, controls, or commands the other. The domineering leader is "authoritarian," and distorts the meaning of Christian ministry. The true authority is one who, of his or her nature, seeks and serves the development, growth, and grace of others. Recognizing a nondominating sense of authority in the potential Christian minister should be an essential part of the discernment of ministerial vocation. Theologically, authority is a char-ism or grace more than it is an office or public role. As Canadian theo-logian Marc Ouellet suggests, "Communitarian leadership requires from each and every person an attitude of service and not a will to power."[133] If the churches could develop a more thoroughly Christian (and consequently less imperial) sense of authority, a more apostolic quality in Christian ministry could result.

The scope of apostolicity: A ministry to all. Catholic communities and their ministers must always undertake their charge to minister effec-tively to all. Canon law charges the local church, its bishop, clergy, and laity, to minister to all men and women without exception. Old atti-tudes die hard and one interchurch couple reports, "The [Roman Catholic] Church seems to want to minister only to one half of the rela-tionships, and prevents effective ministry by those churches which are prepared to nourish both partners."[134] Even if we use the most offensive terms in the old vocabulary, Christ mandates us to seek out and save the lost. The lost ought to include even the "heretics and schismatics."

An ancient example is instructive. In the fourth century, St. Ambrose of Milan composed dozens of the most beautiful Christian hymns during the time that Arianism was popular there. The hallmark of Arianism is the heretical belief that Jesus Christ, the Second Person of the Holy Trinity, is less divine than God the Father. To counter Arian

[132] Marc Ouellet, "Priestly Ministry at the Service of Ecclesial Communion," *Com-munio* 23 (1996) 685.

[133] Ibid., 687.

[134] Melanie Finch and Ruth Reardon, *Sharing Communion: An Appeal to the Churches from Interchurch Families* (London: Collins Liturgical Publications, 1983) 81.

beliefs, Ambrose composed and taught a number of hymns to the Christians who followed him in the Catholic faith. Ambrose's hymns taught orthodox beliefs about Jesus Christ and were wildly popular among the members of his church.

Though Ambrose's hymns mainly helped the faithful members of his own church, we need to look at the other side of the coin. In a curious way, the songs helped the "heretical" members of the Arian church as well. Because Ambrose's community boisterously sang the hymns in public, he had stumbled on an effective means to teach Catholic faith to the Arians. Ambrose understood that he was not only the bishop for faithful, nonheretical Christians. He understood himself as bishop to the whole city of Milan. His ministry to Milanese men and women did not end when he reached the doors to the basilica. Ambrose's story suggests that, when Catholic ministers nurture the evangelical and apostolic life of their own local churches, they will also have been faithful to the ecumenical mission of the Church.

Risk 4:
Expressing a Nonexistent Unity

The most common argument advanced against eucharistic sharing by Catholic authorities is the concern that the Eucharist would be made to express a nonexistent unity. The sacrament, they say, should not be used as a means toward unity. In a word, the argument goes, we must have unity before we can express it in the sacrament of unity. Nonetheless, since the late Middle Ages, Catholic theology has understood the Eucharist as both a means toward unity and a visible expression of the unity we already possess. In this section, I consider the nature and purpose of eucharistic unity. Does eucharistic sharing jeopardize the unity of the Church?

In modern ecumenism, Christians frequently ask one another, "What kind of unity do we seek?" What is the purpose of Christian unity? Catholic theologian Jon Nilson says that God provides Christian unity "for the sake of a world that needs the churches to come together."[135] Vatican II said something similar. In the Pastoral Constitution on the Church in the Modern World, *Gaudium et spes,* the bishops wrote, "the promotion of unity belongs to the innermost nature of the Church."[136] God forms and molds us into the Church for the sake of a world that needs us to become more than merely "human" or "humane." The

---

[135] Nilson, 1.
[136] GS 42.

world does not really need Christians to be "successful" as much as it needs Christians to be faithful. In the end, the quality of our communion with Christ matters much more than the quantity.

Historical considerations. Theologians have taken a variety of positions on the precise relationship between the Eucharist and the unity of the Church. In the ancient Church, eucharistic sharing was the prime expression of unity among local churches. To cease sharing the Eucharist was to cease being united.[137] For example, St. Cyprian of Carthage (ca. 200–58) emphasized the Eucharist as the outward sign of inward communion with God.[138] Reception of the Eucharist strengthens this inward and preexisting unity. Cyprian argued, therefore, that the bishop should refuse Holy Communion to the "lapsed." He thought that Christians who denied their faith in public to avoid persecution had damaged their inward communion with God. For St. Augustine, unity is the inward dynamic *(virtus)* at work in the Eucharist.[139] Likewise, Pope Gelasius I (fl. 492–96) held that the unity of the Church was the precondition of the Eucharist. He did not see unity as the result of the sacrament.[140] Early Scholastic theologians (late twelfth century) generally held that the Church was the realm in which the Eucharist is possible.[141]

Later Scholasticism commuted the relationship between the Eucharist and the unity of the Church. Where ancient writers had stressed the unity of the Church as the context in which the Eucharist occurs, the later authors would note how the unity of the Church is the result of our having received the Eucharist. Late Scholastic theologians like Gilbert de la Porrée and Thomas Aquinas held that the reality of the Eucharist (the *res sacramenti*) results in a network of relationships among all the redeemed with Christ and which comprise them as one Body in the Church.[142] Where the earlier views held that the Eucharist is an expression of unity, the later views held the reverse: The Eucharist is the cause of unity.

The Eucharist As the Means and Ends of Unity

In some fashion, each of these historic viewpoints emerges again in contemporary discussions of eucharistic sharing. The late Scholastic

---

[137] Auer, 343.

[138] Kilmartin, *Eucharist in the West*, 10f.

[139] *Sermon* 272. Aidan Nichols, *The Holy Eucharist: From the New Testament to Pope John Paul II* (Dublin: Veritas Publications, 1991) 54.

[140] Kilmartin, *Eucharist in the West*, 32.

[141] Ibid., 152.

[142] Nichols, *Holy Eucharist*, 83.

reversal points to the great difficulty in attempting to balance Catholic faith. On one side, faith maintains the effectiveness of the Eucharist as a means for creating Christian unity. On the other side, faith holds that eucharistic sharing ought to signify genuine communion and not just a thin veneer of unity. How can Christians claim to signify unity in the Eucharist where unity does not already exist? Modern Catholic catechisms, however, stress the effectiveness of sacraments. Sacraments cause what they signify, we maintain. To divide sacramental means from sacramental ends has the unfortunate result of stranding Catholics in a dilemma. Are the sacraments truly effective to unite us by God's grace or must we do all the work first and achieve complete unity, only after which a common Eucharist will be a kind of reward?

The strongest contemporary responses to the dilemma have sought to balance the means-and-ends approaches. Vatican II notes how the unity of the Church is expressed in the Eucharist and how the Eucharist causes the unity it signifies. *Lumen gentium* states that the "unity of the People of God" is "manifested in a concrete way," it is "signified and caused" by the Eucharist.[143] The Constitution on the Liturgy, *Sacrosanctum concilium*, spoke of how the liturgy—and especially the eucharistic liturgy—is the "summit" (*culmen* or culmination) and "source" (*fons* or spring) of the Church and all its activity. The Eucharist thus expresses the unity of the Church, like a summit; and, at the same time, is its cause, like a source.

In subsequent statements about eucharistic sharing, however, Catholic authorities have tended to stress one side of the dilemma over the other. The Eucharist expresses our unity, they say. If we do not already have unity, how can we express unity through the sacrament? For example, a 1980 statement of the Catholic Bishops of England and Wales, *Easter People,* speaks of the "achievement of unity." The bishops then judged that it would be counterproductive to use the Eucharist, "the perfect symbol of unity achieved as a means of achieving it." "This," they said, "could defer indefinitely the full corporate union for which we all pray."[144] The most significant difficulty with the English bishops' statement is their use of the term "achievement." "Achievement" seems a less-than-apt word to describe Christian communion.[145] Christian communion is not the "achievement" of a human community; it is an act of God.

---

[143] LG 11. Richstatter.

[144] Finch and Reardon, 22. They cite Catholic Bishops of England and Wales to the National Pastoral Congress, *Easter People,* Liverpool (1980).

[145] Richstatter.

Unity Is Not a Human Achievement:
The Risk of Pelagianism

When authorities require that there be no eucharistic Communion before there is full communion, they imply that the unity human beings can create among themselves is analogous and preparatory to the kind of unity that only God can create among us. Gerard Austin helps us clarify the problem. Discussions of eucharistic sharing tend to emphasize either what is accomplished by Christ or what is accomplished by ourselves. Protestant theologies have generally stressed the active role of Christ in the Eucharist. Since the Counter-Reformation, Catholic theologies have generally stressed the active role of the minister and the Church, what they do to assist in presenting Christ before us in the Eucharist. Austin recommends, "We must dig deeper and try to see inside both views . . ."[146]

Pelagianism is the view associated with the early fifth-century British monk, Pelagius, that human actions can be effective means of salvation apart from God's grace. The Pelagian believes we can work our way to salvation. Sometimes we like to think that Christian unity will happen only when we make it happen. The result is a kind of ecumenical Pelagianism, the idea that, by force of will alone, we can unite the Christian family.[147] Instead, a more thoroughly Christian direction would be to emphasize God's unique and intrinsic role in establishing Christian communion.

Several key ecumenical voices point in this direction. In the late 1960s, Cardinal Bea, one of the chief leaders and shapers of the Second Vatican Council, reminded his students that they must always treat the Eucharist with confidence. While the Eucharist is certainly the "seal of unity," he said we must also trust this gift. It is also the means of unity.[148] Vatican II confirmed Cardinal Bea's insight. As long as it was not used indiscriminately, *Unitatis redintegratio* recommended sacramental sharing as a sign of God's gracious drawing of Christians together into unity. Therefore, to trust in the power of the Eucharist to unite Christians from divided churches in full communion is not alien to a proper understanding of the sacrament.

Many other Christian voices join Cardinal Bea's to point the way beyond the means-versus-ends distinction. As prominent Protestant

---

[146] Gerard Austin, "Identity of a Eucharistic Church in an Ecumenical Age," *Worship* 72 (1998) 33.

[147] Falardeau, 11.

[148] Pierre Beffa, "Intercommunion: Some Personal Reflections and Testimonies," *The Ecumenical Review* 44, no. 1 (1992) 41.

theologian Wolfhart Pannenberg observes, eucharistic communion is not only the goal of Church union. It can also be, he wrote, "the present power of Christ by which we travel the path toward that goal."[149] The experience of several South African Churches confirms the effectiveness of eucharistic sharing for the restoration of full communion.[150] Thus Pannenberg's point has been proven time and again in the lived experience of uniting churches around the globe—in India, South Africa, the Netherlands, Canada, to name but a few places, where eucharistic sharing has led the way to church union.

Different Kinds of Unity

Marriage offers a helpful analogy to our understanding of unity. As a respondent to a study of interchurch couples in Great Britain noted: "For us [the Eucharist] is both a means to and a symbol of unity, and we think the distinction is to some degree artificial." "Means" versus "ends" ways of thinking, she remarked, "do not work very well within a successful marriage." The writer concludes, "In one respect unity means service, and that is when the two aspects [means and ends] come together. We think the churches should be each other's *servants* at the Eucharist."[151]

The respondent helps us remember that, in a marriage, the process of growing united in love consists of a covenant that both parties make to perform uniting actions on behalf of the other: sexual intercourse, conversation, dialogue, argument, holding hands, pleasantries, mutual support, and protection. The list extends indefinitely. The point is this: In a marriage, most actions and most words perform a dual function. In the first place, words and deeds simply mean what they mean: "I will pick up the children from soccer practice." In the second place, they create and perform the union of the two parties: "My concern for the well-being of our children signifies that I am united with you and for you in faithfulness." Such expressions within a marriage are both the means (cause) and the ends (result) of the couple's loving communion. Over the course of a lifetime, those who are one in marriage may become even more deeply united.

---

[149] John M. Russell, "Pannenberg on Eucharist and Unity," *Currents in Theology and Mission* 17 (1990) 118. He cites Wolfhart Pannenberg, *The Church*, trans. Keith Crim (Philadelphia: Westminster, 1983) 117.

[150] Dirk J. Smit, "Spirituality, Worship, Confession, and Church Unity: A Story from South Africa," in *Ecumenical Theology in Worship, Doctrine, and Life*, 277.

[151] Finch and Reardon, 91, emphasis original.

Christian unity is a process. When Christians ask about the kind of unity they seek, we sometimes forget that unity may be understood either as an end state or as a process. To understand "unity" as a process makes sense when we recall that "unity" can as easily be a verb as a noun in Greek. *Henosis*—"to make one"—is weakly translated into English as "union." *Henosis* refers to a dynamic dance of movement toward the object of union. In this sense, for Christ to pray that his disciples may be made one is clearly a dynamic prayer with powerful movement and energy (John 17:22). Unity is not achieved "once and for all." It is an ongoing process of movement in concert with another.

Catholic theologian Theresa Berger follows up on the ancient understanding of unity as a process. God's promise of wholeness, she says, is more about restored networks of relationship than it is about unity. These restored relationships are focused on "well-being for all." They are fluid, unstable, and constantly in transition. God creates and sustains these relationships and invites us to join them, to become united.[152]

On the one hand, if one understands that unity is a process of growing ever more united in love, then we can be more optimistic about prospects for Christian ecumenism. From this perspective, Christian union consists of an ongoing commitment to a plan of action: the intent to share ministry, faith, worship, wealth, and, of course, sacraments. The process of growing united in love is no guarantee that both parties will remain faithful forever. It does not mean they will never "commit adultery," will never "lie, cheat, or steal." It simply means, "For better or worse, I am with you." On the other hand, if one imagines that unity is the final state of a thing (the thing is in union with itself), then short of the full coming of the kingdom of God, one doubts that Church unity can ever become reality.

In the context of the Catholic Church—or any Church for that matter—the word "full communion" is a shorthand way to refer to the intent of Christians to live together within an institutional framework (more or less successfully) along with the countless actions they perform in order to signify and express their intent. Full communion is the result of a commitment to a process more than it is the description of a state of being.

Two types of unity in Holy Communion. Therefore, one can identify at least two types of unity in the Eucharist. The kind of unity that results from receiving Holy Communion differs from the kind of unity that can be required before Holy Communion. This is true for a very simple reason. Christian faith understands that we should not be the same kind of people before we received the sacrament as afterwards.

[152] Berger, 229.

If we expect that Christians must be equally united before and after receiving the sacrament, then we have argued our way out of supposing that the Eucharist has anything to do with unity. It might provide some other sort of grace, but it would not have increased our unity. That conclusion, however, is inconsistent with Christian tradition and conflicts with Catholic teaching on the Eucharist.

If our doctrine of sacramental efficacy—the idea that sacraments cause what they signify—means anything, it must mean that full communion is both signified in Holy Communion and caused by it. Therefore, we should not expect people already to be in full communion before they may receive its principal cause. We should expect only that they be disposed to receive the cause of the unity they intend to join. In presenting ourselves for Holy Communion, we unite in intent to receive a unity that transcends our hopes and dreams.

Before receiving Holy Communion, our unity consists of an indication of prior commitment. This is similar to the unity of a prenuptial agreement. It is the unity of a promise, an engagement to be united. After receiving Holy Communion, our unity ought to have been extended from commitment into reality. Coming away from the reception of Holy Communion, we might speak of the unity of the nuptial bed. It is a unity of fulfillment, of mutual intimacy with Christ and one another. Therefore, eucharistic unity must be understood as our capacity for relationship as transformed by Christ into the reality of relationship with others. It means becoming, repeatedly over the course of a lifetime, a community of "men and women for others."[153]

Administrative unity. Several Protestant churches have moved very far on the way toward sharing an open Communion. For example, in July 1997, the Religious News Service reported that the United Church of Christ had approved full communion with the Evangelical Lutheran Church in America and two other denominations in the Presbyterian and Reformed tradition. The formula of agreement allows ministers to "cross denomination lines," subject to the rules of each Church body.[154]

From a Catholic perspective, the full communion described by this report differs from the full communion we seek in Christian ecumenism. From our perspective, full communion would also include an administrative unity. The key phrase "subject to the rules of each Church body" would not be necessary in full communion, since it would amount to there being only one Church body and only one set of rules.

---

[153] Ibid., 150f.

[154] Religious News Service, "UCC Approves 'Full Communion' Proposal," *Christian Century* (July 16, 1997).

Jurisdictional unity and unity of faith stand and fall together from this perspective.

In the Church, administrative unity exists to serve and nurture our intent to live in communion. Administrative unity and full communion are otherwise quite separate realities.[155] Administrative unity exists because there is already a communion with Christ and the Spirit that needs protection and sustaining. With their emphasis on apostolic succession and the historic episcopate, recent statements from the Vatican suggest that Catholic authorities understand ecumenism as a quest for administrative unity rather than for life in communion.

At other times, some Church authorities have come to define unity narrowly, but apply it universally. They take a very narrow and idiosyncratic understanding of what it means to be the Church of Christ and deny its narrowness and particularity. Then, they insist that anyone with genuine piety or intelligence will agree with them. When Christian authorities or churches speak this way, "unity" amounts to a code word for the false universalization of a particular and narrow outlook.[156] It is the unity of a sect.

Because of the heavy-handed approaches from some religious authorities, more than a few have given up on the quest for administrative unity and for convergence in Christian doctrine. They say the quest amounts to a "desperate enterprise."[157] In a word, the requirement of full communion is impossibly burdensome, if it amounts to assent both to an unabridged catechism of dogmatic principles and to faraway and unaccountable authorities who are empowered to alter, abridge, or add to those principles without advice or consent.[158]

Unity in truth. Having concerns about the heavy-handed, authoritarian approach to the ascertainment of Christian doctrine is not the same as giving in to a laissez-faire relativism. It remains true that any form of Christian unity worth its salt will not be a relativist's, "you believe your thing, I'll believe mine," kind of affair. Unity in truth is an essential factor for Christian communion. The experience of South Africa is

---

[155] Maxcey, 92.

[156] Cf. Miroslav Volf, *Exclusion and Embrace: A Theological Exploration of Identity, Otherness, and Reconciliation* (Nashville: Abingdon Press, 1996) 202.

[157] Raimon Panikkar, "The Fragment and the Part: An Indic Reflection," in *The Church in Fragments*, 86.

[158] Additionally, many women rightly fear that administrative unity is inevitably an asymmetrical unity. In ecumenical dialogue, narrow and inflexible configurations of Church unity systematically disadvantage women and other groups. Ecumenical dialogue groups like the World Council of Churches have experienced difficulty speaking to these concerns (Berger, 224).

particularly instructive. South Africa's history of apartheid originated in the refusal of some white Christians to share the Lord's Supper with nonwhite (African, Indian, and mixed-race) Christians. Their refusal eventually led to some of the many rationalizations offered in support of South Africa's former practice of apartheid.

Dirk Smit summarizes the story of apartheid for us. "In a way, it started with the Eucharist," he writes.

> In 1855, white worshipers in a rural Dutch Reformed congregation refused to share the Lord's Supper with colored believers. In 1857, the Synod decided that it was "preferable and Scriptural" that all believers shared the same worship and the same congregation, but where these measures, "as a result of the weakness of some," obstructed the Christian cause, "Christian privileges could be enjoyed in separate buildings and even separate institutions." The "weakness of some" soon became the norm. In 1881, a separate "church" or denomination, the Dutch Reformed Mission Church, was established for colored people, and during the twentieth century several others would follow, all divided according to race or ethnicity. Although they all belonged to the so-called "Dutch Reformed Church family," almost without any structural or visible unity, white believers in the (white) Dutch Reformed Church were gradually made to believe that having separate Churches for each nation *(volkskerke)* was the norm, according to Scripture and the divine will. This church policy of separate Churches would later form the religious roots of the ideology . . . of apartheid.[159]

The history of South African Christians demonstrates how Christians risk and diminish their own unity—their relationship to Christ—whenever they stave off fellow Christians from receiving Holy Communion. In the words of the apostle Paul, we effect a judgment against ourselves if we ever fail to discern Christ in these baptized men and women who stand and pray among us. The desire to stand together in the unity of truth must always be balanced against the need, first, to stand together in charity. At times, when we try too hard to preserve a doctrine, we end up having enacted its negation instead.

Christian unity is not fascist. The Church is a gathering and a unity of men and women in faith. It is not, however, the result of a "fascist binding of many into one" within the domination of a single human will. There is no room, in the Church, for the exclusion of "otherness."[160] A more thoroughly Christian understanding of unity asserts the oppo-

[159] Smit, 271.

[160] William T. Cavanaugh, *Torture and Eucharist: Theology, Politics, and the Body of Christ* (London: Blackwell Publishers, 1998) 271.

site. The unity of the Church is not totalitarian; it is always a "unity in diversity." The unity of the Church is dynamic and full of life; it is not static or motionless. The unity of the Church is always a unity in multiplicity. The unity of the Church is always catholic.[161] Christians' unity is not the result of a "logic of identity."[162] It is not the result of the manufacture of interchangeable parts, where every ecclesiastical widget looks, behaves, and thinks like every other ecclesiastical widget.

The search for Christian unity must not result in absorption or fusion. Christian communion must go deeper than institutional merger. It is a "meeting together" in truth and in love.[163] Christian unity is not the result of a "concession" to the other person in his or her otherness. It is the result of our having "welcomed" one another with the love and truth God gives us in Jesus of Nazareth.[164]

Christian unity is never merely sociological. Unity is foremost a characteristic of God. We know, understand, and experience "unity" only when God has given it to us as a gift.[165] Unity transcends the Church. It is larger and deeper than any chimera of "union" that men and women—even well-meaning Christian people—could construct on their own.[166] In the words of Carl Braaten, "In a certain sense we cannot create unity, we can only recognize it."[167] Unity is something that God does to us; not something we can do for ourselves. To attempt a unity on our own can only result in a "simulated communion."[168] It would amount to another Tower of Babel. It could hardly compare to the rich unity in diversity of a New Pentecost.

Consequently, Christian communion is always a gift of the Holy Spirit. Christian communion is possible only because of the paschal mystery. God invites us, through baptism, to participate in the death and resurrection of Jesus and to receive his Spirit. Because the Eucharist is the place where the paschal mystery is extended sacramentally into our own place and time by the agency of the Holy Spirit, Christians must always enact their intent to live in full communion through the Eucharist. Christ offers us no other more effective way to be uniting and united.

---

[161] Brosseder, "Towards What Unity," 133.
[162] Ruggieri, 151.
[163] Power, "*Koinonia, Oikoumene,* and Eucharist," 122.
[164] Ruggieri, 150.
[165] Ruggieri, 149.
[166] Ibid., 150f.
[167] Braaten, 32.
[168] Cf. Monika Hellwig, *The Eucharist and the Hunger of the World* (New York: Paulist Press, 1976) 75.

The unity we seek is a communion. How long must we wait for full communion among the churches? Can we enjoy full communion tomorrow or must we wait for the end of time? On the one hand, several theologians have suggested that nothing the Church can do on earth will restore unity among Christians. The best we can muster are "interim statements, for at every point they are clouded by our ignorance, our pride, our partial histories, and our lack of trust in the power of God . . ."[169]

Those who follow this mode of thinking imply that Christian unity is not real unless it is perfect. They are waiting for the Christian churches and other communities to be united to a superhuman degree. In these circles, the eschatological reality of the Church, its perfect end, is what matters most. Perhaps, then, the Christian churches cannot be united until the kingdom comes.[170]

On the contrary, *Lumen gentium* offers a far more optimistic perspective on the quest for Christian unity. Christian unity exists at the level of sacramentality and Church unity is not a goal in its own right. Instead, it is an effective sign of God incarnate within the human community.[171] Jurisdictional unity and unity in the expression of faith are sacramental signs of the unity God grants us, the unity we can scarcely signify on our own. God gives us unity not simply because unity is a good thing, but because it is an attribute of God's very being. God communicates God's self to us in Christ and the Spirit. We can become one only because God is One.

In the words of one theologian, unity is not a mark of the Church. It is a mystery of God. It is manifested to us through the ability to discern God the Father in the person of Jesus of Nazareth, the Son.[172] Therefore, paradoxically, we wait but we do not need to wait for Christian unity. Because of God's ongoing communication of grace, the Church of Christ is already one. It is already becoming more one. The task of Christians, their ministers, and authorities is to receive the grace of unity in each time and place. They must bring this unity to visible form.[173] Just as they are experts at making the Gospel audible in preaching, Christian

---

[169] Bernard Thorogood, "Coming to the Lord's Table: A Reformed Viewpoint," *The Ecumenical Review* 44, no. 1 (1992) 12.

[170] Matthias Klinghardt, *Gemeinschaftsmahl und Mahlgemeinschaft: Soziologie und Liturgie frühchristlicher Mahlfeiern,* ed. Klaus Berger et al. (Tübingen: A. Francke Verlag, 1996) 331.

[171] LG 1. Ruggieri, 148.

[172] Ruggieri, 150.

[173] Martin Reardon, "Intercommunion and the Meissen and Porvoo Agreements," *One in Christ* 37, no. 1 (2002) 64.

ministers need to help Christians to become visible words of Christ's Gospel.

Why Expressing a "Nonexistent Unity" Is a Risk

As it is typically stated, we must have unity before we can express it in the sacrament of unity. The risk in eucharistic sharing is that we would have expressed a lie. With the reception of Holy Communion, we would have said we are one without really being one.

If you have to possess unity before you may express it, and if the cause of unity is the expression of unity, then we have fashioned the Eucharist into a chicken-and-egg problem with no foreseeable resolution. This formulation overlooks the cause of our unity: God and not ourselves. It overlooks the kind of unity we seek: authentic relationship in Christ and not an institutional unity alone. It fails to recognize the different kinds of unity expressed in Holy Communion: the unity of intention and the unity that only God can give us. As a result, this formulation of the problem is not particularly helpful for our understanding of the Eucharist and it does not nurture the conditions for greater Christian unity.

Instead, we should focus on the intent to be united. In the presence of an intent to unite, Christians can join in Holy Communion trusting that God will overcome their differences, if not today, then in the actual future. Christians should not need to wait for the end of time to join in Christian communion; but they do need to be open for God's grace to change them and make them fit for a life shared in the Body of Christ. Therefore, Christian ministers should nourish and nurture unity wherever unity exists. They should nourish and nurture the intent to join in unity wherever unity does not exist. As another respondent to the previously mentioned survey of interchurch couples wrote,

> If God is love, and if a Church, in love, helps a couple or family to grow together in love, can it be accused of "indefinitely deferring unity"? If it nourishes unity where unity exists rather than causing division where unity exists, can it be doing anything other than the will of God? How can unity be achieved by fostering division?[174]

The unity offered to disciples of Jesus is a "oneness of total presence" to others and to God. The resurrection alone can make this sort of "total presence" possible for us. The Church is a response to Jesus' request for

---

[174] Finch and Reardon, 92.

God to restore the unity of humankind. God offers the Church to the world as the ordinary means of its restoration to wholeness.[175] God calls us to become one so that we can be uniting. Eucharistic sharing in the absence of the desire to hear and respond to God's call to unity is a risk. A high priority for ecumenism, then, will be to hear God's call together and to learn trust for one another in our responses.

Risk 5:
Indiscriminate Reception of Holy Communion

At the funeral for a trusted aide, former U.S. President Ronald Reagan and his wife, Nancy, received Holy Communion in a Catholic Church in the Archdiocese of New York during the early 1980s. President Reagan was formerly Catholic and Nancy is not. In addition, Reagan's marriage to Nancy is his second marriage and is invalid according to Catholic norms. Unlike the case of President Clinton, there was no public commotion, no communiqués from the Vatican. Andrew Greeley wondered in print whether Reagan's conservative political views had been his Communion ticket.[176]

This example points to the significant challenges faced by pastors who, in good conscience, formulate the policies and procedures that limit or open access to Holy Communion. Because St. Paul wrote that those who receive the Lord's Supper unworthily eat and drink to their own destruction (1 Cor 11:27), Church authorities understand they hold a solemn duty to protect men and women from receiving Holy Communion unworthily. Historically, this has led many Christian churches to practice what is sometimes called "fencing the table." This means that they enact specific policies and procedures to restrict admission to Holy Communion. Such measures range from simple forms of "gate-keeping" to excommunication. In this, the final section of chapter 2, I briefly examine what it may mean to receive the Eucharist worthily. What rites, procedures, and policies has the Church formulated to protect potential communicants from their own unworthiness?

---

[175] Sekretariat der Deutschen Bischofskonferenz, *Einheit der Kirche und Gemeinschaft im Herrenmahl: Zur neueren ökumenischen Diskussion um Eucharistie und Kirchengemeinschaft* (September 25, 2000).

[176] Andrew Greeley, "Clinton-Bashers and the Eucharist," *The Denver Post* (April 11, 1998) B-07. Cokie Roberts and Steven Roberts, "Sacrament Should Serve to Include, Not to Exclude," *The Denver Rocky Mountain News* (April 12, 1998) F-3B.

Worthiness to Receive

As noted above, I do not believe the Eucharist is a laissez-faire free-for-all. At the same time, I do not believe we should be overly protective of the sacrament. Most of the people who would deliberately harm the Church probably do not want to receive Holy Communion. Sinful people know what's good for them. Even if a few wolves in sheep's clothing slip into the communion procession, if they attempt to harm the Church and receive the Eucharist, is Christ powerless to defend himself and us?

This does not mean that worthiness is a trivial issue. For most Christians, it is not. They receive communion with reverence and awe. For example, my father tells me that his mother, my grandmother, made her profession of faith and received the Lord's Supper for the first time in her middle age. He says that, for the longest time, my grandmother felt she could not make a public profession of faith. She had to know with certainty that the Lord had found her worthy to receive him. For her "Blessed Assurance, Jesus is Mine" was not simply the title of a hymn. For her the phrase had great personal meaning only because, later in life, she received an experience of God's assurance and her own worthiness.

Worthiness is not niceness and decency. Sometimes North American Christians confuse words like "decency" and "niceness" with Paul's sense of worthiness as found in 1 Corinthians. We, twenty-first-century Americans, remain the children of bourgeois and Victorian values and we still place a high value on refinement of character. As good as these values are, we should take care not to confuse them with worthiness. Unfortunately, when we read Paul's warning against receiving Holy Communion unworthily, we think he refers to especially sinful men and women alone. We form a mental image of people of ill repute. Communion, we think, is for nice folks.

Kofi Asare Opoku, an African theologian, helpfully distinguishes between Gospel values and culturally relative values. "If the church," he writes, "is seen . . . to be the place for only 'decent' problems, then it is not meeting the real needs of the people, social and spiritual. Such an understanding dichotomizes our lives; decent problems go to church on Sunday, and during the rest of the week, when we are engulfed in 'indecent' problems we take them to other places for solutions."[177] Thus, Opoku suggests that our interest in niceness and decency blinds

---

[177] Primavesi and Henderson, 69. They cite Kofi Asare Opoku, "The Church in Africa and Contemporary Sociological Challenges," *The Ecumenical Review* 40, no. 2 (1988) 250.

us to the role of Christian community in resolving our indecencies and meanness. We ought to bring them to church and pile them high upon the altar so that our meanness and indecency can be healed and transformed into genuine worth.

Unworthiness as the intent to undermine Christian communion. Paul's letter to the Corinthian Christians demonstrates that the manner in which Christians eat and drink the sacramental signs can undermine Christian community. Paul insisted that the quality of eucharistic sharing is essential to the possibility of our eucharistic sharing. In a sense, he was asking the Corinthian Christians, "How can you receive the Body and Blood of Christ when you are receiving it in a manner that undermines the Body of Christ?"

Put another way, you cannot both receive Communion and destroy communion at the same time. This paradox is at the heart of our problem. About this paradox, biblical scholar C. K. Barrett says that the Corinthians contradicted the sacrament, "not by liturgical error, or by undervaluing it, but by prefixing it to an unbrotherly *[sic]* act."[178] In the context of the problem of eucharistic sharing, erecting too strong a fence around our altars may be no less "unbrotherly" an act.

Worthiness as concern for the whole. We should recall the condition of those to whom Paul wrote his words of warning. Paul's emphasis on worthiness to receive the Lord's Supper was directed to men and women who thought they had a very good handle on who is worthy and who is unworthy. These Corinthian Christians were full of themselves; they knew that they had to be the worthy ones. After all, they were blessed with more wealth, higher status, greater knowledge, and power. Who could overlook such overwhelming signs of God's favor? The same group was no less certain of the identity of the unworthy. It was obvious! They were poor, slaves, and merchants. Who was Paul, they thought, to insist and demand that everyone should share Holy Communion at the same time and place?

In speaking about worthiness to men and women who presumed they were already worthy, Paul redefined the notion of "worth." In the eyes of God, worth does not correspond to outward signs of success. Following Paul's argument, worth ought to be measured instead in degrees of accepting and embracing others, especially society's untouchables. Therefore, when people discern whether they are worthy to receive the Lord's Supper, they should consider how well they are accepting

---

[178] Francis J. Moloney, *A Body Broken for a Broken People: Eucharist in the New Testament*, rev. ed. (Peabody, Mass. & Blackburn, Victoria, Australia: Hendrickson Publishers & HarperCollins Religious, 1997) 167. He cites C. K. Barrett, *The First Epistle to the Corinthians*, 264.

and embracing their neighbors—all of their neighbors—without exception. To the extent that one is less accepting and less embracing, and would prefer to dine alone, one is unworthy. To the extent that one is growing in love along with the rest of the Church, one is worthy because he or she has discerned the Body of Christ.

Worthiness as a death to self. At the heart of Paul's eucharistic teaching one finds also the element of a death to self or a commitment to a life given for others. For Paul, a worthy reception of the Body and Blood of Christ amounts to a pledge or oath of loyalty to Christian companions. Our pilgrimage through time leads every Christian through the paschal mystery of Jesus' death, resurrection, and gift of the Spirit.

In the words of Francis J. Moloney, "To celebrate Eucharist is to commit oneself to a discipleship that 'remembers' Jesus—not only in the breaking of the ritual bread and the sharing of the ritual cup but also in 'imitation' of Jesus, in the ongoing breaking of one's own body and spilling of one's own blood 'in remembrance' of Jesus."[179] In baptism, therefore, Christians have made a martyrdom oath. This oath is not a pledge to kill infidels. It is not an oath to slay sinners. Far less is it a suicide pact. The suicide and the martyr are quite different creatures. Rather, it is a pledge to be faithful to Christ and to one another. In baptism, we commit to the Body of Christ, both head and members—no matter the cost.

Disposed to Receive

In his encyclical on the Eucharist, *Dominicae coenae*, Pope John Paul II focuses on the ordinary means to become disposed to receive a worthy Communion. He understands the disposition to receive primarily in terms of confessing one's sins and shortcomings in the context of the sacrament of reconciliation.[180] Being disposed to receive entails freedom from mortal sins (preferably, freedom from lesser sins also). If the Pope emphasizes sacramental reconciliation in preparation for Holy Communion, I would also mention how the liturgy itself prepares men and women to receive the Eucharist in good faith.[181] God calls baptized men and women to assemble. There they hear God's Word. They respond with acclamations and intercessions. They profess the ancient and apostolic faith as expressed in the Creeds. They bless and thank God in the prayer over the bread and wine. With vigorous assent, they announce the "Great Amen" at the conclusion of the eucharistic prayer.

[179] Moloney, 169.
[180] Kilmartin, *Church, Eucharist, and Priesthood,* 49.
[181] ESOU, 21.

They share a sign of peace and reconciliation. When they are offered the consecrated bread and wine, they respond, "Amen." What other "signs of unity" ought to be required of the prospective communicant?

Consequently, when non-Catholics attend the Catholic liturgy, how should we interpret their expressions of faith along with us? When non-Catholics pray with us for the pope, the bishops, and clergy, do we assume they are "crossing their fingers"? Non-Catholic guests respond with no less vigor to the eucharistic prayer at the "Great Amen." Unless they tell us so, we may not assume that they have bracketed out whole sections of the prayer, the parts that may or may not conform to their understanding of the Eucharist. When they share a sign of peace and reconciliation with their Catholic hosts, I believe we should presume our guests' good faith. Non-Catholic Christians desire the peace and reconciliation of Christ no less than we do. If their "yes" does not mean "yes," if their "yes" means "maybe," perhaps they have a duty to tell us so. They tell us this by refraining from receiving Communion; no other words required. But if their "yes" really means "yes," if Catholics question their commitment this may be perceived as indication of a lack of trust and an offense. For all we know, their faith is deeper and more substantial than any other member in our community. What more can we ask from communicants? If more questions need to be asked, we should first look to the liturgy for more detailed commitments.

The Communion of Penitents and Excommunicated Christians

Lingering behind our discussion of the disposition to receive, we must consider if there are any proper reasons to deny Holy Communion to baptized Christians. From the earliest sources, Christians have argued in favor of denying Communion to Christians who had committed adultery, murder, or apostasy, the original capital sins.

Consider the HBO drama series, *The Sopranos*. Perhaps the character of Tony Soprano—who occasionally attends worship and whose wife and family receive Holy Communion—illustrates the casual attitude that some Christians may have about their own disposition to receive Holy Communion. Certainly, membership in a non-Catholic Church bears no similarity to the moral stature of a man whose business is vice and murder or whose wife condones it! If men and women like those on *The Sopranos* are receiving Communion in the Catholic Church, why should morally virtuous non-Catholics be prevented? Some readers will protest that "Tony Soprano," because he is fictional, is not a fair representation. To them I offer the example of General Augusto Pinochet, one-time dictator of Chile. Pinochet did not hesitate to request and receive Communion from the archbishop of Santiago even while his government operated death squads, torturing and assassinating Chilean men and women, Catholic and non-Catholic alike.[182]

If some Church authorities are so loose with respect to regulating access to the sacraments among their own, why are they so strict with respect to regulating access to the sacraments among other baptized Christians? One of the aims of this book is to show that membership in an ecclesial community is, by itself, an insufficient norm for admission to Holy Communion. Indeed, it may not be a satisfactory norm at all.

To encourage the "Tony Sopranos" or authoritarian dictators of our world to receive Holy Communion undermines the integrity of Christ's sacraments. It is to undermine the Eucharist as a visible sign of God's justice. Whenever we do so, we invite contradiction between the sign of God's loving and just dominion and our eucharistic covenant to live on earth in a communion of love and justice.

Excommunication

The strongest ritual of limiting access to the altar occurs in a solemn declaration of excommunication. Some readers will be familiar with the Brother Cadfael mystery novels and television series. On several occasions, the monks of Brother Cadfael's abbey were called on to excommunicate a public sinner or heretic. At least on television—which rarely manages to get Christian rituals quite right—the decisive gesture was the simultaneous extinction of candles as the monks quickly turned their large tapers upside down. We should not imagine that bishops who publicly excommunicate dissident Christians still call on monks to perform these rituals. The symbolism remains fitting. For the monks to extinguish their candles is the ritual equivalent of snuffing the candle that had once been given the excommunicated Christian when he or she was baptized.

In the main, modern theologians hold that excommunication should be seen as a pastoral act. They say it is a healing wound. Excommunication is a juridical act of the Church. We perform it with reluctance, recognizing that a baptized Christian has lost his or her communion in Christ, even in the eschatological dimension of God's ultimate future.[183] Viewed positively, excommunication excludes for the sake of protecting the communion of the Church. Excommunication does not divide the Church. It manifests and makes visible a division already created by the offending parties.[184] Excommunication is not exclusionary,

---

[182] Cf. Cavanaugh, *Torture and Eucharist*.

[183] Ibid., 57.

[184] Cavanaugh, *Torture and Eucharist*, 262.

because the goal of excommunication is reconciliation. The intent of the ban is not to "forsake the sinner but to cure him."[185]

Excommunication wakes up the offender to the seriousness of his or her fault. It "clarifies for the sinner . . . the seriousness of the offense."[186] The Church should excommunicate only after less drastic attempts at reconciliation are unsuccessful. The motive for eucharistic excommunication is to "move one to amendment of life before the Lord has to intervene in his own way in order to *save the sinner from destroying all* that is qualitatively Christian in himself."[187] When done well, excommunication can be an "act of hospitality." It consists of an acknowledgment of an objective condition of brokenness and includes an invitation to its resolution through healing and reconciliation.[188] There is no such thing as an "absolute" or "irrevocable" excommunication.[189]

If the Church is an expression of God's desire for relationship with all humanity, then there are good reasons to protect it. At the same time, we bear unique obligations to the men and women who want to injure or destroy God's relationship to others.[190] In the context of Christian ecumenism, however, there is no reason to believe that baptized non-Catholics want to injure God's covenant. Quite the reverse, most non-Catholic churches assembled in order to preserve and enhance the quality of Christian life. For this reason, the positive and pastoral aspects of excommunication do not seem to fit the problem of eucharistic sharing. Church authorities pronounce an excommunication for the purpose of reconciliation because it assists the sinner in the transition to penitence. By contrast, the bans on eucharistic sharing reassert ecclesial division and do not provide hope for reconciliation. The bans do not clarify an offense or sin on the part of the non-Catholic.

Excommunication amounts to a judgment on the moral character of the Christian; but the bans on eucharistic sharing do not judge the moral character of the non-Catholic Christian. The excommunicated Christian can choose the way of penitence. The non-Catholic Christian could be the greatest of saints, but still not receive. With a word, the excommunicated Christian possesses the power to change his or her status as a noncommunicant. Without self-contradiction, the non-Catholic cannot.

---

[185] Ibid., 240.
[186] Ibid., 243.
[187] Hein, 439f.
[188] Cavanaugh, *Torture and Eucharist*, 243.
[189] Hein, 417.
[190] Lev 26:14-43. Hein, 5.

Gate-Keeping Short of Excommunication

For many Christians, to say a person is worthy to receive the Eucharist refers to a vague moral or religious sensibility. For others, the notion of worth is a useful means of social control. It functions as an "anxiety-producing means of moral gate-keeping."[191]

Churches communicate limitations on access to Holy Communion through a variety of means. For example, in some Reformed and Presbyterian churches, Communion tokens were distributed by Church elders during interviews held in the homes of prospective communicants during the week prior to the Lord's Supper. In many Lutheran churches in the United States, "Communion registration" is a serious undertaking. To register for Communion usually involves signing a brief profession of faith and identifying one's home congregation. Catholics, too, have their own forms of gate-keeping. Meinrad Scherer-Edmunds, a columnist for *U.S. Catholic* magazine, reports, "When it was time for Communion during the installation Mass for a Catholic bishop in Massachusetts, ushers were posted to guard the front pews to make sure the Episcopalian, Lutheran, Baptist, and other Protestant 'honored guests' stayed in their place."[192] Perhaps the ones who prepared for this liturgy believed they were inviting these honored guests to witness a ceremony and not to join in common worship. Perhaps they imagined that Protestant guests are like ambassadors from foreign lands. We invite them to witness the ordination just as foreign countries invite ambassadors to witness inaugurations and coronations. In the political metaphor, the reception of Holy Communion is like voting. It is offered to citizens alone.

The political metaphor fails, however, since entrance to Holy Communion is not a matter of legal right or entitlement. Receiving Holy Communion, rather, signifies entrance into mutual obligation. The reception of the Eucharist is the sign of a covenant relationship between God and God's people. It is a covenant in Christ's Blood. What purpose is served by preventing other Christians from jointly affirming with us this covenant, the same covenant into which they were baptized? Guarding the Eucharist from non-Catholic Christians does little to protect the Eucharist from profanation. It does nothing to advance Christian unity.[193]

I could multiply the number of egregious examples of poor eucharistic practice. Every liturgy professor carries a satchel of horror stories

---

[191] Welker, 70.
[192] Scherer-Edmunds, 24.
[193] Ibid.

like this one. Horror stories about worst practices, liturgical behaviors that nearly everyone hopes to avoid, help if your goal is to spur liturgical planners to consider the potential misunderstandings that a ceremony might stir up for people. Bishops, popes, and the best theologians in the world will misunderstand the liturgy and implement problematic rites and ceremonies from time to time. Even the best intentions will result, at times, in offensive words or deeds. The problem is that horror stories do not make for good theology.

Why Indiscriminate Reception of Holy Communion Is a Risk

Lutheran theologian Dagmar Heller points to divine law and wonders why laws of human origin are usually more restrictive. Heller asks, "Will God condemn the priest who has given the Lord's Supper to a Protestant?" If no, then we must ask why any Church maintains canonical penalties for this priest. If yes, then we must wonder whether God is just and merciful. She concludes that God's openness scandalizes our sensibilities. Divine law, properly understood, threatens the human instinct to construct social relationships by distinguishing insiders and outsiders.[194]

The reception of Holy Communion should not be a test-case for the assertion of self-righteousness on the part of any portion of the Christian community. "It is not an opportunity to grant or refuse moral or juridical recognition to other human beings."[195] Nonetheless, a huge and silent host of people who did not come to worship this Sunday were easily more worthy to receive Holy Communion than those who did. Faith tells us there is far more sanctity in the world than there is sinfulness; and there is more sinfulness in the Church than we should ever care to think.

Where is the moral equity in this strange and ironic situation? If this were not a tragedy, we would laugh at the strangeness. Millions are invited to a banquet but cannot attend because several hundred others, whether invited or uninvited—we cannot be sure—have barred the doors to the dining room. After a time, the ones left out in the cold gave up knocking. They went home to bake their own meals.

Church hopping, commitment, and loyalty. Catholics have special difficulty with limited relationships in religious matters. Our folklore is full of expressions related to this difficulty. "You are Catholic for life,"

---

[194] Dagmar Heller, "Eucharistic Fellowship in the Third Millennium? The Question of the Eucharist in Future Ecumenical Discussions," *The Ecumenical Review* 51 (1999).

[195] Welker, 83.

"Once a Catholic, always a Catholic," "You are a priest for ever," "Until death parts us," "What God has joined, let no one divide." Our difficulty with temporary commitments comes to the fore in the problem of eucharistic sharing as usually conceived. When some folks show up for Mass only occasionally, it is as if they were saying, "I will dine with you today; but not necessarily tomorrow." The Catholic intuition is that authentic Communion must mean something less fleeting.

Church hoppers. A more open eucharistic sharing risks that we might offer hospitality to the "church hopper." The church hopper is the person who moves from church to church, feeding off the hospitality of local communities. Church hoppers live in a community for a time. They find nurture and comfort there. When the local community asserts a transforming effect, most people will remain, endure, and mature as a result of deepening relationships. The church hopper, by contrast, flees from the pressure to change. They leave for another community. How churches and church authorities respond to the church hopper is a far more serious risk than whether churches allow church hoppers to receive Holy Communion. We must always negotiate a balance between openness and commitment.

On one side, to the extent that churches protect themselves from church hoppers by less open eucharistic sharing, they risk their own injury. If the local church works endlessly to preclude the church hopper from latching on to the community, that Church will only kill itself in the process. The Church will have had to erect substantial barriers to joining. They risk their own marginalization and retreat into sectarianism.

On the other side, to the extent that churches fail to challenge the church hopper because they observe an open Eucharist without any expectations from the communicant, they risk their own mission. For example, Jesus seized a moment of conversion when he invited himself into the home of Zacchaeus. If the local church does not work at all to include the church hopper and to follow up after the church hopper detaches from the community, that church will have failed its mission "to seek out and to save the lost" (Luke 19:10).

Commitment and loyalty. Catholic folklore sometimes gives the impression that our first loyalty is to our bishop, to the pope, or to the Vatican. I do not question the value of loyalty to bishop, pope, or the Vatican Curia. The difficulty, though, is how one understands the proper place of that loyalty within the context of Christian faith. Christians do not make a one-sided or unilateral commitment to Christ. As Catholics, we cannot presume to limit our loyalty oath to bishops or clergy. Our pledge is to the whole Church—Christ and all his members. Nowhere in the baptismal rites do we hedge our bets or cross our fingers. Baptismal promises, confirmation, professions of faith, and eucharistic acclamations are made in public, before the Church. Our loyalty is first to Christ and then to his Body.

Instead, our problem has been to ensure that the ones who minister to us—our clergy in particular—are the sacramental embodiment of Christian unity. For us, they must function in fact and not simply in theory as apostles of Jesus Christ. Of course, our bishops are answerable to the pope and to his assistants. Catholics are experts at deferring to higher authorities. Our churches, bishops, and popes have had a much more difficult time, however, learning to listen for and respond to the promptings of the Holy Spirit among the laity, among non-Catholics, and among non-Christians. The matter of eucharistic sharing may be one of those issues where Catholic authorities may profit from tuning their ears to the voices and hearts of non-Catholic Christians and other men and women of good faith.

Conclusions

In this chapter, I have examined five reasons for caution in eucharistic sharing. When we carefully examine and understand them, each of these reasons has significant merit. In other ways, often from the perspective of the more typical interpretations, they seem far less compelling.

A brief summary of each risk as I have defined them:

1. In recent ecumenical dialogue, Christians have created genuine convergence in eucharistic doctrine. Failing to agree on the meaning of the Eucharist is not a significant risk for eucharistic sharing. The more significant risk is that we would fail to enact our doctrine in eucharistic worship, that we would fail to be present to Christ or to enter into the act of his self-offering.

2. The Church is both visible and invisible. In the order of visible things—sociologically—the churches are woefully divided. In the order of invisible things—theologically—the Church of Christ cannot be divided. The risk in a more open eucharistic sharing is that we would unite as the visible Church of Christ in the wrong way. On the one hand, we risk uniting in an oppressive way; on the other hand, in an ephemeral way.

3. One risk in a more open eucharistic sharing is that we would send members of our community to receive ministry from men and women who are not accountable to the Gospels and to the Christian tradition. The doctrine of apostolic succession seeks to certify

Christian ministry. While Catholics are well disposed to recognize the institutional manifestations of apostolic succession, we are less able to recognize how many non-Catholic communities manifest apostolicity in a broad sense, apart from the ministry of bishops.

4. Instead of focusing on the Eucharist as the expression and cause of Christian unity, we will more fruitfully focus on the intent to be united by means of God's grace. A more open eucharistic sharing in the absence of this intent to be united in truth (indifferentism) is a serious risk for the Church. At the same time, when Christians share the intent to unite in full communion (ecumenical desire), the Eucharist can be an effective means to bring those intentions to fruition. When this happens, to restrict eucharistic sharing may instead foster division and indefinitely defer Christian unity.

5. The problem of worthiness to receive Holy Communion touches on the problem of eucharistic sharing, but does not resolve it. In particular, we should not equate the status of the baptized non-Catholic to the status of the penitent or excommunicated Christian. Catholics will not endorse indiscriminate Communion. However, they must be prepared to minister to men and women whenever they present themselves to us. We must learn to respond like Jesus who seized the moment of conversion for Zacchaeus, not by condemning him, but by inviting himself home. Jesus' actions point out how hospitality is the genuine antidote to ostracism, how God's generosity heals human miserliness. At the Eucharist we learn to forgive by being forgiven, to love by being loved, and to abandon ourselves by receiving others.

Questions for Reflection and Dialogue

1. *Risks in general:* In your own view, what is the most serious concern raised by the possibility of a more open eucharistic sharing? How do your views compare to the views of others? Are you aware of risks not mentioned in this chapter?

2. *Delaying Christian unity:* Some have suggested that a more open eucharistic sharing would actually delay and hinder Christian ecumenism. Do you agree with this assessment? Why or why not?

3. *Looking for deeper reasons:* In each category of risk, I have suggested how the "risks on the surface" are less significant than are the "risks beneath the surface." How would you describe some of these "risks beneath the surface" to a friend who had not read this book?

4. *Disposition to receive Holy Communion:* How do you prepare to receive Holy Communion? How have your attitudes about receiving Holy Communion changed as a result of reading this chapter?

For Further Reading

Cavanaugh, William T. "'The World in a Wafer: A Geography of the Eucharist as Resistance to Globalization." In *Catholicism and Catholicity: Eucharistic Communities in Historical and Contemporary Perspectives,* edited by Sarah Beckwith. Oxford: Blackwell Publishers, 1999, 69–84.

_____. *Torture and Eucharist: Theology, Politics, and the Body of Christ.* London: Blackwell Publishers, 1998.

Hellwig, Monika. *The Eucharist and the Hunger of the World.* New York: Paulist Press, 1976.

Huels, John M. *One Table, Many Laws: Essays On Catholic Eucharistic Practice.* Collegeville, Minn.: The Liturgical Press, 1986.

Smit, Dirk J. "Spirituality, Worship, Confession, and Church Unity: A Story from South Africa." In *Ecumenical Theology in Worship, Doctrine, and Life: Essays Presented to Geoffrey Wainwright on His Sixtieth Birthday,* edited by David S. Cunningham, Ralph Del Colle, and Lucas Lamadrid. Oxford: Oxford University Press, 1999, 271–82.

Sullivan, Frances A. *From Apostles to Bishops: The Development of the Episcopacy in the Early Church.* Mahwah, N.J.: Newman Press (Paulist Press), 2001.

Chapter 3

Challenges or Some Reasons for a More Open Eucharistic Sharing

LONDON (March 28, 2001): Until 1996, Tony Blair, the British Prime Minister, had received Communion regularly with his family at St. Joan of Arc Catholic Church, Islington, England. Blair's wife, Cherie, and his children are Catholic; though Blair is Anglican. As a biographer notes, "Since his days at Oxford, Blair's commitment to Christianity has been genuine and active."[1]

Blair explains his decision to worship in the Catholic Church with his family: "I believe it's important for a family to worship together. I wouldn't want to go to an Anglican or Protestant church when my wife and kids are going to a Catholic one."[2] Blair's biographer elaborates, "The sacrament of the Eucharist, taking bread and wine as the body of Christ, was, and is, important to Blair, although he held that it was a universal Christian service rather than the rite of a particular church."[3]

In 1996, new guidelines for eucharistic sharing—*One Bread, One Body*—coincided with the arrival of a new pastor in Islington. Because Blair was likely to become prime minister, Blair's practice of receiving Holy Communion with his family was referred to Cardinal Basil Hume. Blair was asked no longer to receive Communion with his family in Islington. Cardinal Hume, who died in 1999, communicated the decision to Blair. "It is alright," Hume wrote, "to [receive Communion] when in Tuscany for the summer holidays . . . as there is no Anglican

---

[1] John Rentoul, "Blair Part 2—The Battle for Power: A Twist of Faith: Mr. Blair and the Cardinal," *The Independent* London (March 28, 2001) 7.

[2] Ibid.

[3] Ibid.

church near by, but there are plenty in London."[4] At the launch of *One Bread, One Body,* Cardinal Hume maintained that Blair's receiving Communion while on vacation would comply with Canon Law 844.[5]

For his part, Blair accepted Hume's decision. Blair promised to stop receiving Communion "if his presence there caused a problem for Catholic authorities."[6] In the reply to Hume, Blair also wrote, "I wonder what Jesus would have made of it."[7]

Tony Blair's question is important. What would Jesus make of our restrictions on eucharistic sharing? As they consider the state of the divided churches, many people like Tony Blair point to the love and compassion of Jesus when they ask, "What would Jesus do?" They point to phrases from the Gospels that illustrate the breathtaking liberty of Christian faith. They quote the beautiful verses like, "The Sabbath is made for humankind, not humankind for the Sabbath" (Mark 2:27).

"What *would* Jesus do?" When the bishops of the United Kingdom and Ireland considered this question, they responded that we must also mind "the hard words of Jesus." The Gospels contain many stories of people who left Jesus behind because they could not accept his teachings. According to John 6, Jesus' hard sayings about the "Bread of Life" caused a number of people to be scandalized and to walk away from him. In *One Bread, One Body,* the bishops state that Jesus was also a "cause of division."[8] In fact, there are equally many hard words of Jesus to recommend the opposite. In this respect, Blair's intuitive recourse to the words and deeds of Jesus was no less valid than the bishops' was.

Reasons for more openness. In this chapter, I consider six reasons in favor of a more open reception of Holy Communion. By challenges, I refer to situations in the life of the Church where the reception of Holy Communion would seem recommended. They are realities that confront Church authorities and challenge them to extend Holy Communion more broadly than the current norms permit. They are situations that challenge the status quo of ecclesial division.

---

[4] Andrew Grice, "As the PM Said to the Cardinal, Jesus Wouldn't Have Approved," *The Independent* London (March 28, 2001) 1.

[5] Patsy McGarry, "Still 'Sham' If Catholics Take Eucharist Outside Own Church," *The Irish Times* (October 1, 1998) Opinion 16.

[6] Grice.

[7] Rentoul.

[8] Catholic Bishops' Conference of England and Wales, Bishops' Conference of Ireland, and Bishops' Conference of Scotland, *One Bread, One Body: A Teaching Document on the Eucharist in the Life of the Church, and the Establishment of General Norms on Sacramental Sharing* (1998) 119.

At the outset, there are many more bad reasons for a more open eucharistic sharing than there are good ones. Here are a few examples. First, we might resign ourselves to suppose that division is forever and eucharistic sharing is the best kind of unity that we could ever hope to muster. This view amounts to a sin against hope. Second, we could suppose that division is not serious and it has no real impact on our ability to share the Eucharist. If the ecumenical problem is so simple, then we might as well resolve the negligible obstacles to unity without a delay. This view amounts to a naïve relativism. Third, we might think that division is not real. It is an "epiphenomenon" and the result of historical or psychological distortions. This view does not see unity as anything more than an internal or invisible feeling good about one another. If this is true, then why bother with eucharistic sharing either, for it is both external and visible? This view amounts to a "neo-Gnosticism."[9]

Instead, the Eucharist offers us a way of life because it is not a thing.[10] Communion is not an ephemeral feeling good about each other. Division is not forever, it is serious, and the communion of the Church—however much we are divided—remains historical and tangible. In the context of divided churches, then, what is the role of the Eucharist in establishing the conditions for full communion? Can we see the signs already? Where is God challenging us—because God is offering us signs in contemporary experience—to share the Eucharist more freely?

If one favors a more open eucharistic sharing, but lives in a Church that refuses it, what challenges can one pose to legitimate pastoral authority on this question? How can Christians, in good conscience, keep their "pastor's toes to the fire" for the advance of full communion? Churches may be free to refuse Holy Communion to other baptized Christians. They are not free to evade the consequences of that refusal.

Seen as a whole, the challenge is to recalibrate our sense of the ecumenical status quo. A more open eucharistic sharing could reduce our tolerance for ecclesial division. It may increase our desire for full communion.

Challenges

In this chapter, I examine six "challenges" that recommend a more open eucharistic sharing. These challenges include:

---

[9] Jean-Jacques von Allmen, *The Lord's Supper,* ed. J. G. Davies and A. Raymond George, trans. W. Fletcher Fleet, *Ecumenical Studies in Worship* (London / Richmond, Va.: Lutterworth Press / John Knox Press, 1969) 68.

[10] von Allmen, 20.

1. *To share Communion because of Christian baptism.* While Christians generally recognize each other in baptism, they do not equally recognize one another as full members of the Body of Christ. Apart from baptism, what accounts for membership in the Body of Christ? Several unusual developments in the practice of Christian initiation during the twentieth century impair the ability of the Catholic Church to recognize the value of confirmation for admission to Holy Communion.

2. *To serve the pastoral needs of all Christians.* The Catholic Church already recommends eucharistic sharing in cases of pressing need and pastoral necessity. Catholic ministers have a duty to offer the sacraments to baptized Christians in serious situations. This practice is especially challenging for Orthodox Christians, who have difficulty coordinating the concept of pastoral need to their own understanding of the economy of God's grace *(oikonomia).*

3. *To effectively signify the grace of unity.* Christians are challenged to signify the grace of unity (communion) in every Eucharist. While some authorities argue that eucharistic sharing will delay ecumenism, experience has shown how eucharistic sharing has enhanced Christian unity in a variety of contexts. Vatican II recommended that eucharistic sharing signifies unity—and so should not normally be permitted. Nevertheless, it also offers effective means to the grace of unity—and so should be commended. Since Vatican II, Catholic norms have emphasized the cautioning and prohibiting side of this equation; they have minimized the commending and permitting side. This section focuses on the power of the Eucharist to cause what it signifies: Christian unity.

4. *To discern the Body of Christ in one another.* For St. Paul, the single most important factor in receiving Holy Communion is the ability to discern the Body of Christ. Scholars agree that discerning Christ in the entire Christian community was central to Paul's idea. This biblical norm offers the strongest recommendation for a balanced approach to eucharistic sharing. When we fail to discern the Body of Christ in the assembly of baptized Christians, we jeopardize our own status in his Body.

5. *To share genuine Christian hospitality.* Biblical scholarship demonstrates the centrality of meal sharing for the ministry and message of Jesus. The Gospels establish definitive norms for Christian hospitality. They challenge us to offer hospitality at the Eucharist in continuity with Jesus and his ministry of meal sharing.

6. *To avoid further hurts and injuries.* Failing to share the Eucharist has psychological and social consequences for us and for our dialogue partners. Ecumenical pain is real; and those who hold out the strongest hope for ecumenical progress more keenly feel it. Maintaining the discipline of a less open eucharistic sharing risks offending our closest friends and jeopardizes ecumenical progress.

Challenge 1:
To Share Communion Because of Christian Baptism

Being a member of the Church. In his study of Christian initiation, Benedictine liturgist, Aidan Kavanagh writes, "Degrees of belonging to [the Church] are real only antecedent to baptism."[11] The bans on eucharistic sharing create and maintain "degrees of belonging" among the baptized. Because of the bans, we have stumbled into a situation like George Orwell's *Animal Farm*: "All Christians are baptized; but some are more baptized than others."

While Christians recognize each other in baptism, they do not equally recognize the consequences of baptism. They have difficulty seeing one another as full members of the Body of Christ. In chapter 2, we saw how Robert Bellarmine established conditions (the *vincula*, the bonds of membership) apart from baptism to account for membership in the Body of Christ. To the extent that we remain limited by Bellarmine's categories, Catholics may continue to have difficulty recognizing that no Christian is more baptized than any other.

Catholic norms for eucharistic sharing seem to want it both ways. They fiercely maintain the status of all who are validly baptized; yet they deny certain rights and obligations to some of the baptized but not to others. Thus, a document from the CDF like *Communionis notio* makes this stunning claim: In the Church, "no one is a stranger."[12] Every baptized member of the Body of Christ, "especially during the celebration of the Eucharist, is in his or her Church." The CDF understands that every baptized person is, they say, "at home" in every particular Church. This remains true regardless of "whether or not he or she belongs, according to canon law, to the diocese, parish, or other particular community where the celebration takes place . . ."[13]

---

[11] Aidan Kavanagh, *The Shape of Baptism: The Rite of Christian Initiation* (New York: Pueblo Publishing Co., 1978) 174.

[12] Congregation for the Doctrine of the Faith, Letter to the Bishops of the Catholic Church on Some Aspects of the Church Understood as Communion *(Communionis notio)* 1992, 10.

[13] Ibid.

Liturgical practice, however, can appear to contradict the sense of belonging celebrated in *Communionis notio*. For example, a respondent to the 1990 poll in *U.S. Catholic* magazine compared membership in the Church to "rushing a fraternity."

> I find certain parts of the current RCIA program reminiscent of pledging a fraternity, e.g., leaving the church before the offertory. This game playing is especially apparent in those instances when the convert's spouse is Catholic and they have attended Mass together for some years. It appears to me that we are play-acting that they now are not worthy to witness and participate in the consecration.[14]

The respondent points to the confusion—widespread among Catholics—between nonbaptized catechumens and baptized non-Catholics. In the reform of Christian initiation and the Eucharist, for a variety of reasons, we have received rites that do not help us signify our conceptions of Christian unity. In some cases, as in the case of dismissals, they tend to confuse us and many perceive them as an insult.

These confusions require that we sort out the essential, ecclesial nature of the sacraments. How we worship inevitably expresses our understanding of the Church. Orthodox theologians, for example, remind us that every liturgical act is an "act of the Church."[15] When my father, a Reformed pastor, baptized me, the *Church* baptized me. When I was confirmed by the Catholic bishop of Grand Rapids in 1982, the *Church* confirmed me. When I receive Communion, I do so in the name of the *Church*. As an individual at worship, I am always located inside the communion of the whole Church. That is why, as a Christian, I am catholic.

Baptism, confirmation, Eucharist, and the rest are catholic acts because the *whole* Church is present in every performance of the sacrament. The Church performs it, receives it, and brings about its effects as an agent of Christ and the Spirit. In a strict sense, we can say that only the Church receives the Eucharist in Holy Communion. By his Spirit, Christ works through me (and others) to receive himself and to give himself in and through his entire Body.

Consequently, when Catholics fail to share the Eucharist, we end up celebrating a partial and wounded catholicity. By excluding whole portions of the baptized community from Holy Communion, we in-

---

[14] Richard T. Szafransky, "Let Everyone Come to Communion," *U.S. Catholic* (June 1990) 19.
[15] Peter C. Bouteneff, "Koinonia and Eucharist Unity," *The Ecumenical Review* 52, no. 1 (2000).

evitably wound the Church. Catholics (and others) must come to recognize the fullness of baptismal communion. Central to the recognition of one's self as a member of the Church will be the recognition of others. In this, there remains a pivotal, yet often unrecognized, role for the sacrament of confirmation.

Initiation

Historical considerations. In the ancient Church, baptism was the domain of the bishop. The bishop was the chief catechist. The bishop determined when a catechumen was ready for baptism. The bishop oversaw the final days of preparation and, himself, handed over the great symbols of faith: the Creed and the Lord's Prayer. While male and female deacons administered the immersion in water, the bishop gave the final anointing with chrism and welcomed the newly baptized into full communion by offering them Holy Communion and the sign of peace for the first time.

Scholars believe that, in the ancient Church, this was the first time the newly baptized were ever allowed to attend the liturgy of the Eucharist. Scholars call the practice of limiting attendance at the Eucharist to baptized Christians the "discipline of the secret" *(disciplina arcani)*. Some propose that the discipline of the secret was a necessary response to Roman persecution.[16] More importantly, because of the discipline of the secret, this was the first time they were ever allowed to discern the Body of Christ, and to discern themselves within the Body of Christ. This discernment was negotiated exclusively through the ministry of the bishop.

The ancient pattern of Christian initiation points to several important observations. First, clearly distinguishing baptized noncommunicants from catechumens is important and valuable.[17] Second, the ability to discern the Body of Christ intrinsically relates to the ability to join in receiving the Body of Christ and vice-versa. Remaining for the liturgy of the Eucharist was less a privilege than it was a duty, for, if baptized members failed to stay, the rest of the community would have that much more difficulty discerning and receiving itself as Christ's Body. Finally, the newly baptized person enters into the communion of the universal Church in and through his or her entry into a particular church.

---

[16] Later scholarship points to the origins of the discipline of the secret long before extensive persecution had begun. Kenneth Hein, *Eucharist and Excommunication: A Study in Early Christian Doctrine and Discipline* (Frankfurt am Main: Peter Lang, 1973) 10.

[17] Maxwell Johnson, *The Rites of Christian Initiation: Their Evolution and Interpretation* (Collegeville, Minn.: The Liturgical Press, 1999) 388.

They join the communion of the whole Church of Christ by communion in their own local church and by relationship to their own local bishop.[18]

Baptism

The doctrine of the validity of baptism does not divide the Church of Christ. For the most part, Christians agree on the validity of baptism, with water, in the name of the triune God.[19] However, the consequences of baptism remain a pivotal issue for the question of eucharistic sharing. As Dagmar Heller notes, to recognize the baptism of a fellow Christian, but to fail to admit her to the Eucharist imposes on her a contradiction and an ambiguity.[20] If the mutual recognition of baptism will adequately form the basis for further growth in Christian communion, it must amount to something more than the recognition of the validity of a merely human action.[21]

In the view of some theologians, the mutual recognition of baptism is minimal. It is merely a "technical and outward matter," and "hardly anything to celebrate."[22] For example, Danish theologian Peder Nørgaard-Højen writes, "What really leaps to the eye is not unity but disunity in the area of baptism."[23] Either we have to abandon our present opinion on the high potentials of baptism for Church unity, he says, or we have to take our own high estimation seriously and content ourselves with baptism as prerequisite for being a full member of the Church of Christ—without reservation and with no other ecclesiastical act intervening.[24] Nørgaard-Højen concludes,

> What the highly praised and celebrated mutual baptismal recognition amounts to, in the end, is in reality the declaration of the *validity* of baptism when administered in the name of the triune God and with use of water in the form of immersion or pouring.[25]

---

[18] *Communionis notio* 10.

[19] von Allmen, 74.

[20] Dagmar Heller, "Eucharistic Fellowship in the Third Millennium? The Question of the Eucharist in Future Ecumenical Discussions," *The Ecumenical Review* 51 (1999).

[21] Gerard Kelly, "Intercommunion—Critical for the Future of the Ecumenical Movement and Church Unity," *One in Christ* 34, no. 4 (1998) 523.

[22] Ibid., 519.

[23] Peder Nørgaard-Højen, "Baptism and the Foundations of Communion," in *Baptism and the Unity of the Church*, ed. Michael Root and Risto Saarinen (Grand Rapids, Mich. / Geneva: Eerdmans Publishing Co. / WCC Publications, 1998) 69.

[24] Ibid., 71.

[25] Ibid., 68.

Some ecumenical directions in theology of baptism. Fortunately, the declaration of the validity of baptism is not the end of the matter. Ecumenical dialogue has led the way in deepening appreciation for the meaning of baptism. As the Catholic bishops of the United Kingdom and Ireland state, baptism is a common bond of unity among all Christians.[26] All the baptized already belong to the same Church, the Church of Jesus Christ.[27] The unity of Christians that is created in baptism is deepened and continued through eucharistic communion.[28] Baptism and the Eucharist are inseparable.[29]

Lutheran liturgical scholar Max Johnson extends these conclusions. Baptism, he writes, is a "great equalizer" among Christians. It reduces and enlarges us.[30] Baptism reduces us in the sense that we are made to die to self. When people are true to their baptism they are always engaged in pouring themselves out in love for God and others. Baptism enlarges us in the sense that we are made to rise with Christ. When we are true to our baptism we are always engaged in being children of God and the brother or sister of all, even with respect to our biological parents.

In this sense, baptism is not its own end; we do not baptize for the sake of the forgiveness of sins alone. Christians receive baptism with a variety of other ends in view. Baptism is, in a certain sense, "incomplete" in itself. It is incomplete in the way that the gateway to a garden exists for the purpose of entering and enjoying life in the garden. One of the main reasons we may think of baptism as incomplete is firmly to maintain the propriety of infant baptism. Because the infant is unable to make a profession of faith, and because the infant is thought to be unable to participate in the Eucharist fully, consciously, and actively, these other sacramental acts are delayed or postponed.[31]

Profession of faith is integral to the sacrament, according to Catholic ecumenist Jean-Marie Tillard. In our baptism, he says, we give a twofold assent to Christian faith. On the first level, we say "Amen" to

[26] Catholic Bishops' Conference of England and Wales, Bishops' Conference of Ireland, and Bishops' Conference of Scotland, *One Bread, One Body: A Teaching Document on the Eucharist in the Life of the Church, and the Establishment of General Norms on Sacramental Sharing* (1998) 22.

[27] Maxwell Johnson, 387.

[28] Hein, 67.

[29] Thomas Ryan, "Eucharistic Sharing: Why the Churches Act Differently," *Ecumenism* 110 (1993) 32.

[30] Maxwell Johnson, 366.

[31] Cf. Susan K. Wood, "Baptism and the Foundations of Communion," in *Baptism and the Unity of the Church*, ed. Michael Root and Risto Saarinen (Grand Rapids, Mich. / Geneva: Eerdmans Publishing Co. / WCC Publications, 1998) 45f.

Christ himself, as we know him. Every baptism is alike in this first level. No one is baptized who does not, in some fashion, give his or her "Amen" to Christ in the Spirit. On the second level, we say "Amen" to Christ, as he is known in this Church, in this assembly. On this level, no two baptisms are exactly alike. Tillard maintained that assent to Christ occurs on a personal and on a communal level. He seemed to say that I cannot give an "Amen" to Christ without also giving an "Amen" to a community of others who understand and know Christ in a particular fashion. In a word, the "Amen" we make to the particular Church is a sacrament of the "Amen" we make to Christ.

Baptism is directed always toward profession of faith. It always points the way to confirmation and the Eucharist. Restoring the fullness and logic of the sacraments of initiation would better clarify and express their character as professions of faith.[32] As the Catholic bishops of the United Kingdom and Ireland noted, first Communion initiates Christians into a "new and deepened communion with the Catholic Church."[33]

Confirmation

Catholic sacramental theology understands that confirmation more fully expresses the communion between the Catholic and his or her bishop. Additionally, this relationship is one basis for the reception of Holy Communion in the Catholic Church. Several unusual developments in the practice of Christian initiation during the twentieth century impair the ability of the Catholic Church to recognize the value of confirmation for admission to Holy Communion.

In the ancient churches, the baptismal candidates were baptized in the nude, in the baptistery, by male or female deacons, apart from the main congregation. Then, the deacons and other clergy led the newly baptized people, now clothed in white robes, before the bishop and the whole assembly for another anointing with oil or chrism. Only after the anointing with chrism could they take part in the intercessory prayer of the Church and the eucharistic prayer. As scholars examine this ancient pattern of Christian initiation, they see that confirmation is an episcopal and public ratification of the pouring of water that had taken place in private. It is a rite of welcome into the eucharistic communion.[34]

---

[32] Pontifical Council for Promoting Christian Unity, Directory for the Application of Principles and Norms on Ecumenism (March 25, 1993) 92.

[33] OBOB, 64.

[34] Maxwell Johnson, 84. Cf. Paul Turner, "The Origins of Confirmation: An Analysis of Aidan Kavanagh's Hypothesis," in *Living Water, Saving Spirit*, Max Johnson, editor (Collegeville, Minn.: The Liturgical Press) 255.

Now joined to Christ, having risen with him in baptism, they are admitted as "priests into the Holy of Holies," where Christ in the person of his assembly is always interceding before God.

In the Catholic Church, the practice of admitting children to Holy Communion who had not yet been confirmed dates no earlier than 1917 with Pope Pius X's encyclical *Quam singulari*. Pius X held that children who had reached the age of reason could be admitted to Holy Communion. Pius X understood the age of reason to be at or around seven years old. In his drive to encourage an earlier and more frequent reception of the Eucharist, Pius X did not encourage the early reception of the sacrament of confirmation. The effect of Pius X's new regulation was to stress the rational over the spiritual and sacramental preparation of children for the Eucharist.

For all the positive benefits of early and frequent reception of Holy Communion, *Quam singulari* left confirmation dangling without a theology. We risk losing our collective memory on this issue when confirmation is fashioned into a rite of passage for adolescents. We jeopardize our sacramental theology and gerrymander our ecclesiological perspective as well, especially in the context of eucharistic sharing. In Aidan Kavanagh's words, confirmation became "bereft of its psychological consummation in the experience of first communion."[35]

When seen from a long-range historical perspective, the sacrament of confirmation is the missing link in the sacramental initiation of Christians. Confirmation is the public ratification of baptism. It is the sacrament of public recognition of baptism. It is the sacrament of admission to Holy Communion and it includes the public discernment of the gift of the Holy Spirit in the life of the Christian. Sacramental confirmation is the normal ritual form of establishing relationship with the bishop. Through the laying on of hands in confirmation, every Christian—not just ordained Christians—are initiated into a relationship of apostolic succession. This amounts to a real, if implicit, apostolicity that pervades and enlivens the entire local church.

If we were clearer on the sacrament of confirmation as the sacrament of admission to Holy Communion, then many of the theological problems that have arisen in the ecumenical context could be avoided. Perhaps the most viable theological reason to prohibit baptized non-Catholics from receiving Holy Communion is that their local Catholic bishop has not validly confirmed them. If the sacrament of confirmation were restored to its historic location, the Code of Canon Law could simply state, "Ordinarily, only those who have been confirmed by a Catholic bishop (or his delegate) may receive Holy Communion." This

---

[35] Kavanagh, 69f.

is a much simpler and inviting norm. It does not require the Catholic to make negative judgments as to the validity of the sacrament of baptism or confirmation among non-Catholics. It does not distinguish among non-Catholics based on the validity of their ordination. It amounts to a simple and positive assertion of an important element of Catholic faith: Catholic bishops are ordained in apostolic succession and the sacrament of confirmation is the ordinary means for baptized men and women to participate in the apostolicity of the Catholic Church.

First Communion

Since Pius X, Catholic practices surrounding First Holy Communion represent a significant departure from the ancient pattern of Christian initiation. Our churches limit access to Communion by heightening the rituals that accompany First Holy Communion. We may not normally think of the festivities that surround the first reception of Holy Communion as a limitation. On First Communion Sunday, we celebrate the access of young Christians to Communion, not the reverse. Speaking primarily of Catholic parishes in the United States, we must carefully consider how First Communion is less a celebration of access to Communion than it is a ceremonial lifting of limitations to Holy Communion.

In a study of French parishes, anthropologist Laurence Hérault noted that most of the preparation of the children involved the communication of ceremonial procedures. Priest and parents were far more concerned to instruct children how to receive Communion. The adult authorities appeared less concerned to convey emotional, spiritual, or intellectual attitudes to the first communicants. First communicants signal their membership in the community by approaching the altar as a group, by appropriate gestures and decorum. By folding their hands and bowing their heads at certain moments, the young Christians signal that they can receive Holy Communion properly.[36]

Mostly, the rites and customs that accompany First Holy Communion (white dresses, veils, suits and ties) function as social constraints. These social constraints can never fully and completely indicate the faith or spiritual capacity of the young Christians. The symbols and rites that we presently use to surround first communicants are more about establishing cultural expectations of gender, race, age, or childhood. This phenomenon is quite distant from the practice and understanding of the ancient Christians. It involves us in several burdensome ambiguities.

---

[36] Laurence Hérault, "Learning Communion," *Anthropology Today* 15 / 4 (1999) 4–8.

For instance, canon law in the Roman Catholic Church recommends a kind of prevalidation before one is admitted to Holy Communion. For Catholic youngsters, this prevalidation is either the sacrament of confirmation or of reconciliation. (For non-Catholics, it is the rite of profession of faith.) In the United States, the bishops require that first reconciliation (confession or penance) precede First Holy Communion. This requirement forms a significant gate to the Eucharist. Behind the bishops' gate-keeping lies the presumption that an articulated self-awareness of one's self as a sinner—as a forgiven sinner—is prerequisite to a worthy reception of Holy Communion.

In many respects, the membership status of a baptized non-Catholic is similar to that of a baptized Catholic who is preparing for First Holy Communion. As Catholic sacramental theologian Susan Wood maintains, someone who has not received First Communion is no less than "fully Christian." That person is no less a "member of the Church."[37] Both are baptized, neither is confirmed. While one is being prepared for Holy Communion, the other is held off from it. In both groups, we see a population of the baptized who are not permitted access to the Eucharist. They are not held off because they are exceptional sinners. They are not necessarily heretics, though their faith may be partial, faulty, confused, or incomplete. In both cases, they are limited in their access to Holy Communion based on an assumption about their understanding of the meaning of the sacrament. The ritual barriers reinforce a presumption of ignorance on the part of the first communicant.

Why Christian Baptism Is a Challenge to Share a More Open Communion

In light of our reflections on Christian initiation, we see that admission to Communion is often a function of social and cultural factors to which theological and spiritual concerns are only loosely attached. Perhaps it matters more to us that communicants are members of our own particular community than that they understand our eucharistic theologies. Because of the recent confusion in our practice of Christian initiation, valid theological concerns seem only vaguely attached to the way we practice eucharistic gate-keeping. Therefore, some Catholic authorities may understand admission to Communion as a cultural and social marker more than they see in it an expression of faith in Christ coming home to dwell among us. Yet Christian initiation is far more than a visible token, it is an expression of ecclesial will with respect to including others in ultimate realities.

[37] Cf. Wood, 47.

To deny the Eucharist to a baptized Christian amounts *to denying them to ourselves. It signifies also our determination to deny them to Christ.* The bans on eucharistic sharing limit access to Christian communion on every level. On the horizontal or visible dimension, we have excluded them from our communities, our fellowship, our ministries of caring and compassion, study, and concern. On the vertical or invisible dimension, we implicitly express before God the will to exclude them from the ordinary means of sanctification and salvation. When we deny access to the horizontal dimension of communion, we also symbolize our will (but not necessarily God's will) to deny the other person access to the vertical dimension of Christian communion.[38]

Because the Eucharist always has an open-ended quality, we are challenged especially to abandon the will to deny others before God. Every time I receive Holy Communion, there is an unfinished edge. With every Holy Communion, I am called to a deeper maturity and commitment. In the words of Aidan Kavanagh, the Eucharist is the true sacrament of Christian maturity because it is "the way Baptism comes home to rest in us at every stage of life."[39] We approach the Eucharist in a state of incompletion and, changed for the better ever so slightly, we leave the Eucharist in a state of incompletion. The Eucharist is the sacrament of God's not being finished with us yet. No less is it the sacrament of accepting that God is not finished with others.

Challenge 2:
To Serve the Pastoral Needs of All Christians

The Catholic Church already recommends eucharistic sharing in cases of pressing need and pastoral necessity. Catholic ministers have a duty to offer the sacraments to baptized Christians in serious situations. This practice is especially a challenge for Orthodox Christians, who have difficulty coordinating the concept of pastoral need to their own understanding of the economy of God's grace *(oikonomia).*

What Is Pastoral Need?

Christians need the Eucharist. When Catholics discuss their need for Holy Communion, we should be sure to understand need not only in terms of personal and spiritual growth. Need for the Eucharist arises out of a deep and existential need for Christ and one another. It con-

[38] Cf. Hein, 57.
[39] Kavanagh, 177.

cerns the need to "enter more deeply into Christ's church."[40] Canon law recognizes that, normally, baptized non-Catholics can meet their need for the Eucharist from their own ministers, "as their conscience dictates." Catholics are especially concerned, therefore, to provide norms for those times when baptized non-Catholics need the Eucharist, yet cannot seek out or approach their own ministers, and when they seek out a Catholic minister on their own initiative.[41]

The bishops of Great Britain help limit our understanding of pressing need. Grave and pressing need, they say, is more than a "passing desire." It is more than an "impulse arising from the sadness of feeling 'left out.'"[42] Defined more positively, situations of grave and pressing need include imprisonment, captivity, natural disaster, or social disturbance. They include ministry at the time of serious illness and death. In the opinion of canon lawyer John Huels, cases of grave necessity include spiritual need as much as material need or grave bodily illness.[43] Therefore, we may also encourage ministers to consider times of serious emotional or psychological anguish under the category of pastoral need.

In *One Bread, One Body,* the bishops reserve the right to determine in each case what amounts to a pressing need.[44] Each decision forms an exception in its own right, the bishops say. A positive decision on one case does not establish a precedent or create a category of exceptions to the general prohibitions. In his study of *One Bread, One Body,* however, Bhaldraithe says that the Code of Canon Law is more liberal with respect to exceptions. Once the conditions of need are met, Bhaldraithe concludes, the minister may not refuse the sacrament, the permission of the bishop notwithstanding.

Frankly, in most cases of serious pastoral need—especially near the time of death—delaying the sacrament to put a call in to the local bishop would make the bishop's permission a moot point. The time of need would have expired in the interval. When carrying out the requirement to seek permission, Catholic ministers should prudentially

[40] Secretariat for the Promotion of Christian Unity, On Admitting Other Christians to Eucharistic Communion in the Catholic Church, *In Quibus rerum circumstantiis* (1972) 3.

[41] Ibid., 4.

[42] OBOB, 108.

[43] John Huels, *One Table, Many Laws: Essays on Catholic Eucharistic Practice* (Collegeville, Minn.: The Liturgical Press, 1986) 91. Cf. Secretariat for the Promotion of Christian Unity, Instruction, June 1972 in AAS 64 (1972) 518–25, n. 6 (*Documents on the Liturgy,* 1050).

[44] OBOB, 113.

weigh the time of need against the time needed for communication with episcopal authority. In most conceivable cases, the objective need of the person *in extremis* outweighs the need of the Church to express authority beforehand.

Pastoral Need and the Economy of God's Grace

Orthodox Christians are puzzled when Roman Catholic authorities allow people to receive Holy Communion on the basis of need.[45] They wonder how persons could be the members of a church only for the time of their extreme necessity. When the grave situation is resolved— the person recovers or returns to their homeland—why is he or she, in a sense, "re-excommunicated?"

The Orthodox Church does recognize the value of leniency or *oikonomia* to facilitate the return to the Church by particular groups or individuals. *Oikonomia* is a prudential judgment of the Church meant to facilitate reconciliation with dissidents. In extending lenience, the prudential judgment of the Church imitates the philanthropy of God in anomalous and troublesome situations.[46] The principal pastoral need thus recognized by Orthodox Christians is the need to be united to the one Church of Christ where the only real sacramental sharing ever takes place. Every other need, they say, is secondary.

For instance, Orthodox priest and theologian Paulos Gregorios focuses on the eucharistic economy. Gregorios states that the Church offers itself to God through bread and wine while God offers God's self to us through Christ's Body and Blood. This is the exchange of goods at the heart of the eucharistic economy. In terms more familiar to Roman Catholics, the eucharistic economy is a miraculous exchange *(admirabile commercium)* by which God and humankind are joined at the Eucharist through Jesus Christ and the Spirit.

It is not my intent, in this section, to fully compare the Orthodox conception of *oikonomia* to the Roman Catholic concept of pastoral need. However, I would like to make a few observations. First, just like the idea and practice of *oikonomia*, pastoral need involves the prudential recognition of an anomalous situation in pastoral practice. Second, just like *oikonomia*, our practice of recognizing pastoral need stems from the desire to imitate God's philanthropy through a more lenient application of canon law during difficult situations encountered by baptized men and women.

---

[45] Robert G. Stephanopoulos, "Implications for the Ecumenical Movement," *The Ecumenical Review* 44, no. 1 (1992) 19.

[46] Ibid., 25.

The Special Needs of Interchurch Families

As we consider pastoral need, interchurch families raise special concerns. According to Catholic teaching, valid marriage gives rise to a domestic Church. The spouses and their family are called to model the union and ministry of the entire Church of Christ.[47] On the face of it, these affirmations should make the question of sharing the Eucharist with non-Catholic spouses in interchurch marriages a simple matter. It would seem that the non-Catholic spouse lives in communion with the Catholic Church by means of two sacramental relationships: by baptism and by marriage. The bond of marriage would appear to confer a unique status on the non-Catholic partner.

To the contrary, in many places—in the past and presently—Catholic communities and ministers have treated non-Catholic spouses in interchurch marriages poorly and with disdain. The mistreatment of non-Catholic partners has become for many a barrier to faith and a source of alienation. Many older Catholics remember the days of "sacristy weddings" when the wedding ceremonies of Catholics to non-Catholics were held in the sacristy and could not be performed in the sanctuary. One partner in an interchurch marriage reports that, prior to Vatican II, "a nuptial mass for a mixed marriage was not permitted and the Roman Catholic Church did all it could to make the sacrament as mean and cold as possible."[48] Even today, interchurch couples report that their children are no longer interested in attending either church. In another case, the couple attributes their children's lack of enthusiasm to "the Catholic Church's attitude to the non-Catholic parent."[49]

Our accommodation, in pastoral practice, for the spiritual growth and nurture of interchurch Christian families remains at the beginning stages. At present, it may be that we can go no farther than the principles enunciated in *One Bread, One Body*. There, the Catholic bishops of the United Kingdom and Ireland state that marriage does not remove the incompleteness of communion between the Churches of the interchurch spouses. Interchurch marriage, they say, is constituted within the framework of division and not above it.[50] Marriage alone does not make a couple one in faith, and interchurch families are not in communion with one another to the extent that their Church communities

[47] Myriam Wijlens, *Sharing the Eucharist: A Theological Evaluation of the Post Conciliar Legislation* (Lanham, Md.: University Press of America, 2000) 350.
[48] Melanie Finch and Ruth Reardon, *Sharing Communion: An Appeal to the Churches from Interchurch Families* (London: Collins Liturgical Publications, 1983) 27.
[49] Ibid., 45.
[50] OBOB, 81.

remain divided.[51] Nonetheless, in Ireland and the United Kingdom, at special times in the life of an interchurch family—e.g., at a wedding, First Communion, confirmation, or funeral—with the permission of the local bishop, the non-Catholic spouse or parent may receive Holy Communion along with the rest of his or her family. Perhaps North American bishops could find a way to make similar allowances for interchurch families here.

Pastoral Need and the Evidence of the "Internal Forum"

When I watch people receiving Holy Communion, I do not usually presume to think that they are rejecting certain key articles of faith when they say, "Amen" and receive the host or drink from the chalice. My instinct is to think the best and to understand that they are saying "Amen" to Christ and to his Body—both head and members—as well as they can. What about the less clear situations when non-Catholics receive Holy Communion from Catholic ministers? Perhaps they willfully defy our norms. Perhaps they misunderstand our ministers when they encourage non-Catholics to come forward at the time of Holy Communion to receive a blessing. Some have suggested that eucharistic ministers should become more cautious, more wary, of the men and women who come forward to receive Holy Communion. We should simply refuse access, they say, or we should quiz the ones who do not look familiar.

There is a significant difference between refusing Holy Communion to those who seek it and being careful in granting permission to non-Catholics beforehand.[52] At present, very few Catholic ministers would be comfortable giving Holy Communion to non-Catholics who request it, except in the extreme cases foreseen by canon law. On the other hand, there is no external difference between Catholic and non-Catholic Christians. In most situations, short of requiring baptismal and confirmation certificates in the Communion procession, there are few ways a Catholic minister of Holy Communion could knowledgeably refuse the sacrament. To help understand these situations, canon law distinguishes between evidence of the internal forum and of the external forum.

In general, whether or not a communicant is disposed to receive the Eucharist is a matter of internal forum.[53] The internal forum consists of matters that have a bearing on the valid or licit reception of a sacrament known only to the recipient. In most cases, only I can decide if I ought

---

[51] Ibid.
[52] Finch and Reardon, 56.
[53] Huels, 89.

to receive (or abstain from) Holy Communion on any given Sunday. Were I to ask a minister, however, to help clarify my situation, were I to seek permission to receive Holy Communion, the minister would then have evidence from the external forum—the sound of my voice—on which to determine whether or not I ought to receive. The minister could then advise me and suggest appropriate pastoral alternatives.

John Huels concludes, however, that unless there is external forum evidence to the contrary, the Catholic minister must presume the proper disposition in the person who approaches the sacrament.[54] Pre-Communion interrogations are not appropriate during the liturgy in any context. Similarly, we should not be requiring people to make external forum declarations of their ecclesial or spiritual status during the liturgy. As pastoral as it may seem, to invite people to declare their intention not to receive Holy Communion by placing their hand(s) over their heart compels men and women to bring evidence from the internal into the external forum.

Why Pastoral Need Is a Challenge to Share a More Open Communion

Eminent ecumenist Geoffrey Wainwright concludes that eucharistic sharing on behalf of individuals with pressing needs is not the same issue as communion. When churches are joined in full communion one expects to see regular, mutual celebration of the Eucharist, joint presidency, mutual recognition of ordinations, other agreements, and joint commissions on faith and morals.[55] Toward that end, grace challenges us to progress much further.

The Catholic position on pastoral need is helpful at this time for its gracious willingness to administer sacraments in ambivalent and ambiguous situations. It is important that we help Catholic ministers and others become aware of exceptions and of the possibility of pastoral leniency. In this respect, the present guidelines of the U.S. Conference of Catholic Bishops could better elucidate openness to sharing sacraments under the special circumstances envisioned by canon law.

The special circumstances that require leniency *(oikonomia)* help us to recognize that no one Church exists by itself as the sole Church of Christ. The concern of Catholic authorities has been to balance the need of the baptized non-Catholics to pastoral care against the need of those in the communion of the Catholic Church who seek to maintain an

---

[54] Ibid.
[55] Geoffrey Wainwright, "Towards Eucharistic Fellowship," *The Ecumenical Review* 44, no. 1 (1992) 9.

exclusive bond of unity. Nonetheless, canon law seems confused when it does not provide a dispensation for the pastoral need of Catholics in similar extreme circumstances. Why can Catholics receive sacramental rites only from ministers ordained in valid apostolic succession even in the most extreme circumstances? While the Catholic may harbor a modicum of doubt with respect to the efficacy of the sacrament offered by the non-Catholic minister, doubt over the validity of orders should not outweigh the pastoral need of Catholics in grave circumstances.

Challenge 3:
To Effectively Signify the Grace of Unity

Christians are challenged to signify the grace of unity (communion) in every Eucharist. While some authorities argue that eucharistic sharing will delay ecumenism, experience has shown how eucharistic sharing has enhanced Christian unity in a variety of contexts. Vatican II teaches that eucharistic sharing signifies unity—and so should not normally be permitted. The council simultaneously teaches that eucharistic sharing offers effective means to obtain the grace of unity—and so should be commended. In the years since Vatican II, Catholic norms have been strong in prohibiting eucharistic sharing. They have been weak in commending it. In this section, I focus on the role of the Eucharist in causing what it signifies: Christian unity.

The experience of many non-Catholic Churches points to the power of the Eucharist to unite Christian Churches. German Protestants have been vocal in their call for a more open eucharistic sharing. As they prepare for an ecumenical gathering to meet in Berlin in 2003, they have publicly criticized Catholic resistance to the possibility of sharing a common Eucharist at this meeting. The general secretary of the German Evangelical Council of Churches, Friederike Woldt, and the bishop of the Evangelical Church in Berlin-Brandenburg, Wolfgang Huber, asked the Catholic Church to permit eucharistic sharing at the Ecumenical Council of Churches meeting in Berlin, 2003. Evangelical pastor Helga Trosken of Frankfurt am Main remarked on the difficulties, "The Lord's Supper is a token of fellowship with Jesus not a token of the division of Christians." She criticizes "a timid Eucharistic theology" that fails to recognize the efficacy of the Eucharist to heal division and to establish Christian unity.[56]

---

[56] Visser, "Pleidooi op Sacramentsdag voor gemeenschappelijk Avondmaal," *Nederlands Persbureau* (June 14, 2001).

The German Evangelical Church has no difficulty with the participation of Catholics in the Eucharist. For Catholics, however, the request has been received with great awkwardness. Catholic archbishop of Berlin Cardinal George Sterzinsky responded by sidestepping the key issue of eucharistic sharing. He said, simply, that one of the main difficulties is that the meeting takes place over the feast of the Ascension of Jesus. Since this is a holy day of obligation for Catholics in Germany, he said, "they are not likely to be dispensed from the obligation to attend the Mass" on that day, whether or not they had attended the worship services at the ecumenical gathering.[57]

Ecumenical difficulties are not limited to Germany. An organization of Dutch theologians, the *Oekumenische Polderkring*, continues to plead for eucharistic sharing. The failure to share the Eucharist, they say, has led to stagnation in ecumenism and impedes the Church's striving for unity.[58]

Does eucharistic sharing weaken or strengthen the willingness of Christians to resolve differences?[59] This question should not be answered in the abstract. From the testimony of non-Catholic Christians, eucharistic sharing has enhanced their willingness to resolve differences. An example, as Lutherans and Episcopalians in the United States made plans for eucharistic sharing, these plans led to serious soul-searching on the part of Lutherans with respect to their understanding of the role and ministry of bishops.

In their response to *One Bread, One Body*, the Anglican bishops disagree with their Catholic counterparts. They do not believe that eucharistic sharing should be reserved to the end point of unity only. Based on both theology and experience, they contend that interim eucharistic sharing is a particularly effective stage in the advance toward unity.[60] In supporting this view, the bishops restate the traditional doctrine that sacraments both signify what they cause and cause what they signify. In some ways, then, the Anglican bishops hold to a higher doctrine of sacramental efficacy than their Catholic counterparts do.[61]

Catholic authorities resist upholding the power of the Eucharist to cause Christian unity. American Catholic bishop Thomas J. Tobin says that eucharistic sharing is analogous to living together before marriage.

[57] "Protestanten wollen zur Eucharistie eingeladen warden," *Frankfurter Allgemeine Zeitung* (December 28, 2001).
[58] Bakker, "Theologen pleiten voor Intercommunie," *Algemeen Nederlands Persbureau* (October 19, 2001).
[59] Huels, 85.
[60] House of Bishops of the Church of England, *The Eucharist: Sacrament of Unity* (London: Church House Publishing, 2001) 16.
[61] Ibid., 7, 11.

Partners who live together may not have resolved all their differences. Living together demystifies relationships and romance. From the beginning, the partners know the faults and foibles of the other. The demystified person, we fear, may be easier to divorce. Living together risks intimacy with another and, in many cases, partners live together in a premature intimacy. Finally, in their desire for sexual intimacy, unmarried partners may overlook significant future sources of difficulty including their own neediness and weaknesses.

Even so, we should not press the analogy to adultery too far. When a person receives Holy Communion, one is not permanently wed to a local church in the way spouses are wed to one another. We live in a mobile society and even Catholic bishops are transferred from one local church to another. When they prepare to marry, engaged couples are not expected to have resolved all their differences beforehand. The best marriage counselors, instead, help couples to discover and discern broad areas of difference. Marriage requires they negotiate these differences over a long period of time. Similarly, divided churches that seek unity will be more successful if they work hard to discover and discern broad areas of difference while, at the same time, remaining open to negotiating these differences after they complete their formal union.

The Eucharist establishes us in union. The Eucharist is a "church-making sacrament."[62] The Eucharist unites every baptized person to the Church because it first unites them to Christ.[63] In order for there to be a unity that is worthwhile, that has enough positive impact on us, *it must be given to us by God.* When we say this, our words entail that everyone who receives the Eucharist together makes the Church together. All people who receive the Eucharist must want, in some way, to make the Church together. Judging from appearances, this does not happen even within some Catholic Churches. The qualitative standard for Christian unity is established in the Eucharist. Eucharistic communion sets a high standard for our common life.

What kind of unity do we seek through eucharistic sharing? If we understand unity to mean the absorption of non-Catholic Christians and their Churches into the Roman Catholic Church, then eucharistic sharing will be thought of as a final step, and—given human nature—will be deferred indefinitely. However, as one writer notes, "If the aim is 'growing together in Christ,' then surely the more Christians can join together in the Eucharist, the more difficult it will be for them to maintain their divisions."[64]

---

[62] OBOB, 53.
[63] *Communionis notio* 5.
[64] Finch and Reardon, 93.

In Christian theology, unity always means communion and communion is always catholic.[65] Christian unity is never union, uniformity, or monolithic, because the triune God is neither uniform nor monolithic. The one God, for Christians, is a communion of Persons. The one Church, for Christians, is a communion of persons, and because it gathers the many grains into one loaf, it is always catholic. The Eucharist, for Christians, is always a communion of persons in Christ. The Eucharist is a communion in the same sense that God and the Church are one in *many places*, in *many times*, in *many people*, from *many cultures*. The unity comes from God; the diversity, from us. The unity and the diversity together result in catholicity.

Unity of Intention As Sufficient for Holy Communion

Some authorities fear that a few communicants lack the intention to share in actual communion and harbor the intention to reject the leadership and authority of a local church. Can people share communion with Christ and with a Christian community, even if they decide, in conscience, that the leadership or ministry of that community is not authentic?

Occasionally, a communicant will express the intent to share communion, but will later draw back from the local church for a variety of reasons. This is quite understandable. Local Christian communities will exhibit a wide array of woundedness. As a result, some churches are better able than others to initiate and nurture long-term relationships with communicants. Evaluating and increasing the ability of the local church to nurture lifelong communion is one of the chief tasks of pastoral leadership in any Christian community.

On any given Sunday, communicants will manifest significant variety of intent to share communion. One of the key objectives for good pastoral care (and subsequently for the more helpful disciplinary norms expressed in canon law) is to help baptized men and women discern their depth of intent and to lead them, over time, into deeper levels of desire for communion. These difficult pastoral tasks point to a simple observation. The intent to share in communion is not the same as the reality of sharing in communion. The actuality of sharing in communion is not something that men and women attain on their own. In Christian theology, actual communion is not just about communion among ourselves. It is always also about communion with God.

If communion were simply about human community, we would find the task challenging, but not impossible. Since eucharistic communion

[65] Walter Kasper, "The Church as Sacrament of Unity," *Communio* 14 (1987) 8f.

is also about community with God, we find the task impossible for ourselves, and paradoxically easy because it is accomplished for us by the gift of the Holy Spirit. Because of this distinction, actual communion is a nearly impossible standard for admission to Holy Communion. Actual communion is the result, the hoped-for effect of the reception of the Eucharist. Instead, the intent to share communion is a more feasible standard for admission to Holy Communion.

Unity in Doctrine

When we speak of "Christian unity," we must remember that the idea of a "fully united Church" is a myth.[66] Just as the Church was never "fully united" jurisdictionally, so also has it never been "fully united" in doctrine or theology. From its origins to the present, the Church has exhibited tensions and disagreements. These tensions are not always the sign of faithlessness on the part of one side or another. They are, as often as not, signs of differences in emphasis, expressions of cultural difference, or legitimate differences of opinion on matters that no one could ever know with certainty.

Some examples: The book of Acts records tensions between Hellenist and Jewish Christians. In the second century, Christianity was full of strange, Gnostic teachings and Christian communities were rather loose in doctrine. The finding of noncanonical writings during the past century, in Nag Hammadi, Egypt, and elsewhere, confounds any idea of a pristine, apostolic community. The rich doctrinal vocabulary of the ancient Church is astonishing. It is almost as if they refused to settle for one definition or set of terms. That would have implied they had solved the mystery. Therefore we should not be surprised that, among Catholics today, there exist differences in understanding the mystery of Christ's presence and grace in the Eucharist. According to variations in our funds of knowledge, the strength of our faith, and the teachings we have received (whether correct or erroneous), we differ considerably in the emphasis we place on a variety of historical and orthodox eucharistic teachings.

Consequently, in the opinion of canon lawyer John Huels, Catholic authorities should not require a more detailed knowledge of Catholic teaching on the Eucharist from some communicants than from others. Especially in the extreme cases where canon law allows eucharistic

---

[66] Lorenzo Perrone, "In the Footsteps of the Apostolic Churches: Fragmentation and Unity in the Christian West," in *The Church in Fragments: Towards What Kind of Unity?*, ed. Giuseppe Ruggieri and Miklos Tomka, *Concilium* (London / Maryknoll, N.Y.: SCM Press / Orbis Books, 1997) 55.

sharing, Catholic ministers may take a gesture of assent alone (a nod of the head, the lifting of a finger) as a sufficient indication of faith in the Eucharist and of desire to receive Holy Communion. Of course, assent to the teachings of a Church is not the same as a complete and thorough knowledge of those teachings.

Catholic authorities do not normally expect Catholic communicants to be excellent theologians or junior versions of Thomas Aquinas. They do not normally require communicants to manifest a detailed knowledge of Catholic teaching on the Eucharist. In ordinary cases, presence to the liturgy, participation in the prayers and acclamations, and reception of the eucharistic bread and wine—with the very important dialogue between minister and communicants, "The Body of Christ / the Blood of Christ: Amen"—is considered a sufficient manifestation of Catholic faith in the Eucharist.

Saying "Amen" to Who You Are

The mystery of faith includes both an assent to God (the theological dimension) and an assent to the Church (the ecclesial dimension). Faith always asks us to respond, "Yes," in love to God and to God's people. In the order of faith, God is primary, the Church is secondary. Our assent to God must be absolute even if our assent to the Church is partial, passing, and limited by time and place.[67] Consider how people signify assent in the liturgy. The "Amen" they say before they receive Holy Communion ("The Body / Blood of Christ: Amen") is one with the "Great Amen" of the eucharistic prayer.[68] The one "Amen" implies and warrants the other. Augustine said something similar in a sermon to newly baptized Christians:

> You are the body of Christ, member for member.
> If you, therefore, are Christ's body and members,
> it is your own mystery that is placed on the Lord's table!
> It is your own mystery that you are receiving!
> You are saying Amen to what you are—
> your response is a personal signature, affirming your faith.
> When you hear "The body of Christ"—you reply "Amen."
> Be a member of Christ's body, then, so that your Amen may ring true! . . .
> Be what you see; receive what you are. . . .
> Remember, friends, how wine is made—
> individual grapes hang together in a bunch,

---

[67] Avery Dulles, "The Ecclesial Dimension of Faith," *Communio* 22 (1995) 427.
[68] OBOB, 28.

but the juice from them all is mingled to become a single brew. This is the image chosen by Christ our Lord to show how, at his own table, the mystery of our unity and peace is solemnly consecrated.[69]

Hold Augustine's words about the "Amen" in memory, but add to them some contrasting thoughts about the typical "lawyer's 'amen'": Were a modern lawyer to advise us to say "Amen," perhaps she would urge us to attach a lengthy codicil. The lawyer would have us say, "Amen, except that I mean only to refer to the Real Presence and not to the presence of Christ in this assembly, and . . . begging your pardon . . . I'm not too sure that you are a 'real' and 'validly ordained' minister of Christ in apostolic succession, but then, you might be, therefore, because it suits me I will assume, for today, that you are . . ."

Jesus instead urged his disciples to let their "Yes" mean "yes"; and their "No" mean "no." Dissembling and the "amens" of the lawyer—with their lengthy prevarications and codicils—do not advance the cause of Christian unity.

What prevents me from saying, "I believe in God, but do not believe in the Church?" Nothing prevents it; but internal consistency requires me to say something different. Church and faith offer two, unequal sides to the same coin. To assent to the Church is to assent to the adequacy of its reflection of God into the world of human knowing and being. To assent to God, however, is to assent to the divine person as revealed to faith in the person of the Church. The Church is a mirror or lens of the love of God. In contemplating the Church, we see a reflection of God. In contemplating God, we see the human community—transformed by grace.

Why Signifying the Grace of Unity Is a Challenge to Share a More Open Communion

If we conceive of the Eucharist mainly as the means to resolve doctrinal differences or as a powerful jurisdictional lever to stifle dissent, we would not really be sharing the Eucharist. At best, we would have turned the blessing and breaking of bread into a form of ecclesial or family therapy. At worst, we would have made it the brand or trademark of "Church, Incorporated."

On the other hand, if the Eucharist is the best, real source of the grace for Christian communion, then we must do everything in our power to drink deeply from that well together. The love and peace of Christ is

[69] Augustine, *Homily*, PL 38:1246-1248. Trans. Nathan Mitchell, *Assembly* 23, no. 2 (1997) 14.

infinite. Because the Eucharist is a sign of Christ's infinite love and peace, our challenge is to prevent the communion of those who receive the Eucharist from being limited or exclusive.[70] We would be challenged not only to say "Amen" to who we are (as Catholics), we would be enabled to say "Amen" to who we all are together (as Christians and members of the Body of Christ).

Challenge 4:
To Discern the Body of Christ in One Another

For St. Paul, the single most important factor in preparing to receive Holy Communion is the ability to discern the Body of Christ. He wrote that Christians—like those in Corinth—must not celebrate the Eucharist if they are unable or unwilling to "discern the body of Christ" (1 Cor 11:29). Scholars agree that discerning Christ in the entire Christian community was central to Paul's idea. This biblical norm offers the strongest recommendation for a balanced approach to eucharistic sharing. A eucharistic sharing that is too open may weaken our ability to discern the Body of Christ. Yet, when we fail to discern the Body of Christ in the entire assembly of baptized Christians, we risk rejecting Christ when we reject others of his members. We jeopardize our own status in the Body of Christ.

St. Paul and the Church in Corinth

If nothing else, Paul's discussion of the Eucharist in 1 Corinthians points out that receiving Holy Communion touches the core of what it means to be the Church and to be a member of the Church. Theologians consequently say that the reception of the Eucharist has ecclesiological consequences.[71] One of the more important consequences, Paul thought, is that the unity of the Church is the result of communion in Christ and that communion in Christ is received in the Eucharist. An unworthy Communion is one in which the communicant receives, yet despises and neglects the needs of his or her fellow communicants. Paul thought that receiving Communion, while failing to discern the Body, represents

---

[70] Philippe Larere, *The Lord's Supper: Towards an Ecumenical Understanding of the Eucharist*, trans. Patrick Madigan (Collegeville, Minn.: The Liturgical Press, 1993) 77.

[71] Matthias Kilinghardt, *Gemeinschaftsmahl und Mahlgemeinschaft: Soziologie und Liturgie Frühchristlicher Mahlfeiern*, ed. Klaus Berger, et al., *Texte und Arbeiten zum neutestamentlichen Zeitalter* 13 (Tübingen: A. Francke Verlag, 1996) 308.

a serious ambiguity and contradiction.[72] He thought that the Lord's Supper was the worst place to have division surface.[73]

Biblical scholars generally agree that the Christian community in Corinth was not divided in a dispute over eucharistic doctrine. It was not the matter of a disagreement over a matter of eucharistic piety, as earlier scholars once suggested.[74] Moreover, the division of the Corinthian Church was not the result of a simple class distinction. The community of Corinthian Christians is described more adequately as divided between those who had some control over their economic destiny and many others who had no say in their livelihood.[75]

Paul recommended self-lowering and status reversal as the main types of behaviors that would heal the division of the Corinthian Church. Biblical scholars conclude that the elite members of the Corinthian community found Paul's advice a threat.[76] Paul's strong words point less to the possibility that the Corinthians heard them and mended their ways, behaving in a united fashion ever after. They point instead to the reality that, even after Paul's scolding, the Corinthians were misunderstanding the nature of Church unity and Holy Communion.

Discerning the Body of Christ

What is the body? The Greek word for "body" in 1 Corinthians is *soma*. When Paul speaks of the *soma* of Christ, Christians understand that he means several things. In the first place, he means the literal body of Christ, executed by Roman authorities on a cross. In the second place, he means the Body of Christ given to us in the bread and wine of Holy Communion, the sacramental Body of Christ. In the third place, he means the Church as Body of Christ, the composition of a community under Christ as its head.[77]

Paul teaches that the Body of Christ is the location of our unity (1 Cor 10:17). Participation in the Eucharist causes our union in this body.[78]

---

[72] Hein, 63.

[73] Dale B. Martin, *The Corinthian Body* (New Haven, Conn.: Yale University Press, 1995) 75.

[74] Ibid., 194.

[75] Ibid., xvii.

[76] Ibid., 68.

[77] Klinghardt, 306f. Sekretariat der Deutschen Bischofskonferenz, *Einheit der Kirche und Gemeinschaft im Herrenmahl: Zur neueren ökumenischen Diskussion um Eucharistie- und Kirchengemeinschaft* (September 25, 2000).

[78] Johannes Brosseder, "Die ökumenische Bedeutung des Bischofsamtes," in *Christus Spes: Liturgie und Glaube im ökumenischen Kontext*, ed. Paul Berbers and Thaddäus A. Schnitker (Frankfurt am Main: Peter Lang, 1994) 86.

We never lose our individuality in this body, but we come to know ourselves as living within a higher form of life. We become part of an organism that transcends our own means or ends.

A body for others. When we examine the stories of the Gospels, it becomes apparent that Jesus' body was "given for many" (Luke 22:19) long before he surrendered it in death. In ministry of healing and teaching, Jesus put himself at risk for the good of others. This is the proper imitation of Christ: to respond to the bodies of others and to put our own bodies and goods at risk for them and for their good.[79] After Christ has risen and been glorified, once the Spirit has been poured out on the Church, whatever is of God in the world is Christ in his head and members, the Body of Christ, the Church. That is to say, after the resurrection and Pentecost, there is from now on only the whole Christ, the "*Christus totus.*"[80] In the words of *Dominus Iesus*: The Church and Christ are "inseparably united."[81]

Even in his glorification at the right hand of God, Christ is seated beside God in his corporeal form, as Jesus of Nazareth—risen and glorified—and in his corporate form, as the communion of saints—the adopted children of God, sanctified and fully incorporated into the divine Word. In Eastern Orthodox theology, this is called *theosis* or divinization. This doctrine does not suggest that each of us will become mini-deities, but that each of us will be immersed into the divinity of the Word, engrafted into the Body of Christ. Our salvation consists in entering through Christ, with Christ, in Christ, and as Christ into the communion of the triune God.

As glorious as this sounds, one of the more negative ramifications of the doctrine of divinization is the idea that, to the extent a person has rejected incorporation into the Body of Christ, as expressed in a person's rejection of the Church, that person has rejected salvation itself.[82] Since Vatican II, with its decrees on the Church, on ecumenism, and on non-Christian religions, it has become difficult to say that any person's rejection of the Church *ipso facto* amounts to a rejection of Christ or a rejection of God's offer for salvation. Leaving aside the question of the non-Christian, what happens when baptized non-Catholics neither explicitly reject nor explicitly accept the Catholic Church as the Church of Christ?

[79] Theresa Sanders, "The Otherness of God and the Bodies of Others," *Journal of Religion* 76, no. 4 (1996).

[80] Michael Higura, "Church and Eucharist in Light of the Trinitarian Mystery," *Communio* 17 (2000) 239.

[81] DI 16.

[82] Higura, 230.

Since Vatican II, we may not say these "separated brethren" will not be saved, are not members of the Body of Christ, or have rejected Christ. We should not say these "separated brethren" stand entirely outside the communion of the Church, even if they fail to discern the authority and jurisdiction of Catholic bishops within the Body of Christ.

Other reflections on bodiliness. Contemporary conceptions of the body–spirit dichotomy are a recent invention. The body–spirit dichotomy is, in part, an invention of the modern philosopher, René Descartes. It would be anachronistic to equate our own ideas about "body" and "spirit" with those of Paul or other ancient writers.[83] When Paul speaks of the "bodily" *(sarkikos),* he does not refer to our understanding of the corporeal—hunks of flesh, beefcake, and the like. When Paul speaks of the "spiritual" *(pneumatikos),* he does not refer to our understanding of the ethereal or noncorporeal—ghosts, angels, or disembodied voices. Rather, to be bodily for Paul is to be materially organized and structured. For Paul, as for others in the ancient world, the human body was conceived as a microcosm, a world in miniature.[84]

Therefore, when Paul commands the Corinthians to "discern the body of Christ," this is a matter of external forum. Their unity must be tangible and visible. Their organizational principle must be discernible. The discernment requires the Corinthians to work actively to reduce their fractiousness and greediness. In their small community, they must comprise the microcosm of resurrected life, the Body of Christ.

Discerning—diakrinein. Paul's word for "discernment" is the Greek word, *diakrinein.* The term was part of the forensic or legal vocabulary of the Greeks.[85] Paul's letters are full of this sort of legal terminology. The passage in 1 Corinthians is virtually a glossary of terms from the law courts: guilty, judgment, distinguish, judge, condemn.[86] *Diakrinein* comes from the root verb *krineto:* "to part," "to sift," or "to divide." The verb implies evaluation, assessment, and judgment.[87]

Paul does not use the word *"diakrinein"* consistently. At 1 Corinthians 4:7, the verb for "distinguish" *(diakrinein)* means to mark one out as

---

[83] Dale Martin, 15.

[84] Ibid., 16.

[85] Wayne Grudem, "A Response to Gerhard Dautzenberg on 1 Cor. 12.10," *Biblische Zeitschrift* 22, no. 2 (1978) 257.

[86] C. K. Barrett, *A Commentary on the First Epistle to the Corinthians* (New York: Harper & Row, 1968).

[87] Troy Martin, "But Let Everyone Discern the Body of Christ (Colossians 2:17)," *Journal of Biblical Literature* 114, no. 2 (1995). Cf. *TDNT* 3:922–23.

different from others. At 1 Corinthians 6:5, the verb means to decide between two disputing church members, to determine who is right and who is wrong. At 1 Corinthians 14:29, the verb means to give careful attention to the sayings of the prophets.[88] Paul also uses the verb "diakrinein" in a meal context in Colossians 2:16-17. There "diakrinein" carries the implication of disrespect and a negative evaluation.

Discernment, more than just Real Presence. Many, perhaps most, Christians believe that Paul's phrase, to discern the Body, refers to having faith in the real presence of Christ in the elements of bread and wine.[89] In the context of the Eucharist, discerning the Body does mean recognizing, through faith, the presence of Christ's Body and Blood in the sacramental signs of bread and wine. But, Paul says it means something more.

Biblical scholars agree that to discern the Body of Christ does not refer primarily to recognizing the real presence of Jesus in the elements of bread and wine.[90] Instead, for Paul, to discern the Body of Christ means to find him both in the elements of the meal *and* in the communal gathering of Christians. Both high- and low-status Christians equally manifest their membership in the Body of Christ.[91] In a word, discerning the Body of Christ refers both to the sacramental bread and wine and to the Church.[92] To discern the Body of Christ is to judge one's self and others to be authentic members of the Savior's risen and glorified Body.

Discerning the Body means seeing Christ in unlikely people. Imagine, for the moment, that you were one of the "high and mighty" folks in Paul's Corinth. What would discerning the Body mean for you? Since you would have been full of yourself, discerning the Body requires at least a certain amount of self-deflation. To recognize Christ in those lesser folks, the commoners, the *hoi polloi*, demands a potentially painful wound to one's self-conception. Whenever we read 1 Corinthians, we need to remember that sense of woundedness. Paul was not writing to a perfect Church, perfectly gathered, comprised of perfect people, assembled to share a perfect and peaceful banquet with great decorum.

No, the main concern of Paul's first letter to the Corinthians is to establish unity within the Christian community there.[93] Paul was writing

---

[88] Barrett.

[89] Cf. Ernie V. Lassman, "1 Corinthians 11:29—'Discerning the Body' and its Implications for Closed Communion," *Logia: A Journal of Lutheran Theology* 3 (1994).

[90] Hein, 62f.

[91] Dale Martin, 75.

[92] OBOB, 93.

[93] Dale Martin, 39.

to a wounded Church, divided against itself. It was a Church comprised of weak and strong Christians—both egotistical and timid, only loosely assembled to eat a meal, where some of the guests got drunk and others went home hungry.[94] Paul criticizes Christians who use sacramental acts like the Eucharist to distinguish themselves from other Christians. Rather, in sacramental acts like the Eucharist, everyone must discern the Body of Christ in and among everyone.[95] Each communicant must judge whether his or her celebration of the meal is "giving expression to this unconditional acceptance of all participants."[96]

Discerning, both active and passive. For Paul, discerning the Body also takes an active and a passive sense. Taken passively, to discern the Body means to recognize—without reservation—one's self as standing among the Body of Christ sacramentally assembled in worship by a particular group of baptized men and women. Taken actively, to discern the Body means to contribute to its constitution here and now, in this place and time (e.g., by assembling at the right time and place, by bringing bread and wine to share with all who will come, by waiting to partake of the meal).

Passively, discerning the Body means being able to see the Body and Blood of Christ in all who join together in Holy Communion.[97] Actively, discerning ourselves as the Body of Christ means that standing together before the cross, "covered by the blood of the Lamb," we know and love our fellow communicants as simultaneously needy and blessed.[98]

Taken passively, discerning the Body entails self-examination. When Paul says that "a man should examine himself," this is a matter of internal forum. The examination goes on within the person. Paul is clear that right discernment depends on having reflected on the extent of one's commitment to the Body of Christ. How much am I committed to this Christian community? Am I willing to pour myself out on their behalf? If not, have I discerned the Body among them?[99]

[94] Francis J. Moloney, *A Body Broken for a Broken People: Eucharist in the New Testament*, rev. ed. (Peabody, Mass. / Blackburn, Victoria, Australia: Hendrickson Publishers / HarperCollins Religious, 1997) 190f.

[95] Troy Martin.

[96] Michael Welker, *What Happens in Holy Communion?*, trans. John F. Hoffmeyer (Grand Rapids, Mich. / Cambridge: Eerdmans Publishing Co. / SPCK, 2000) 17.

[97] Szafransky, 15.

[98] Syd Hielema, "Recognizing the Body: Discovering That the Church Is Bigger Than My Own Tradition," *Reformed Worship* 48 (1998) 32.

[99] Ibid., 33.

Contingency and self-giving. Therefore, discerning the Body has something to do with "realizing the contingency of one's own status as a member of the Body of Christ." It includes the recognition of one's own vulnerability in the body before dissolution, disease, or death.[100] Paul believes that the judgment of God is real. People, he says, are literally sick and dying. Literally, not metaphorically, they are eating and drinking themselves to death.[101] Discerning the Body, therefore, always has "something to do with paying attention to the bodily needs of other Christians."[102]

Discerning the Body of Christ in the Eucharist relates to the classic doctrine of self-giving. Only as far as I have poured out the gift of my self am I enabled to receive the other with love.[103] Entry into the death of Jesus is the "vital shaping power of one's life." As individuals and as a community, we are best able to discern the Body of Christ in the light of our participation in the paschal mystery.[104]

Dissembling As Failure to Discern the Body of Christ

Bishop Tobin says that a more open Communion risks "papering over our differences with other religions." Leave aside that I am nowhere advocating Communion for the nonbaptized, with people from other religions. Papering over differences remains an important concern. When differences are papered over, this suggests that there was a failure to discern the Body of Christ among fellow communicants. Similarly, other commentators say that a more open Communion has the potential to harm ecumenical relationships. Archbishop Wuerl has said that the non-Catholic receiving Holy Communion in the Catholic Church is "involved in . . . deep personal ambiguity, not to say contradiction." How can this be so? How can he be certain? Wuerl does not say specifically what the ambiguity and contradiction are, but let us try to figure out what he may mean.

By receiving Holy Communion in the Catholic Church, perhaps the baptized non-Catholic is saying, "I would not be one with you, but will perform an act which suggests that I am." Perhaps he or she is even thinking, "I do not believe what you do, but I will perform an act that

---

[100] Dale Martin, 196.

[101] Barrett.

[102] Dale Martin, 195.

[103] Edward J. Kilmartin, *Church, Eucharist, and Priesthood: A Theological Commentary on "The Mystery and Worship of the Most Holy Eucharist,"* (New York / Ramsey: Paulist Press, 1981) 9.

[104] M. Robert Mulholland, "Discerning the Body," *Weavings* 8 (1993) 22.

suggests I do." The result, in this instance, would amount to a lie or a dissembling. Just as Wuerl said, the mental reservations entertained by the non-Catholic in our example add up to deep ambiguity and contradiction.

Evidence to the contrary? On the other hand, many baptized non-Catholic men and women receive Communion quietly, without approval, and in such a way as to cause no offense or scandal.[105] They receive Holy Communion (occasionally and quietly) without any sense of ambiguity or contradiction. In effect, these men and women are saying to us, "I am one with you and I *assert* my baptism among you." Their act becomes a statement: "I will to live in communion with you in a way that you do not yet discern or understand." Others may hold a slightly different point of view: "I do not believe everything you do—who does? Yet I will perform an act that signifies my assent to you. We share the essentials of faith—even if you believe that there are 'more essentials' than I do."

Communion on the sly. This kind of "Communion on the sly" is not without risk. Encouraging baptized non-Catholics to receive Holy Communion risks becoming a communion of subterfuge, an encouraging that they become "anonymous Catholics." Some authors, in describing their willingness to break with Church discipline, do point up their own contradictions.

A study of interchurch couples in England provides the example of Christians who regularly disobey the canonical norms—in order to preserve their marriage. They admit that they nonetheless feel a certain "underhandedness." As one couple writes, "The result of this is that we lead something of a double life, anxious as we are not to hinder full unity either by blindly ignoring the rules, or by hurting other members of our churches."[106] A member of another interchurch couple sounds more embittered, "I . . . feel oppressed by the Roman Catholic official stance that I am not allowed to receive Communion. I feel that it denies the reality of my religious experience . . . I feel that I should be able to receive Communion within a Catholic Church, and sometimes do, but feel because of the official stance that I am being underhand."[107]

Discernment works both ways. When some authorities say that there can be no eucharistic Communion before there is full communion, they suggest that non-Catholics must submit to the authority of the Catholic hierarchy as a precondition to the fullness of our expression of love for

---

[105] Pierre Beffa, "Intercommunion: Some Personal Reflections and Testimonies," *The Ecumenical Review* 44, no. 1 (1992) 40.

[106] Finch and Reardon, 70.

[107] Ibid.

them. Some non-Catholic Christians interpret the Roman Catholic prohibition on sharing the Eucharist with non-Catholics as the expression of a will to dominate the non-Catholic in his or her life of faith and conscience. Thinking of my Protestant friends and family members, most would say they discern the Body of Christ among the Catholic Churches in communion with Rome. However, they would quickly add that they discern the Body of Christ among their own ecclesial communities not one bit less. Catholics may find this point of view perplexing. For these "separated brethren," discerning the Body of Christ is not equivalent to discerning the authority and jurisdiction of a Church's ministers.

We should be clear. If there is sin and deceit here, it does not pertain to the out-of-place communicant alone. To discern the Body cuts in both directions. Clearly, the non-Catholic communicants discern the Body of Christ (in the passive sense) or else they would have no desire to receive the Eucharist in the Catholic Church. Whether Catholics or non-Catholics discern themselves within the Body of Christ is not difficult—we all do. The greater difficulty is whether Catholic authorities are willing to discern the non-Catholic into the Body (in the active sense). Do Christians discern the authority of the ministers to the Body? And, the greatest difficulty of all: Do the authorities within the Body truly discern the membership of all who comprise it?

Indifference As Failure to Discern the Body of Christ

Vatican II understands "indifferentism" as the belief that there is no significant difference between Christians on the teaching and discipline of the sacraments. It may include the belief that "it does not matter where one worships."[108] Indifferentism is a common perception among many of my undergraduate students. For them, personal relatedness to God is all that matters. They have a hard time being anything other than easy, syncretistic, polytheists. For some, the Pope and the Dalai Lama are no less holy and awesome. For others, the initial inclination is to walk away from the discussion of differences in matters of faith or morals. The slogan of indifferentism: "You believe your thing and I'll believe mine." Instead, Church authorities argue strongly against indifference. "Receiving Communion at the same altar," they say, "is not a sign of unity when we do so with the intention of separating afterwards to return to our various Churches."[109]

---

[108] Huels, 95.

[109] Thomas Richstatter, "Eucharist: Sign and Source of Christian Unity," *Catholic Update* (May 2000).

We should not be indifferent to the Body of Christ. Along these lines, discerning Christ in the sacramental signs of bread and wine presupposes that one discerns his Body, simultaneously, in the community that has gathered around that bread and wine to constitute them as sacraments of Christ's Body and Blood. Vice-versa, you could gather Christians of every stripe in a room, building, or arena; but you wouldn't necessarily have a gathering of the Church. We cannot remain indifferent to the men and women who live around and among us and remain participants in Holy Communion. The two dynamics are totally opposed to one another.

Rather, to discern the Body refers always to the ecclesial Body of Christ. When some Corinthian Christians failed to share the Eucharist with other Corinthian Christians, they showed "contempt for the Church of God" (1 Cor 11:22).[110] In constituting the sacrament of Christ's Body and Blood, the Church becomes itself a sacramental sign of Christ's bodily presence. "Discerning the Body" always means recognizing, through faith, the presence of Christ's Body in the sacramental sign of the Christian Church, assembled here and now to receive the Eucharist.[111] It always includes both elements: Christ present in the elements of bread and wine and Christ present in the baptized men and women assembled here.[112] In discerning the Body and Blood in sacramental signs, we come also to discern the Body and Blood in the community of Christians.

A Comment on Catholics Receiving the Eucharist in Non-Catholic Churches

Catholics in the non-Catholic context. One writer to *The Spectator* of London says that he freely communes in Anglican services, though he does not believe Anglican orders are valid. The writer concludes that he understands that the Anglican Eucharist cannot "strictly speaking" be the "Body and Blood of Christ." This same commentator excuses the contradiction between these views and his holding that there is nonetheless a "real presence of Christ" in the Anglican Eucharist, saying "good intentions are what matters."[113]

---

[110] Cf. William T. Cavanaugh, *Torture and Eucharist: Theology, Politics, and the Body of Christ* (London: Blackwell Publishers, 1998) 236.

[111] Moloney, 173.

[112] OBOB, 93.

[113] Paul Johnson, "Why Tony Blair Is Right to Take Communion in Our Churches," *The Spectator,* London (October 10, 1998) 27.

Of course, Catholics have moved far beyond their pre-Vatican II understandings of *communicatio in sacris*. The 1917 Code of Canon Law allowed "passive participation" or "physical presence" at non-Catholic worship only when (1) it was attended out of civic duty, courtesy, or respect; (2) there was a grave or important reason; and (3) there was no risk of scandal in the way that the Catholic presented himself or herself in that context.[114]

Now, when Catholics take part in non-Catholic worship, there is still the risk that this participation might amount to a rejection of Catholic faith. If we were especially fearful, we could think that it amounts to a profession of faith in contradiction to Catholic doctrine. It could mean that the Catholic approves the false faith. It could give rise to a scandal of appearances, where the Catholic appears to condone or profess the non-Catholic faith, causing harm to others by way of a public misimpression.[115] In every case, the Catholic must consider, do the benefits of ecumenical worship outweigh the potential risk of my dissembling or giving a false impression?

A Protestant perception of the problem. In *The Eucharist: Sacrament of Unity,* the Anglican bishops say they find the ban on Catholics ever receiving the Eucharist from Anglican ministers an "ecumenical, theological, and pastoral affront."[116] In *One Bread, One Body,* Catholics are prohibited from receiving the Eucharist from non-Catholic ministers (with the less likely exception that they may receive from Orthodox clergy). The norm implies that, even when the Catholic finds herself in a grave situation or in danger of death, the reception of the Eucharist from the Anglican minister would be positively harmful to her. Otherwise, pastoral need would be sufficient to dispense the Catholic from observing the canonical norm.

Is eucharistic sharing really more risky than idolatry? The greatest irony exists in the ban on Catholics receiving the Eucharist or Lord's Supper from non-Catholic ministers. For example, St. Paul did not prohibit Corinthian Christians from receiving meat that had been sacrificed to idols. The idols, he said, are nothing (1 Cor 8:1). The meat is just meat and to eat with your non-Christian friends is just good hospitality unless it causes offense to Christians with weak faith. On what basis, I wonder, is it possible to suggest that eating bread and drinking wine, consecrated to God by fellow Christians, is more harmful than eating the remains of a non-Christian sacrifice? To sustain this ban requires

---

[114] Wijlens, 72.
[115] Ibid., 66.
[116] ESOU, 16.

that the reception of bread and wine from non-Catholic Christians, a possibly—but not certifiably—valid Eucharist, is inherently more risky than eating the foods that had been sacrificed to non-Christian gods in idolatry.

With the current norms, Catholic authorities risk offending the Body of Christ. Failing to permit Catholics ever to share Communion in the non-Catholic context risks a sin against the communion of saints, for the norms treat the Lord's Supper of these non-Catholic communities —among whom we number many martyrs and saints—to be less effective and more harmful than the sacrificial meals of ancient Corinthian idolaters.

Why Discerning the Body of Christ Is a Challenge to Share a More Open Communion

When we look at Churches today, we must ask how well they do the work of being disciples of Christ. How well do they show forth Christ within—to one another—and without—to nonmembers within their part of the world? Only in this active sense can we meaningfully speak about their discerning the Body of Christ.

For some, failing to see the Eucharist as a source of grace amounts to failing to discern the Body of Christ in the sacrament. For others, seeing the Eucharist as a tool or a means to an end is their own kind of failure to discern the Body of Christ. From either perspective, Christians fail because they have failed to discern the Body of Christ in the sacrament: in the one case, because they failed to recognize its powerful efficacy; in the other case, because they failed to see Christ, but see only a "tool."

Christians discern the Body only when they have taken upon themselves—as a whole Church—the task of being the Body of Christ here and now, in every time and place that they gather for the Eucharist. It is not unfair if our eternal salvation is made to depend on the salvation of others. In a sense, Christians know the Church is an ark—we will sink or swim together. Whenever communities—even worldwide communities—of baptized Christians try to become a Body of Christ all by themselves, isolated and alone, they have already failed. Again they need to fall back on the grace of God and the wider Christian community to draw them into the comprehensiveness of Christian communion.

The sacraments always establish the churches in covenant community with God and with all the baptized.[117] The Eucharist is no excep-

---

[117] Monika Hellwig, *The Eucharist and the Hunger of the World* (New York: Paulist Press, 1976) 60.

tion. In the Eucharist, the Body of Christ takes body in the body of Christ's disciples. This body includes male and female, Jew and Greek, slave and free.[118] Leaving out any bodies is contrary to the gift that Jesus left among us at the Last Supper. The Church does not possess the Body of Christ. It is God's gift for us to comprise Christ's Body.[119]

Being the Body of Christ, knowing it, and loving it require that we work hard to alleviate the sorrow and pain that "afflict others without distinction of rank or group, whatever the cost."[120] To participate in the communion is "to commit oneself to God and to the people he makes his own."[121] Discerning the Body, then, is an awesome commitment. We undertake it at great personal risk.

For Paul, unworthy Communion consists of receiving the Eucharist without regard for the well-being of the whole Body of Christ.[122] William Cavanaugh extends Paul's idea. Cavanaugh says that discerning the Body means "being able to identify truthfully where the body is not whole, where divisions exist."[123] To discern or judge the Body is not an act of differentiating or dividing. For Paul, to discern the Body consists mainly in uniting what only appears to be divided.[124]

Consequently, when some Christians are denied the Eucharist, the person who is doing the denying needs to examine his or her own conscience. Is that person worthily celebrating the Supper of the Lord or drinking to his or her own condemnation?[125] At the end of the day, the fragmentation and disunity of the Church may be as much a matter of our predisposition as it is a reflection of any essential distinction among Christians. Ecumenism and the search for Christian unity transforms how we choose to see, how we decide to regard each other.[126] The dialogue and common ministry that have resulted from the ecumenical movement challenge us to discern again the Body of Christ among our fellow Christians.

[118] David N. Power, "Roman Catholic Theologies of Eucharistic Communion: A Contribution to Ecumenical Conversation," *Theological Studies* 57, no. 4 (1996) 590.
[119] *Einheit der Kirche.*
[120] Sanders.
[121] OBOB, 24.
[122] Hein, 62.
[123] William T. Cavanaugh, "Dying for the Eucharist or Being Killed by It? Romero's Challenge to First World Christians," *Theology Today* 58, no. 2 (2001).
[124] Hein, 63.
[125] Welker, 158.
[126] Raimon Panikkar, "The Fragment and the Part: An Indic Reflection," in *The Church in Fragments: Towards What Kind of Unity?*, ed. Giuseppe Ruggieri and Miklos Tomka, *Concilium* (London / Maryknoll, N.Y.: SCM Press / Orbis Books, 1997) 86.

Challenge 5:
To Share Genuine Christian Hospitality

Contemporary biblical scholarship demonstrates the centrality of meal-sharing to the ministry and message of Jesus. The Gospels establish definitive norms for Christian hospitality. They challenge us to offer hospitality at the Eucharist in continuity with Jesus and his ministry of meal-sharing.

Meal Fellowship and Hospitality in Christian Families

Richard Szafransky helps us explore the analogy between the Eucharist and the family meal. "I have never been in any family's home at mealtime without being invited to eat with them. I've never been told I could join them in the grace before meals, and in conversation, but not the food."[127] Simply stated, North American families do not publish "Guidelines for Receiving Thanksgiving Dinner."

Another example: I am vegetarian and so, at times, I have found myself in the home of a friend who has gone to great expense and effort to prepare a lovely roast (or some other meat dish) for me to share at dinner. Perhaps most vegetarians have found themselves in this awkward dilemma. Should I compromise my principles and eat the meat, or should I disappoint and risk insulting my host while maintaining my diet and my principles? I have tried both solutions, and I confess that neither solution is completely satisfying.

Anglican bishop John Neill continues the analogy to hospitality in one's home. "People who come to our homes," he says, "are offered hospitality, but we do not take offence if they do not accept."[128] In all fairness, the bishop seems far too forgiving. We should consider the analogy to hospitality in one's home in more detail.

Hospitality is an inviting term. Instead of using the term eucharistic sharing as I have, some ecumenists prefer the term eucharistic hospitality. They believe it helps us focus on the relationship of guests to host at the Lord's Table. Eucharistic hospitality is an inviting term. It helps us understand how every Christian is a guest in Holy Communion and the Lord is our only proper host. When Christians gather around the altar in the Lord's Supper—no matter to which Church they belong—they are guests of the Lord, who is the only true host of the Eucharist.

---

[127] Szafransky, 14.
[128] John Neill, "Christians' Desire to Unity in Communion Is Quite Understandable," *The Irish Times* (December 18, 1997) 16.

Hospitality amounts to the offer of a generous welcome to strangers. In the family, "loss of communication results in the loss of communion." The restoration of positive and meaningful interaction is the primary goal of most marriage and family therapy.[129] Consequently, it is instructive to point out that communion in a Christian family does not consist of adherence to doctrinal formulas. It consists of an ongoing commitment to meaningful interaction. There is no expectation of hospitality being granted "on the condition of the acceptance of the beliefs and objectives of the host community."[130]

A variety of understandings. There exists a tension between a variety of understandings of the meaning of hospitality. For some people, hospitality means changing in order to meet the guest. For them, hospitality is like the prodigal father running out to the fields to greet his wayward son. Hospitality is roasting the fatted calf without counting the risks. (Will we starve during the dry months because we slaughtered the calf too soon?)

For others, hospitality means expecting the guests to change. For them, hospitality is welcoming people into their household and expecting them to abide by the norms of the household. Hospitality is being so good a guest as to be nearly indistinguishable from the rest of the family. For them, the story of the prodigal father and his wayward son results in the reconciliation of the wayward son with the norms and expectations of the father's household. No longer would he need to run away to assert his independence. For the others, no matter how hard a guest tries to fit in with the household, he or she will always be the adopted one, the son-in-law, or our daughter's friend. The challenge for every host is to adopt the exuberant hospitality of the prodigal father, without "giving away the roost."

As we become accustomed to speaking of the Church as the "household of God" (in Greek this too is part of the meaning of the word *oikonomia*), we must beware of narrowing this household into something all too manageable and less than mysterious. For example, the Canaanite woman reminded Jesus that "even the dogs eat scraps from the master's table" (Mark 7:27-28).[131] Reformed theologian Bernard Thorogood suggests that no existing institutional Church is now "the household of God in the world." He warns that the household of God

---

[129] Cf. Carl Maxcey, "Roman Catholics and Intercommunion: Unity or Union," *Ecumenical Trends* 16 (1987) 92.

[130] Stuart Williams, "Sharing Communion: A Common Inheritance," *One in Christ* 31, no. 4 (1995) 353.

[131] Cf. Szafransky, 15.

should not be "narrowed down from the breadth that the Holy Spirit has created to mean 'people like us.'"[132]

Some Limitations on Hospitality

Hospitality can be compromised when a household has too strong or too exclusive a sense of family. Suppose I am in the home of a friend, yet I may not share in the family meal. Unless I am willing to be legally adopted, I may sit at the table, but "Please, don't touch the food!" In most families, there are degrees of closeness (anthropologists speak of consanguinity) that must be respected at mealtime. Guests of the family are expected to eat and to share the food that has been prepared. Guests are expected to conform to the minimal behavioral expectations of civilized table-companions: they chew with their mouth closed, in Europe they use fork and napkin; in Asia, chopsticks suffice. On the other hand, most guests do not expect to sign "pre-dining contracts" before they can take a place at the table!

Invitations behind the invitation. Sometimes, perhaps even in Catholic contexts, I am invited to receive a meal, unaware of the invitation behind the invitation. A meal turns into a fundraiser, a banquet becomes political, lunch becomes a meeting, and cocktails become a sales-pitch. Should Catholics ever practice a more open Communion, we need to state upfront our understanding of the invitation behind the invitation to commune with us. To what level does receiving Holy Communion imply assent to Catholic doctrine, to Catholic authorities, or membership in the Catholic Church?

The man who came to dinner. Moreover, in everyday life, continued hospitality eventually implies membership.[133] Eat enough meals at the Smith's and they are going to start expecting you to help with the shopping, the cooking, and the cleaning. A person might be a eucharistic guest a few times; but when do eucharistic guests become members of the family? Just like "The Man Who Came to Dinner," you simply cannot be a good guest forever.

Archbishop Wuerl helps us understand why the analogy to mutual hospitality is overly simplified. Hospitality, he says, is insufficient to frame the "profound issue of the meaning of the Eucharist." "If the issue were truly that clear," he writes, "it would have been solved long ago."[134]

[132] Bernard Thorogood, "Coming to the Lord's Table: A Reformed Viewpoint, *The Ecumenical Review* 44, no. 1 (1992) 13.

[133] Maxcey, 91.

[134] Donald Wuerl, "Serious Issues Prevent Catholics from Sharing the Eucharist," *Pittsburgh Post-Gazette* (April 15, 1998) Editorial, A-19.

I agree. Eucharistic sharing is not simply a matter of conviviality and invitation. Communion is complex. It is offered and expressed. It may or may not be received. Sometimes it is refused.

Analogies drawn from everyday hospitality to eucharistic hospitality are therefore limited. In everyday hospitality, guests are expected to go home. Hosts expect to be left to their own after a reasonable length of time. There is a point when "guests" must cease to be guests. They must either "join the household" or depart for other tables. If we are to understand the difference between everyday hospitality and eucharistic hospitality, we must look to Jesus and his practice of hospitality in meal-sharing.

Hospitality of Jesus Christ at the Heart of Communion

Biblical and liturgical scholars identify many important themes in the accounts of meals shared with Jesus.[135] For the sake of simplicity, I will focus on just three types of meal-sharing in the Gospels, and discuss one especially important characteristic of Jesus' ministry of hospitality: The parable of the Great Banquet, his dining "with tax collectors and sinners," the Last Supper, and meal-sharing as an effective sign of the kingdom of God.

The Great Banquet

Jesus' parable of the Great Banquet is especially instructive (Luke 14:15-24). There Jesus tells the story of someone who gave a great dinner and invited many people. The dinner was ready, yet the invited guests made excuses. For a number of reasons, they sent regrets. The host, with a dining room table full of food but no guests, sent his servant out

---

[135] Bruce Chilton identifies at least six types of meals with Jesus from within the New Testament evidence. First, there are the two meal types originally identified by Hans Lietzmann in the early twentieth century. (1) There is the agapic meal tradition seen in the meals of the kingdom and the multiplication of loaves traditions. (2) There are also the cultic meals that take on the appearance of a substitution for Temple sacrifice. Next, there are four more meal types Chilton adds in supplement to Lietzmann's conception. (3) There are the covenant meals of blessing (*berakah* meals) such as the Petrine, breaking of bread meals. (4) There are the Passover Seder meals central to the annual eucharistic feast of James' Jewish-Christianity, and the Quartodeciman Easter. (5) There are the anamnetic symposium meals evident in 1 Corinthians and the Synoptic Gospels. (6) There are the heroic sacrifice meals (the Hellenistic signs) of John's Gospel and letters. Bruce Chilton, *A Feast of Meanings: Eucharistic Theologies from Jesus through Johannine Circles*, ed. A. J. Malherbe and D. P. Moessner, *Supplements to Novum Testamentum* 72 (Leiden: E. J. Brill, 1994) 148.

to bring in "the poor, the crippled, the blind, and the lame." The host even asked that the servant "compel people to come in . . . so that my house may be filled." Consider the mystery of this banquet and the indiscriminate invitation of the host. Then, look around you during the Communion procession next Sunday.

Have you ever wondered why you were eating with all those other "riffraff"? Perhaps your "Sunday morning guest list" sounds like this: Joe is having an affair, Sally is divorced, Tom is homosexual, Melanie is alcoholic, Peter is verbally abusive; Karen overeats, Jim is a card shark, Joy is a recovering drug addict . . . The list goes on. The room is overflowing with poor, limping, blinded, powerless people. Looking around at the Church, at times, our prayer becomes distorted and we cry out, "But God, why do we have to eat with all these other folks? Please! Couldn't they eat in another room?" For some reason all of them, like you, responded to an invitation to dine at this table.

At one time or another, many Christians have not wanted to believe Paul when he wrote, "God has no favorites" (Rom 2:11).[136] The openness of the invitation to the Great Banquet—God as indiscriminate host—is all the more startling for its great depth. The guests are being invited to a setting where the possibility of social adjustment—today we would call it "upward status mobility"—would have been enormously profound.

Turn this parable around and something a bit more complex is also occurring. Lutheran theologian Dagmar Heller poignantly reflects on her sense of exclusion from the Eucharist in certain contexts: "If I do not go to the Lord's Supper, I feel like one of those people in Jesus' parable who turned down the king's invitation to a feast for all manner of reasons (Lk 14:15-24)."[137] In Jesus' parable the king has sent out servants to invite people to the feast. Perhaps Heller is feeling excluded because the servants were not faithful to the king's directions. Did she receive her invitation? If not, perhaps some of the servants are falling down on the job.

When we think about the parable of the Great Banquet, our slowness to heal the divisions of the churches can begin to sound like "many, many excuses."[138] Together, God invites us to the Great Banquet. We have many important excuses to come late to the feast. If the parable teaches anything, it is this: *Invitation delayed is invitation declined.*

[136] Anne Primavesi and Jennifer Henderson, *Our God Has No Favourites: A Liberation Theology of the Eucharist* (Turnbridge, Wells, England / San Jose, Calif.: Burns & Oates / Resource Publications, 1989) 47.

[137] Heller.

[138] Kondratha M. George, ed., "Eucharistic Hospitality," *The Ecumenical Review* 44 (1992) 3.

Dining with Tax Collectors and Sinners

In first-century Judaism, meals always had a religious connotation. They were organized to express levels of purity and of closeness to the divine. The meal, in the words of Morton Smith, "became an instance of fellowship within a realm that was understood to be divinely mandated."[139] This point was brought home to me one afternoon as I shared lunch with a Jewish student.

"Isaac" is an Orthodox Jew of Sephardic extraction.[140] He keeps *kosher* and diligently observes the Sabbath. He is, in every respect, a very faithful young man. We met for lunch at a kosher restaurant on the west side of Los Angeles. As we sat down to eat on the dairy side of the restaurant, Isaac excused himself to wash his hands. After returning to the table, he took out a small prayer card from his wallet, broke off a piece of bread and began to pray, "*Baruch Adonai . . .*" and so forth. My Hebrew is not very good, but I know the beginning of a table prayer when I hear one.

Isaac's witness tells me that I am far too comfortable with the idea of a secular meal. Here was an ordinary meal, a little tabouleh, hummus, and pita bread, transformed into an occasion for praising and blessing God for the bounty of creation. In Isaac's little prayer, I had the sense of being in the presence of a true "priest," not in the sense of an Aaronic priest—he is not a *kōhen*; nor in the sense of a Roman Catholic priest— he is Jewish; but in the sense of an "Adamic" priest. Here was a young man who boldly holds creation in one hand, faith in the other, and *intercedes* with thanksgiving and praise for these bits of food on our plates. Isaac taught me that it takes great *boldness* to stand in the presence of God and to bless God at mealtime.

The spiritual dimension of a meal. What is the spiritual dimension of a meal? For residents of North American cities and suburbs, it is a challenge to recognize the spiritual dimension of the "quickie-meals" we pick up at one of those nationwide chains of fast-food restaurants. To the contrary, the Scriptures suggest that a meal is never just food. Meals, in Jesus' day, always had a theological dimension.[141]

The social dimension of a meal. Christians too easily forget how we construct social categories in terms of those with whom we will eat versus those with whom we will not eat. In the Gospels, Jesus used mealtime to create and establish solidarity among people and with their God. There was no means-ends distinction. The purpose of a meal, as Jesus

[139] Chilton, 13.
[140] This is not his real name.
[141] Leo Gafney, "Sharing the Meal," *America* (May 17, 1997) 20f.

saw it, was to establish solidarity among broken men and women in light of God's free decision to commune with them.[142] The meal was itself the cause and the sign of its social and theological goals.

When we think about Jesus at table with "tax collectors and sinners," we may need to get several Sunday School or Hollywood images out of our heads first. Jesus was not like the actor Jeffrey Hunter in *King of Kings.* He was not a charming bon vivant! He was rather, in the words of Nathan Mitchell, a "vulnerable vagrant" and a "homeless wanderer."[143]

Purity concerns were central to Jesus' own practice of meal-sharing, but not in the way that self-righteous people usually think. Jesus was concerned about purity in two respects: with respect to what one may eat and with whom one may eat. In both respects, Jesus broke the social conventions of his own day. That is why he was called a "glutton and a drinker" (Matt 11:18, 19 and Luke 7:33-35). That is why the social and religious elites saw him as a threat. He ate with sinners *while they were still sinners.*[144] Our understanding of Jesus' ministry to men and women after the resurrection cannot be radically discontinuous from his ministry to men and women during his earthly life. Therefore, eucharistic Communion must be seen as continuous with Christ's desire to share the table with "tax collectors and sinners."[145]

The Last Supper

In the first century, a wide variety of types of Eucharist existed among Christians. Some would be nearly unrecognizable to modern Christians. The stories about the Last Supper developed later than the actual practice of sharing the Eucharist. As the stories about Jesus' meal-sharing with the disciples come to share uniform features, scholars surmise that this uniformity is a "sign of lateness." They are the result of later authors retrojecting what they knew about their own Eucharist on top of the story of Jesus' meals with disciples and, of course, on top of the story of Jesus' final meal, the Last Supper. In every case, the Gospel writers understood that they were depicting the Last Supper along lines congruent with their own theological aims and messages.[146]

---

[142] Ibid.
[143] Maxwell Johnson, 3.
[144] Chilton, 25.
[145] James Arne Nestingen and Wayne Zweck, "Communio, Inter-Communion with Non-Lutheran Churches, and the Lutheran Confessions / A Response," *Lutheran Theological Journal* (Adelaide) 33, no. 1 (1999).
[146] Chilton, 13.

The novel view of Bruce Chilton is that, after the failed occupation of the Temple, Jesus' meals took on the tone of a substitution for the sacrifices that were performed there.[147] In any event, the last meal Jesus shared with disciples before his death must have occurred within a highly charged and complex situation. Full of danger, the meal took place in a room surrounded by—and filled with—risk.[148]

The Gospels offer evidence of a variety of levels of commitment in the meals that Jesus shared with others.[149] The stories of the multiplying of loaves, for example, suggest there was no particularly deep level of commitment on the part of those who received the barley loaves and fish. With the exception of Judas, the stories of the Last Supper suggest an unusually deep level of commitment. Here, the disciples are engaged in "eating unto death." Their covenant meal implied a high degree of personal risk—notwithstanding Jesus' imminent abandonment by everyone who took part in that meal.

A note on Judas as the model for excommunication. In the Synoptic Gospels, Judas received the Last Supper along with the other disciples. According to John, Jesus dismissed Judas before the meal; but John's account of the Last Supper is not typical in many other respects.[150] In Christian antiquity, preachers rarely used Judas' dismissal from the Last Supper as an argument for excommunication. More often, they simply understood the case of Judas as an example of "unworthy reception."[151]

Meals As Effective Signs of the Kingdom of God

Renowned Bible scholar Norman Perrin observed that table fellowship was the "central feature of the ministry of Jesus." In Jesus' life and ministry, table fellowship was an "anticipatory sitting at table in the Kingdom of God."[152] The preaching of the kingdom of God was central to Jesus' ministry and message. All the meals of Jesus recorded in the Gospels anticipate the great Messianic Banquet.[153] The Eucharist, no less a meal with Jesus than those other meals, must also anticipate the Messianic Banquet. To join in a meal with Jesus was to anticipate the

---

[147] Ibid., 148.
[148] Welker, 46.
[149] Hellwig, 70.
[150] Hein, 42f.
[151] Ibid., 49.
[152] Maxwell Johnson, 107. Norman Perrin, *Rediscovering the Teaching of Jesus* (New York: Harper & Row, 1967).
[153] Hellwig, 46.

kingdom "in the manner delineated by him."[154] The Church, therefore, ought to comprise a continuous table fellowship with Jesus.[155]

However, within a generation, Christians had turned to Jesus himself as the central focus of their message and ministry. The message had become the messenger. Adolf von Harnack, an early twentieth-century biblical theologian, encapsulated this progression of messages and messengers in a noteworthy phrase. "Jesus preached the kingdom of God as good news, but the apostles preached the Lord Jesus Christ."[156] In the millennia since the time of the apostolic Church, in some places and times Christians have turned to a new central focus. They have turned to the Church as central focus. The message has become the community and its leaders.

In exploring the matter of Jesus' practice of meal-sharing, several tensions have emerged. These tensions, I believe, ought to remain in tension; we ameliorate them at our peril. For example, when we consider the Eucharist under the sign of table fellowship with Jesus, we see a table fellowship that was both open and intimate. Jesus invited many people to join him in meals; yet many of the meals we see in the Gospels were intimate gatherings of close friends and disciples. There is a simple lesson in the Gospels to be learned from all this. In the Eucharist, the unlikeliest folk will become our table-companions.

Meal-Sharing in Continuity with Jesus Christ

Like Tony Blair, when confronted by the problem of eucharistic sharing, many people point to the words of Jesus or they ask, "What would Jesus do?" In response, the bishops of the United Kingdom and Ireland said that we must mind the hard words of Jesus and recall the many people who left him behind because they could not accept his teaching on the Bread of Life.[157] There is a problem with the bishops' comment. In the time of the author of the Gospel, this analogy helped to distinguish Christians from others who could not accept Jesus' teachings (Jews, followers of other religions, and so forth). In the modern ecu-

[154] Chilton, 39.

[155] Welker, 29.

[156] Carl E. Braaten, *Mother Church: Ecclesiology and Ecumenism* (Minneapolis: Fortress Press, 1998) quoting Willi Marxsen, *Mark the Evangelist* (Nashville: Abingdon, 1969) 145. In our zeal to protect and preserve the historic episcopate and the ordained priesthood, Catholics might take a lesson from this page. We must avoid the next logical step in von Harnack's phrase: "but the bishops and priests preached themselves."

[157] OBOB, 119.

menical context, however, the analogy is less apt. I hope the authors of *One Bread, One Body* did not think that non-Catholics are departing from Jesus because of his teachings. I hope they do not think that the division of baptized Christians from one another is caused by Jesus himself.

In John 6, the author of the Fourth Gospel marks the point at which "the Christian practice of Eucharist self-consciously and definitively parted from Judaism."[158] We should compare this view to the one found in *One Bread, One Body*. The author of John was writing against Jewish-Christians, people who believed in Jesus, but could not accept the Johannine teaching on the Eucharist. They were the ones who left Jesus because they were scandalized.

The implication is not that *Jesus* used the Eucharist to separate believers from nonbelievers. Rather, the importance of this passage is that *John* uses an exaggeratedly harsh teaching on the Eucharist to separate real Christians from those *he* viewed as fakes. We should not suppose that John's group of fakes ever really departed from Jesus, scandalized by his teachings. Rather, this story can be read as an invective against other Christians of good faith, Christians who could not accept the authenticity of John's teaching about Jesus.

Continuity in table fellowship. Continuity between the table fellowship of Jesus in the first century and the table fellowship of Jesus in successive centuries is essential. The continuity between the meal sharing of Jesus and our own table fellowship in the Eucharist is best thought of in qualitative and spiritual terms. When I speak of "qualitative terms," I mean to emphasize that the most essential characteristics of the table fellowship of Jesus during his earthly ministry must be transposed into our own table fellowship or else we are not celebrating an authentic Eucharist. When I speak of "spiritual terms," I mean to stress the role of the Holy Spirit in helping us be hospitable in the manner of the radical and scandalously open meal fellowship of Jesus.

Sharing food is central. The central act of the Eucharist is the sharing of food.[159] When a church offers a share in the Eucharist, it acknowledges that all the baptized are already members of a single family, the household of Christ. These are not strangers but long-lost cousins, aunts, and uncles, who seek to dine among us. They are as much family members as they are guests. And, we are as much hosts as we are siblings for them.

Whenever we fail to share the eucharistic food, we also fail to complete our Eucharist. Completing the Eucharist means that we have entered into Christ's own spirit of lavish generosity and, without a

[158] Chilton, 142.
[159] Hellwig, 10.

trace of self-consciousness, share the eucharistic meal as if we were Jesus Christ himself, here, today, blessing, breaking, pouring, and giving the meal to all of his disciples. Christ's eucharistic mandate was for every Christian to "Take and eat." His implicit eucharistic mandate to every Christian minister should also be heard: "Give and let them eat."

Why Christian Hospitality Is a Challenge to Share a More Open Communion

When we look at patterns of human meal-sharing, we understand how meals satisfy our hungers—and change us—not just for their nutritional sustenance, but also for their power to form social connections. Meals nourish our hunger for human relationships. At some meals, on the road, at fast-food joints, we arrive, we eat, and we leave. At other meals, the consumption of food *causes us to become new persons and to inhabit new social roles*. In North America, meals associated with graduations, *quinceañeras*, weddings, retirements, and funerals often perform these kinds of social adjustments for us.

Likewise, the Eucharist continues the table fellowship of Jesus and causes us to become *new persons*.[160] The table fellowship of Jesus, as seen in the Gospels, invited the most unlikely men and women of his day into a radical transformation of life and character. The Eucharist, as seen in real life, similarly invites and transforms the men and women of our day. In both sorts of meals—the meals of Jesus then, the Eucharist of Jesus now—the invitation is open; the transformation is radical.

In the parable of Jesus, it is telling that the riffraff off the street are invited to a wedding banquet. From stories of meal-sharing like these, we see that Jesus proclaimed three conditions sufficient for eating in his company and for entry into the kingdom of God: (1) a willingness to provide for the meals; (2) to join in the fellowship; and (3) to forgive and to be forgiven.[161]

Who may invite whom God has not? Orthodox priest and theologian Paulos Gregorios asks whether the Church can "invite some more people to the Eucharist."[162] Implicit to his critique is the idea that the Church may not act on its own in contradiction to the desire of God. In sharing the Eucharist, the Church can never invite some more people in addition to the ones whom God has already invited. Rather, in providing access to Holy Communion, the Church is "ratifying the permanent

---

[160] Maxwell Johnson, 374.

[161] Chilton, 146.

[162] Paulos Mar Gregorios, "Not a Question of Hospitality: A Comment," *The Ecumenical Review* 44, no. 1 (1992) 46.

invitation" which that person received in baptism. In the eucharistic economy, Gregorios says there is no question of hospitality.[163]

However, I would call attention to those whom God offers God's self. The question of hospitality emerges in the eucharistic economy only after we think about who is included and who is excluded from the Church. The Holy Spirit entrusts the Church to offer and to receive Christ's Body and Blood to all and from all whom God has chosen. If Church norms stand in the way of this offering and receiving, have they not damaged the eucharistic economy and created a tragic climate of inhospitality? They would have made us inhospitable because we would have been made to enact false beliefs about our neighbors and their relationship to God—that they do not love us, that they are asking us to violate our beliefs, that God has not chosen them, or that they do not share in the benefits of Christian baptism.

Recalling the meal Jesus shared with his disciples at Emmaus, Rev. John Muddiman, an Anglican member of the Anglican-Roman Catholic International Commission, asked, "What assurance did the risen Christ have that Cleopas and his companion had the right beliefs and were in good standing before he celebrated the Eucharist for them?" The simple invitation, he says, to "stay and eat" was "sufficient for the divine grace to comply."[164]

Eucharistic hospitality amounts to the determination not to stand in the way of God's grace. The inherent risk to a closed Communion is that God has invited men and women into communion, but they cannot get in because we—in willfulness and not obedience—have barred the doors and closed the gates. When the Church shares the Eucharist with an individual, however, it exercises the collective will (the discernment) *not to stand in the way* of God's saving grace for that person, to his or her becoming a member of the Body of Christ.

Challenge 6:
To Avoid Further Hurts and Injuries

Failing to share the Eucharist has psychological and social consequences for us and for our dialogue partners. Ecumenical pain is real; and those who hold out the strongest hope for ecumenical progress more keenly feel it. Maintaining the discipline of a less open eucharistic

---

[163] Ibid.

[164] Meinrad Scherer-Edmunds, "Let's Stop Posting Bouncers at the Table of the Lord," *U.S. Catholic* (June 2000) 28.

sharing risks offending our closest friends and jeopardizes ecumenical progress.

For the moment, assume that eucharistic sharing is not a significant problem for most non-Catholic, non-Orthodox Christians. Even if it is a non-issue for most Protestants, there remains one significant area of difficulty. Christians from churches with an open Communion stand at their altars every week to welcome Catholics in good faith to share in the Lord's Supper. Likewise, a significant number have no difficulty receiving the Eucharist with us.

In failing to share Holy Communion with all the baptized, we risk sinning against the conscience of those who recognize Christ in our Eucharist, who desire to receive him with us, and yet are warned away by rubrics. In turn, this can lead to a hardening of ecclesial divisions on many levels.

For example, an interchurch couple reports that a period when they attempted conscientiously to follow Church discipline nearly destroyed their marriage.

> Unhappiness at a division led to a series of quarrels, depressions, resistance to practice, anguish and finally a realization that if our marriage was to be preserved as a loving relationship there must be a way through dogmatic attitudes. . . . Our practices have the feel of being surreptitious. We have to be careful in speaking about them in certain circumstances.[165]

The couple now receives Holy Communion regularly in each other's churches. The essential question raised by such reports is whether the theological and ecclesiological benefits of the present statutes outweigh the psychological and spiritual burdens they place on faithful Christians.

People know when they are not welcomed, and inhospitable incidents can lead, in some cases, to a lifelong prejudice. While vigilance in protecting the quality of our Communion is essential to good pastoral care, inhospitable practices can thwart the best intentions of good pastors. Occasionally, ministers model inhospitable behaviors without being aware of having done so. In each of these cases, we must ascertain whether our pastoral practices follow the gracious and transformative hospitality modeled for us by Christ or whether our guests are seeking false friendliness in the guise of genuine hospitality.

Recall too, that our inability to be hospitable also reflects a negative judgment on the validity and apostolicity of non-Catholic ministers

---

[165] Finch and Reardon, 71.

which is perceived as a grave insult. The bishops of the Church of England find that the Catholic discipline on eucharistic sharing is both "hurtful and unhelpful."[166] When the Anglican bishops report this finding, Catholics must not dismiss their statements as the result of strong emotional reactions only. When the bishops said there was "hurt," this is not only the indication of a feeling or an intuition. It is the result of deliberation and reflection by responsible and charitable Christian leaders. These statements confront and challenge Catholics and Catholic authorities who defend the present statutes on eucharistic sharing. The present norms have serious psychosocial consequences.

Our failure to share the Eucharist may ultimately jeopardize the potential future unity of Christian communities. Ecumenism stagnates when the ban on eucharistic sharing continues to be repeated. The ban itself will not be the problem. The willingness of Catholics to engage in ecumenical dialogue will not be the problem. The continuing offense and hurt that is felt by our closest ecumenical dialogue partners will be the problem. They will have walked and they will work to unite the Church without us. Catholic hesitation would have resulted in our marginalization within the community of baptized Christians.

Current Norms, Blowback

The example of the Swiss Conference of Catholic Bishops illustrates this difficulty. During their synod of 1972–75, the bishops of Switzerland formulated the principle that a "believer cannot be deprived of the spiritual fruit of the sacraments without good reason." The bishops also determined that the decision of a non-Catholic to receive Communion in a Catholic Church cannot be interpreted as a decision to "break with his own Church." These policies and understandings of the Swiss bishops were considerably more open than what has come to be expressed in the Code of Canon Law or in subsequent Ecumenical Directories.

In 1986, under pressure from Rome and from other European bishops, the bishops of Switzerland abandoned their earlier norms. Swiss Protestants report they felt the reversal in norms for eucharistic sharing as though it were a "douse of cold water" on ecumenical progress.[167] What had been a sign of an ever-closer union progressively attained among divided Christians was changed overnight into a means of asserting and creating division. The moral of the story: In their zeal to

---

[166] ESOU, viii.

[167] Hugh Cross et al., "Eucharist Experiences Today," *The Ecumenical Review* 44, no. 1 (1992) 55f.

promote the Eucharist as a "sign of unity attained," Catholic authorities must not change the Eucharist into a "means of disunity sustained."

The problem of "blowback." When Church authorities assert or reassert sacramental discipline, they sometimes encounter puzzling and disappointing reactions. Military and political strategists call the unintended results of a policy decision "blowback." Blowback may not be the most appropriate word for the unintended consequences of the decisions of Church authorities. Nevertheless, Catholic authorities often fail to weigh the impact of their decisions on the sensitivities of baptized non-Catholics, their churches, and communities. This can result in unintended harm to ecumenical relations. The solution, of course, is simple. We must be ecumenical in the formulation of Church discipline. No Church law prohibits bishops to consult with non-Catholics as they formulate sacramental norms.

As it happens, the discipline of the sacraments can be helpful for us in our quest to become better disciples of Jesus. Sometimes, however, discipline is imposed by Church authorities with little consideration for consequences. It then seems to diminish the graciousness of God's mercy. On the one hand, too loose a discipline and we are not transformed by grace. On the other hand, too strict a discipline and we are made to think that God's desire to save us is very limited indeed. The sacraments, it should be noted, are accommodations to our humanness. They accommodate to our fallenness. We should be wary, however, to avoid turning sacramental norms into limitations on God or God's grace.

Repeating Bans and Prohibitions

Catholic theologian Gerard Austin reports the experience of a friend who attended a wedding that "lasted more than two hours." Considerable time was spent on the Communion rite since the pastor "asked each person approaching Communion whether he or she were Catholic."[168] The repetition of canonical restrictions during the liturgy does nothing to serve the spirit or intent of true worship. Good pastoral practice requires, instead, that ministers presume the good faith of those who present themselves to receive the sacraments. A pre-Communion quiz is an obvious misinterpretation of the canonical norms. It damages the liturgy. It insults and injures the ecumenical goodwill that has been nurtured so carefully in the decades since Vatican II.

[168] Gerard Austin, "Identity of a Eucharistic Church in an Ecumenical Age," *Worship* 72 (1998) 26.

Cokie Roberts, a Catholic, reports that many of her Protestant friends perceive the statement of the U.S. bishops as "hurtful" and "exclusionary." In their view, says Roberts, "It's *designed* to hurt."[169] Whether we like it or not, some Christians will experience the reiteration of unilateral statements on the Eucharist as painfully tactless.[170]

In April 1998, archbishop of Canterbury George Carey stated that it is hurtful to be denied the Lord's Supper by a fellow disciple of Jesus Christ. Focus for a moment on the verb "denied." In Carey's remarks, "denied" is shorthand for a very complex social exchange. Every Sunday, in Catholic Churches around the world, members of the Body of Christ are turned back at the altar or warned off from receiving the Eucharist well in advance of the Communion procession. In many Catholic Churches, non-Catholics are forewarned not even to try to receive the Eucharist. They are not merely denied the Eucharist, they are prohibited, in the very technical sense of having been inhibited from taking an action before they could consider whether it was a good or a bad thing for them to do. These actions, words placed on the back of missalettes or good-natured directions from well-intentioned priests and hospitality ministers, seem directed less to putting the guest at ease than they are to protecting the Catholic minister from finding him or herself in the awkward position of having to actually deny the Eucharist—as Archbishop Carey finds so hurtful.

Which is more hurtful—to actively deny the Eucharist to a non-Catholic or to prohibit and inhibit the non-Catholic from coming forward so as to avoid facing the uncomfortable reality of Christian division at the altar rail? I suggest that prohibition is more hurtful because it is more cowardly and no less divisive. When prohibitions are printed in bulletins and missalettes, they are self-serving insofar as they serve the desire of the one who prohibits. The one who prohibits desires to be protected from the position of awkwardly denying the Eucharist to the non-Catholic.

Ecumenical Pain

Many Christians feel strong emotions because of the division of the Church. These strong emotions should not be dismissed. Christians especially feel the pain of division when they feel they are called to receive the Eucharist although they are barred from receiving it. Church authorities and others should be wary to wave away these feelings of

---

[169] Cokie Roberts and Steven Roberts, "Sacrament Should Serve to Include, Not to Exclude," *The Denver Rocky Mountain News* (April 12, 1998), emphasis added.

[170] Larere, 67f.

anger, dismay, or disaffection. While reason strongly assists the life of faith, emotions also have an authentic place.[171] For instance, in the parable of the Prodigal Son, the father followed his emotions much more than his reasons in running to embrace his wayward boy. The emotions, the good pastor realizes, can orient our reasoning along lines of true and genuine empathy and therefore in potentially more fruitful directions.

The anecdote of a non-Catholic spouse in an interchurch marriage illumines the problem of the pain of separation. An Anglican spouse reports she had been receiving Communion with her spouse at a Roman Catholic abbey in England. A novice reported to her, subsequently, that several members of the community would be disgruntled if they knew an Anglican was receiving Communion with them. The woman brought up the matter with the abbot, who both articulated the official Catholic position while affirming that she should follow her conscience. She reports that after she stopped receiving Communion, so as not to upset others, "The whole thing was brought into the open and the Roman Catholics tried to make a virtue of the pain of separation." Several monks came to the Eucharist at the Anglican Church and did not receive Communion, "so that they could experience the pain of separation themselves."[172] This report causes me to wonder. Who understood the virtue of the pain of separation most keenly, the non-Catholic spouse or the monks who attempted to understand her pain?

The view of the Catholic bishops of the United Kingdom and Ireland is that eucharistic sharing is not justified solely to remove the sense of pain or sorrow that divided Christians may feel.[173] They insist that *disunity* is the source of pain, not the sacramental norms. Pain, they say, is a sign of a need for healing. When people are injured, they feel pain. In most cases, the injury needs a cure more than the pain needs an analgesic.[174] *One Bread, One Body* thus follows a typical strategy: to turn pain into a virtue. The bishops imply that the deeper our pain the more urgently we will pray to be united.[175]

Recently, Cardinal Simonis of Utrecht, Netherlands, has also remarked on the pain of disunity. He says that the ban on eucharistic sharing has become one of the "greatest points of pain" for ecumenism in the Netherlands. It is a matter, he said, "of not pretending a unity

---

[171] Beffa, 42.
[172] Finch and Reardon, 29f.
[173] OBOB, 77.
[174] Cf. OBOB, 76.
[175] OBOB, 119.

which does not really exist."[176] Look behind the words and read the implications. These authorities are saying that if we share the Eucharist too soon we will not feel the pain and the malady will remain uncured. Their words suggest that eucharistic sharing (despite division) is only a placebo and not a cure. They deny the power of the Eucharist to restore human community and to create reconciliation.[177]

To the contrary, in a discussion of martyrdom, William Cavanaugh reminds us that pain and suffering are not goods in themselves. They are, he writes, the "to-be-expected by-products" of faithfulness and witness "to the re-creation of the world through Jesus Christ."[178] Perhaps we *should* feel more pain over the division of the Churches. But only because we could be better "martyrs"—in the *original* sense of the word: as stronger and more faithful *witnesses* to Christ.

Ecumenical Woundedness

According to the Congregation for the Doctrine of the Faith, we must always reckon with the "woundedness" of the Church. In the view of the Congregation, Christian communities vary in their "wounds." Some (primarily the Orthodox Churches) are wounded only because they lack communion with Rome. Others (primarily the Protestant Churches) are wounded because they also lack the apostolic succession. Even the Catholic Church (the communion of Churches in communion with Rome) is wounded because it "fails to manifest its own inherent universality." As the CDF states, "This [the woundedness of these other particular churches and ecclesial communities] in turn also injures the Catholic Church, called by the Lord to become for all 'one flock' with 'one shepherd,' in that it hinders the complete fulfilment of its universality in history."[179]

The analogy of woundedness is both helpful and troublesome. The analogy is troublesome because the language of several CDF statements suggest that the woundedness of the Catholic Church is an injury—a tort—for which non-Catholic Christians are liable. For this reason, Protestant and Orthodox authorities and theologians will configure the "woundedness" analogy quite differently from the CDF.

The analogy is helpful for it suggests that something is truly missing in the communion of Catholic Churches that can only be resolved

---

[176] Bakker, "Simonis: Intercommunie blijft Pijnpunt in Oecumene," *Algemeen Nederlands Persbureau* (January 18, 2002).

[177] Primavesi and Henderson, 10.

[178] Cavanaugh, "Dying for the Eucharist."

[179] *Communionis notio* 17.

through full communion with the historic Orthodox and Protestant Churches. Because of its "woundedness," the Catholic Church remains unable to comprise in full the unity of the universal Church understood as the communion of all the baptized members of Christ's Body.

When Catholic authorities acknowledge that even the Catholic Church is wounded by the division of the Church, included is a reluctant understanding that the Catholic Church has a relative lack of comprehensiveness, a certain loss of wholeness. Among the non-Catholic Churches there exists an enormous treasury of grace and wisdom. The Catholic Church is wounded when it remains unable to draw upon that treasury in its common life and ministry.

The woundedness of the Catholic Church does not mean that our Church does not save people. It does not mean that the Catholic Church is not rich with integrity. It does not mean that the Church of Christ does not subsist in the Catholic Church. It means there is simply a lack; the table is set but many places are empty. In the words of David Power, it means that the Catholic Church needs also to cultivate, in itself, an understanding of its own "lack of fullness."[180]

Ecumenical Desire

Roman Catholics sometimes feel a very strong sense of completion. The Church, we say, is one. We live within the sphere of true Christian teaching. This sense of completeness is a great gift for it shields us from much doubt, many conflicts, and controversies. This sense of completeness is also a liability for it is difficult for us to desire other Christians. Desire for the missing members will teach us two things. It will teach us the pain of their absence. It will teach us the joy we hope to find when we are restored to communion with one another.[181]

If anything, the failure to find non-Catholic Christianity sufficiently desirable is one of the more significant obstacles to ecumenical progress in Catholic circles. The tale of Narcissus and his self-absorption is perhaps cautionary in this regard. Narcissus could find no one more desirable and alluring than himself. Catholics may need to work hard to avoid the ecumenical equivalent of narcissism. What can we do to both burn with desire to share the Eucharist with one another and to assist others to burn with desire to share communion with us?[182]

[180] Power, "Roman Catholic Theologies of Eucharistic Communion."

[181] Cf. Miroslav Volf, *Exclusion and Embrace: A Theological Exploration of Identity, Otherness, and Reconciliation* (Nashville: Abingdon Press, 1996) 141.

[182] von Allmen, 74.

By contrast, the narcissist, one who is full of himself or herself, has no room for others in his or her life. When a person is full of himself he cannot offer genuine hospitality because there is no room for anyone else within his world. That is reason enough to be wary of people and groups overly confident in their sense of self or in their sense of mission and identity. The more a group is clearly defined and unambiguous in its perspectives, the less that group seems desirous of including others.

Monika Hellwig reminds us that those who do not hunger are "dead."[183] When we feel self-sufficient, we no longer hunger for relationship with others. We become calloused to our own sense of neediness and ignore the hunger for relationship. Hunger, like many other essential human desires, helps us experience and acknowledge our dependence on others. The risk for churches is to think that they are independent. Some churches seem to have lost the hunger for relationship with other churches. In their sense of self-sufficiency, these churches forget that, as the Body of Christ, they once cried out from the cross, "I thirst!"

Which is worse? A Christian could feel no urgency toward reunion with other Churches and nonetheless share the Eucharist with them. Or a Christian could feel no urgency toward reunion with other Churches and avoid eucharistic sharing at all costs. The problem is not with eucharistic sharing; it lies in the indifference to unity. Indifference to Christian unity is the deeper of the two problems. Over the long haul, communities and neighborhoods have hardened to ecclesial division and accept these divisions as part of the status quo.

Ecumenical Reconciliation

In Catholic theology, we hold a rather high view of sacramental reconciliation. Catholic theology emphasizes the reconciling power of confessing our sins before a priest and receiving the absolution with a firm purpose of amendment. Because of our emphasis on confession, Catholic theology has tended to downplay—at times even overlook— the reconciling power of the Eucharist. Historically, Catholic theology has always recognized and never denied the power of the Eucharist to restore relationships that have been damaged, wounded, or destroyed by sin. We have always known that the Eucharist creates a shared world of grace where we might live together in peace.[184]

---

[183] Hellwig, 15.

[184] John M. Russell, "Pannenberg on Eucharist and Unity," *Currents in Theology and Mission* 17 (1990) 119.

The risk here is that Catholics may fail to do anything at all to restore the unity of Christians. To cooperate with God's grace offers a solution. We need to do the ecumenical tasks that are in our power, all the while acknowledging our limitations in comparison to what the infinite power of God's love can do among us really, now, and not at the end of the world.

Why Ecumenical Hurts and Injuries Are a Challenge to Share a More Open Communion

As our liturgy teaches us, the Eucharist is a *sacrum convivium,* a holy meal-sharing. It is an *admirabile commercium,* a miraculous exchange. The Eucharist saves us not because it helps us, but it helps us because it saves us. If the Eucharist were merely an aid, it would be of no help at all; for it would more or less leave us in the same sinful conditions we started in. Rather, we need to consider how Christ saves us (and so helps us) by drawing us into communion with God and one another. The saving element is that we are drawn out of ourselves. The Eucharist *substitutes* my ego with Christ. In a very traditional sense it is correct to say, "I am not saved, but Christ is saved in me."

The economy of the Eucharist is part of the economy of salvation. In the economy of God's grace, the most abundant and ordinary things are the most valuable. As Christians have said since the time of Augustine, "Where there is sin, grace abounds all the more." For Christians to limit access to God's grace does not make the grace more amazing. The disciples made this mistake when they thought that limiting the access of children to Jesus enhanced his social standing. Abundant and nearly unlimited access to the Eucharist, instead of cheapening its worth, rather enhances it. Instead of enhancing or protecting its value, to limit access to the Eucharist distorts and cheapens it.

Conclusions

In this chapter, I have examined six challenges to the present norms for eucharistic sharing. A brief summary of each challenge as I have defined them:

1. Christians are challenged to recognize the fullness of baptism. The modern, average view of baptism is insufficient, for it leaves us stranded in an odd theological limbo. Baptism frees from sin, but our average view leaves the Christian strangely powerless with respect to the promptings of the Spirit. The link between confir-

mation and the Eucharist should be restored and would rightly point to the relational character of the episcopate and of Christian communion.

2. The connection between the economy of salvation and serious pastoral need should be drawn more carefully. It is true, as the Orthodox say, that the only real pastoral need is the need for salvation. At the same time, God works out our salvation in and through human relationships. The principle of pastoral need recognizes our responsibility to minister to all men and women, especially in times of crisis.

3. Christians are challenged to unleash God's power in the Eucharist to create unity among men and women who are divided. The sacraments, we must remember, signify Christian unity precisely because they bring it about in every context of human life.

4. The most basic challenge is for us to discern the Body of Christ in one another. Christ lives among us in the baptized Christian, in the person in need, in the community that gathers for prayer and worship. Discerning the Body of Christ is perhaps the greatest challenge for contemporary Christians. The division of Christianity is a result of our refusal or failure to discern the Body of Christ in one another.

5. Biblical scholars agree that Jesus' ministry of meal-sharing was an effective proclamation of the kingdom of God. The challenge for Christians is to ensure that our fears do not blunt the message of the Eucharist. The Eucharist is the continuation of Jesus' ministry of meal-sharing and must be no less effective in proclaiming the kingdom of God. This—not vague or warm feelings of sentimentality—must be the source of all genuinely Christian hospitality.

6. Finally, we are challenged to a deeper empathy. The repetition of bans and prohibitions harms and injures the prospect for Christian unity because it hurts the feelings of real men and women, whether or not that was our intention. No matter how well grounded are the reasons for caution in eucharistic sharing, we ought to be tender and generous when expressing those concerns. The decision not to share the Eucharist must always be expressed in temporary terms—it is a prudential decision and an interim solution. The refusal to share should be stated in the most generous terms possible because it is "the best we can muster for now."

Questions for Reflection and Dialogue

1. *Challenges in general:* In your own view, what is the most serious challenge to the current norms on open eucharistic sharing? How do your views compare to the views of others? Are you aware of challenges not mentioned in this chapter?

2. *Discerning the Body of Christ:* Saint Paul wrote that discerning the Body is one of the most critical elements in the ability of a community to share the Lord's Supper. Has your understanding of discerning the Body changed as a result of reading this chapter? What does discerning the Body of Christ mean for you now?

3. *Christian hospitality:* How do you practice mealtime hospitality in your own home? How do you understand the difference between mealtime hospitality in the home and mealtime hospitality at church? Some would say that the norms of mealtime hospitality do not apply to the Eucharist. Do you agree or disagree? Why or why not?

4. *Hunger and thirst for Christian unity:* How do you view the problem of Christian unity? Is it a goal worth striving toward? In the context of a world in need, what priority should ecumenism be given in comparison to the many other needs that people face (e.g., poverty, illness, abuse, exploitation, and so forth)?

For Further Reading

Chilton, Bruce. *A Feast of Meanings: Eucharistic Theologies from Jesus through Johannine Circles.* Edited by A. J. Malherbe and D. P. Moessner, *Supplements to Novum Testamentum 72.* Leiden: E. J. Brill, 1994.

Johnson, Maxwell. *The Rites of Christian Initiation: Their Evolution and Interpretation.* Collegeville, Minn.: The Liturgical Press, 1999.

Martin, Dale B. *The Corinthian Body.* New Haven, Conn.: Yale University Press, 1995.

Moloney, Francis J. *A Body Broken for a Broken People: Eucharist in the New Testament.* Rev. ed. Peabody, Mass. / Blackburn, Victoria, Australia: Hendrickson Publishers / HarperCollins Religious, 1997.

Scherer-Edmunds, Meinrad. "Let's Stop Posting Bouncers at the Table of the Lord." *U.S. Catholic* (June 2000) 24–28.

Welker, Michael. *What Happens in Holy Communion?* Translated by John F. Hoffmeyer. Grand Rapids, Mich. / Cambridge, Mass.: Eerdmans Publishing Co. / SPCK, 2000.

Wood, Susan K. "Baptism and the Foundations of Communion." In *Baptism and the Unity of the Church*, edited by Michael Root and Risto Saarinen, 37–60. Grand Rapids, Mich. and Geneva: Eerdmans Publishing Co. and WCC Publications, 1998.

Chapter 4

Opportunities or Some Reasons for Sharing the Eucharist in Hope for Full Communion

TEGWITZ, GERMANY (July 29, 2001): Ms. Arnhild Ratsch, a member of the German Evangelical Church (EKD), began a 2,000-kilometer pilgrimage to Rome. She set out on foot using an early sixteenth-century map and would reach Rome in mid-November. When in Rome, she hoped to deliver her appeal to the Pope in a private audience.

Her petition states, "We find it deeply painful that we are still divided at the Lord's Table. We ask and hope that we will soon be granted the possibility of coming to an understanding in which our differences lose their church-divisive character and we are able to celebrate the presence of our risen Lord together."[1] The appeal welcomed John Paul II's "unflagging dedication to the cause of ecumenism," but added, "Local Christians need more signs of encouragement."[2]

Catholic and Evangelical bishops from the region of eastern Germany endorsed Ratsch's pilgrimage and provided her a "letter of safe passage." The former German Democratic Republic is widely recognized as one of Europe's most secularized populations. Frequent writer for *The Tablet*, Jonathon Luxmoore reports, "A quarter of its 16 million inhabitants nominally belong to the Protestant church, and a further five per cent belong to the Roman Catholic Church."[3]

Thomas Kruger, representative for the EKD, said that the condition of the local churches made ecumenical cooperation especially important.

---

[1] Jonathon Luxmoore, "Protestant Pilgrim Hopes Walk to Rome Will Lead to Ecumenical Progress," *Ecumenical News International Daily News Service* (September 17, 2001).

[2] Jonathon Luxmoore, personal correspondence (April 25, 2002).

[3] Luxmoore, 2001.

Kruger's view is seconded in the remarks of Leo Nowak, Catholic bishop of Magdeburg. "It's very important that Catholics and Protestants can tell society of our common faith in Jesus Christ, by praying together and engaging in dialogue. But we have said clearly that the conditions are not right for inter-communion."[4]

Writing in the March 2001 edition of *Evangelische Verantwortung (Evangelical Responsibility)*, Bishop Joachim Wanke, Catholic bishop of Erfurt and chair of Germany's Council of Christian Churches, allowed that pressure for eucharistic sharing was "not just intended to annoy church leaders." "Admittedly," he wrote, "some pressure is meant to be provocative and [is] sometimes based on naive theological reasoning, but the desire is understandable." Not necessarily referring to Ms. Ratsch, he concluded, "The people of God are the legs of the ecumenical movement, and these legs should walk in the right direction."[5]

What Do We Do in the Meantime?
Some Future Directions

What is the right direction for the ecumenical movement in our day? Why must men and women of faith, like Arnhild Ratsch, courageously walk the road to Rome to seek "more signs of encouragement"? These are important questions for the ecumenical future, and the ecumenical future is the theme of this chapter.

In this book, I have presented several important reasons to remain cautious in eucharistic sharing. I have presented several other reasons for a more open eucharistic sharing. While I would personally prefer a more open eucharistic sharing, I acknowledge that many Catholics and many Catholic authorities do not agree with me. On the one hand, I agree that an open Communion is not a good idea. The Eucharist is not a free-for-all; there must always be an element of discernment. On the other hand, I argue for a more open access to Holy Communion for baptized Christians, both Catholic and non-Catholic. Continuing along the way of bans and prohibitions is not necessarily a "walk in the right direction." Faithfulness to Christ's prayer for unity demands that we take up the burden of ecumenism with diligence, good will, and integrity.

Members of the Body of Christ must work hard to discern one another into the Body of Christ. The days of dismissing one another from the Body should be set behind us. People become members of Christ's

---

[4] Luxmoore, 2002.
[5] Ibid.

Body not for their own benefit alone, definitely not for the augmentation of an institution, but *for the benefit of a needful world.* Therefore, an eventual eucharistic sharing must not be needlessly delayed. It represents an essential pastoral opportunity: for reevangelization, for renewal and sharing of faith, for recognizing the legitimate breadth of Christian faith.

What to do in the meantime? For the near future, all signs point to the Catholic Church continuing to restrict admission to Holy Communion.[6] Concerned Christians can do several things in the meantime to foster an eventual full communion and not to delay it. They can help people in their churches and in other churches to discern the Body of Christ in their midst.

In the first place, as Catholic authorities reconsider the norms for eucharistic sharing, it is important to prevent the harsh, judgmental, and unforgiving side of our personalities to set the agenda.[7] Ecumenical dialogue partners are likely to make errors in judgment as they walk together toward unity. They must learn to respond to mistakes from the position of charity and patience. Wisdom suggests that ecumenical listening should take priority over unilateral declaring. For example, at this crucial time, Catholic authorities could refrain from making irrevocable statements about admission to Holy Communion. They could listen carefully to the concerns of non-Catholic leaders, especially to the judicious remarks of groups like the Anglican bishops.

In the second place, Catholics and non-Catholics should continue to worship with one another. We should find ways to worship together more often—on a weekly and even a daily basis. Let us end the days when common worship is limited to a few festivals and special events. This may entail giving local Catholic churches freedom to adapt liturgical structures to the Christian culture of non-Catholic communities. Our local churches—Catholic and non-Catholic—may need to learn new songs, to pray with new words and in new tongues, to listen to more Scripture, to celebrate the sacraments more frequently, to preach more competently, to evangelize more effectively.

In many places, we can find ways to share resources such as buildings, schools, even the nonordained personnel—choir directors, janitors,

---

[6] Archbishop Tarcisio Bertone, secretary of the Congregation for the Doctrine of the Faith, reports that CDF is preparing a new teaching document on the Eucharist in relation to the Church. "Congregation for Doctrine of Faith to Focus on Natural Law and Eucharist: Two Key Topics for Ecumenism and Dialogue with World," *Zenit.org* (January 14, 2002).

[7] Cf. Andrew Greeley, "Clinton-Bashers and the Eucharist," *The Denver Post* (April 11, 1998) B-07.

secretaries, Christian education teachers, and so forth. Canonical communities could revise their statutes to allow non-Catholic men and women to become full members and to hold positions of leadership in their communities (provincial, prior, abbot, and so forth). In the United States, if not elsewhere, pastoral cooperation on every level—neighborhood, region, and nation—remains at the stage of "possible dreams." With effective leadership, ecumenism could move out of the realm of dialogue and into the realm of shared ministry. We would learn to trust the authority in the ministry of others as a way of moving toward recognizing their validity.

What should we do when we worship together? When Catholics and non-Catholics worship together, they can participate in the worship of the other community in nearly every way, short of receiving Holy Communion.[8] R. T. Halliday has enumerated at least six ways to fully, consciously, and actively participate in the Eucharist of Catholic and non-Catholic Churches under the current norms and limitations.

1. We *remember* the saving deeds of Christ *(anamnesis).*[9]

2. We *offer* a "sacrifice of praise" through the great eucharistic prayers of our various traditions (sacrifice and oblation).

3. We *intercede* through Christ and the Holy Spirit on behalf of the whole world, through litanies, through sung "Kyrie eleisons," through the prayers and petitions of the liturgy, and through the intercessions embedded in many eucharistic prayers (intercession and *epiclesis*).

4. We lay claim to *participate* in the communion of saints, the "Church triumphant." As we sing the "Holy, Holy, Holy," we beg to join prophets, saints, and angels in the heavenly liturgy (the *communio sanctorum*).

5. We may *discern* the Body of Christ in the place where we are, even if we cannot affirm and proclaim this discernment through the reception of Holy Communion. We can know and recognize one another as knit together into the Body of Christ (as baptized members of the "Mystical Body of Christ").

---

[8] The *Ecumenical Directory* of 1993 articulates norms for these situations. For Catholics, there remain some limitations on reading from Scripture, sponsors for baptism, and other leadership roles in non-Catholic settings.

[9] Without including a burdensome amount of detail, behind each of the six ways I have added a technical term in parentheses to help readers correlate these modes of participation to the underlying theological concepts.

6. Finally, we share in *being sent forth* in mission, blessed to be a blessing for others (*diakonia* and evangelization).[10]

While the reception of the Eucharist together would offer a unique strengthening for mission, we may draw upon these other spiritual resources to accomplish our vocations in the world. Indeed, few spiritual resources are more effective than the gift of the Holy Spirit and the inherent power of our shared baptism into Christ's death and resurrection. Because of our shared baptism, Christians already know and practice real eucharistic hospitality—short of receiving the Eucharist in Holy Communion—whenever they join in common worship and prayer.

In the remainder of this chapter, I will offer some thoughts on two problems we might wish to avoid as we walk together toward unity. These I call the problem in blessing noncommunicants and the problem of ecclesial disobedience. I then turn to focus on two opportunities, or reasons to share the Eucharist in hope for the ecumenical future. We must take the opportunity to embrace one another in Christian charity. We must take the opportunity to receive salvation from God through the ministry of one another. I close the chapter with several thoughts on the inherent relationship between eucharistic communion and salvation as Christians conceive of it.

The Problem in Blessing Noncommunicants

Gestures conceal as much as they reveal. At one of their meetings, Pope Paul VI gave his episcopal ring to Anglican archbishop of Canterbury Michael Ramsey. The city of Milan had given the ring to Pope Paul when he was the archbishop there. At the time, an observer reports that the Pope's gift outraged many Scottish Catholics. They felt he was "handing over the very symbol of his authority."[11] Reflecting upon this action, one wonders why Paul VI would give his ring to Archbishop Ramsey but not the Eucharist?

Assume, for a moment, that Paul VI *had* shared the Eucharist with Archbishop Ramsey. If so, they would have been committing all their churches and all their bishops to eucharistic sharing. After all,

---

[10] For a full explication of the "six forms of participation" see R. T. Halliday, "Visiting Each Other's Worship," *The Ecumenical Review* 45 (1993) 46.

[11] John S. Pobee, "Bread and Wine: See of St. Augustine and See of St. Peter," *The Ecumenical Review* 44, no. 1 (1992) 31f.

Communion with one is Communion with all. It would have amounted to a stunningly grand ecumenical act.

Instead, when Paul VI shared a ring with Ramsey, from the perspective of a certain bureaucratic mentality, he had made no explicit commitment to the future. To this way of thinking, he had made a lovely personal gesture. It denoted the creation of a more relaxed public atmosphere surrounding the relationship of Rome and Canterbury. Nevertheless, the gift did nothing to shorten the theological distance between the two sees. No one is going to say that Pope Paul's gift of the ring conferred validity on Archbishop Ramsey's ordination.

As we know, heads of state often exchange gifts. These gifts help to warm relationships between the men and women who must negotiate difficult and delicate agreements. They are the tokens of diplomacy. Political gifts do not erase borders or disagreements. They do not mean that the hard-nosed and hard-edged negotiations that will take place the next day will be any easier or less burdensome. In a certain sense, diplomatic and political gifts conceal significant disagreements. They create the impression of good will where good will, in fact, may be strained.

What does this have to do with blessing noncommunicants? Increasingly, in many Catholic churches, ministers invite noncommunicants to enter the Communion procession. They are asked to cross their hands over their hearts, and signify their intention to receive a blessing in place of Holy Communion. I would argue that, like the diplomatic gift, the routine blessing of noncommunicants at the time of the Communion procession amounts to concealment, a well-meaning attempt to minimize pain and division at the time of Holy Communion. It creates the impression of inclusion where inclusion, in fact, is still prohibited. If Holy Communion is the worst time to manifest our divisions, it is no less the worst time to conceal them. It is important, when we treat the topic of eucharistic sharing, not to distort the Eucharist into a diplomatic token.

Blessing noncommunicants: some historical considerations. The Catholic bishops of the United Kingdom and Ireland now encourage reciprocal blessings at the time of Communion "until such time as full communion can be attained."[12] Catholic ministers in the United States and elsewhere are encouraging non-Catholics to enter the Communion procession to receive a blessing instead of Holy Communion. Since no official form of Catholic liturgy provides a warrant for the practice, it is not possible to know the form of blessing ministers use in these contexts. These prayers of blessing may differ considerably from place to place and from minister to minister in each place. Quite apart from the legal-

---

[12] OBOB, 84.

ity or permissibility of the practice, there remain important concerns about its appropriateness.

An anecdote told by Max Johnson is a helpful starting point, for it reminds us that how people perceive our actions is not necessarily congruent with the meaning we intend our actions to convey.

> I was recently told by one of my graduate students of her experience where a young child she knew had flatly refused to go forward any longer for a "blessing" at the time of communion distribution. When asked why, the child responded that the last time he had gone he had been "X'ed" out by the communion minister, who, instead of giving him bread, had traced an "X" over him (obviously the sign of the cross in blessing), telling him by this gesture that he did not belong.[13]

Historical forms of the liturgy allow for the blessing and dismissal of penitents and catechumens, but not at the time for Holy Communion. Ancient Christian churches routinely dismissed penitents and catechumens from the assembly before the liturgy of the Eucharist. This was a practice associated with the "discipline of the secret" mentioned in the last chapter. At the time of their dismissal, the penitents and the catechumens received a blessing. These blessings and dismissals remain in Byzantine and other Eastern Rite liturgies. There, extensive litanies of intercession precede the dismissal. In light of this historical background, the observation of the Anglican bishops makes sense. Blessings, they say, are appropriate for penitents and catechumens. They are less appropriate for "those who are . . . spiritually prepared to receive Holy Communion."[14] The historical practice of the Churches affirms this. The blessing and dismissal of baptized Christians—whether or not they received Holy Communion—has always been given at the conclusion of the liturgy.

The point in this historical pattern of blessings and dismissals was so the gathered assembly could better *discern itself as the Body of Christ.* The practice recognized that some men and women—notably the catechumen and the penitent—are not able to do this. In the case of catechumens, they are not yet members of the Body. In the case of penitents, while members of the Body, the Church recognizes that they are not yet ready to be discerned (in the active sense) back into the Body.

The Catholic Rite of Christian Initiation of Adults (RCIA) provides blessings and dismissals for catechumens. The Roman Missal and the

---

[13] Maxwell Johnson, *The Rites of Christian Initiation: Their Evolution and Interpretation* (Collegeville, Minn.: The Liturgical Press, 1999) 376.

[14] House of Bishops of the Church of England, *The Eucharist: Sacrament of Unity* (London: Church House Publications, 2001) 20.

Rite of Reconciliation do not. After Vatican II, the Consilium reformed the liturgy according to historical patterns as best could be ascertained and accepted at the time. The Mass was revised first; other rites were prepared later. Therefore, the Roman Missal does not include the dismissals because the need for their restoration was not foreseen at the time of its revision. Only later, when the rites for baptism were revised, did the Consilium recognize the benefits of blessing and dismissing catechumens. Similarly, the Rite of Reconciliation does not include a blessing for penitents because the Consilium was unsuccessful in attempts to restore the concept of an order of penitents in the reform of the rite.

These unfinished reforms leave pastoral ministers in a difficult position. One set of rites (the RCIA) calls for the routine blessing and dismissal of penitents and catechumens, whereas another set of rites (the Missal) does not. In addition, many Catholics and their communities have yet to restore the practice of blessing and dismissal for catechumens.

Blessing as a sign of exclusion, a sign of contradiction. We should not doubt the good intentions of those who bless noncommunicants during the Communion procession. It is important to note that this blessing, however meaningful and good, is always exclusionary. It is, in a curious way, an "anti-sacrament."

It is sometimes helpful to put ourselves in the shoes of the non-Catholic. When non-Catholics come forward for a blessing, they signal their desire for a blessing by crossing their heart. If we were non-Catholic and came forward in the Communion procession "for a blessing," we would be *submitting to our own exclusion.* In effect we would be saying, "Yes, I agree that I have no place in your Eucharist—even though I am baptized and I know myself to belong to Christ and to his Body by right and by duty." We have contradicted our sense of faith and baptismal identity.

"Crossing the heart" as a sign for requesting a blessing instead of Holy Communion puts the non-Catholic in the position of needing to decide: "Should I stay in the closet and simulate Catholic faith or should I come out and participate in my own exclusion?" At best, to instruct people to hold their hands over their heart amounts to instructing people to reveal their disposition not to receive the Eucharist to the external forum. Instructing people to reveal matters of internal forum in public raises serious ethical questions.

Communion of desire. In considering what Catholics and non-Catholics should do when they are present to one another's worship, some authorities also appeal to the concept of a "communion of desire" to fit this new situation. Recall how the Catholic was not supposed to participate in non-Catholic worship prior to Vatican II. If the Catholic had to be physically present (for social or political reasons), she was required to refuse herself any spiritual participation in the ceremonies. A communion of desire moves in exactly the opposite direction. Spiritual communion refers to an inward participation in the sharing of Holy Communion without physical presence to the consecrated elements, that is, without actually moving one's body to receive them.

The English Catholic bishops propose that spiritual communion is an appropriate option for baptized noncommunicants, both Catholic and non-Catholic.[15] The U.S. guidelines for reception of Holy Communion similarly recommend prayer in place of receiving the sacrament. Catholics are not alone in seeing the value of communion by desire. For example, the Anglican bishops admit there are many conceivable occasions when Christians will need the spiritual benefits of the Eucharist, but it is not available. A twentieth-century classic in Catholic spiritual literature, *The Mass on the World (La Messe sur le monde)*, by Pierre Teilhard de Chardin, consists entirely of a meditation in the context of spiritual communion.[16] In situations like these, the presence of Christ available to us through spiritual communion is valuable, helpful, and comforting.

Spiritual communion is apt whenever we find ourselves in a situation where Holy Communion is impossible. By contrast, several point out that the concept of spiritual communion is far less fitting in situations where one could receive Holy Communion, but does not. The Anglican bishops maintain that, when the Eucharist is available, a Christian desires to receive it, and he or she is properly disposed, the rubric of a communion by desire should not normally apply.[17]

Deep spiritual communion is best expressed only in Holy Communion. The Catholic bishops of the United Kingdom and Ireland propose that receiving a blessing in the place of Holy Communion "emphasizes that a deep spiritual communion is possible even when we do not share together the sacrament . . ."[18] To the contrary, Catholic ecclesiology maintains that sharing the sacraments is the principle means of sharing in deep spiritual communion with one another. To speak of communion separate from the act of receiving baptism or Holy Communion

---

[15] OBOB, 43.

[16] One could argue that, because he was a priest, Chardin's meditation amounted to an entire spiritual Eucharist. Chardin's desire was not simply to receive Communion, but to consecrate the entire world in a fashion similar to consecrating the eucharistic elements. His desire was not simply to be a recipient, but to exercise his priestly ministry in the absence of altar, bread, and wine.

[17] ESOU, 20.

[18] OBOB, 43, emphasis added.

results in an etherealizing or a "de-sacramentalizing" of the idea of Christian community. We make Communion the product of a secret desire rather than the effect of a public action performed in common. Instead, eucharistic sharing is the source of Christian community. To seek and find deep spiritual communion with non-Catholic Christians requires that we discern them into the Body of Christ and that they discern themselves among us. Whenever this happens, we *must* share the Eucharist with them or we will not have shared a Eucharist at all (1 Cor 11:17-20).

The Problem in Ecclesial Disobedience

Irish Times reporter Billy FitzGerald states that Sheila Brown, then a recently ordained Anglican priest, received Communion "in her collar at a private Mass in the Vatican."[19] Another example: The prodigious scholar of American Christianity and Lutheran pastor Martin E. Marty says there has been a "quiet smuggling of communion elements" among American Christians for decades. He says that he has given and received Communion with Catholic cardinals and bishops. These were not covert acts, he says, but they were also not "joyful public signs of realized common life in the body of Christ."[20]

The Catholic bishops of the United Kingdom and Ireland put it this way: Some Catholics attempt to practice an open Communion in opposition to the present norms. They have experienced open Communion elsewhere and "negatively evaluate the present discipline" of the Catholic Church.[21]

This kind of "Communion on the sly"—although, if pope, cardinals, and bishops are doing it, it cannot be very secret—amounts to a form of "ecclesial disobedience." By ecclesial disobedience, I mean to draw a parallel to the concept of civil disobedience and nonviolent resistance. Just as men and women of conscience resist and disobey the unjust law created by civil authorities, some men and women of faith will also resist and disobey the unjust norm created by Church authorities. In this section, I want to point up several serious difficulties associated with ecclesial disobedience.

[19] Billy FitzGerald, "Tentative Advance in the Sharing of Communion," *The Irish Times* (April 21, 1998) 14.
[20] Meinrad Scherer-Edmunds, "Let's Stop Posting Bouncers at the Table of the Lord," *U.S. Catholic* (June 2000) 25.
[21] OBOB, 98.

The Church as gated community. In my part of the world, we find many gated communities. Los Angeles County and Orange County, California, have many gated communities, but they are not alone in North America for this popular trend. The gated community is an entirely enclosed subdivision, with secure entrances maintained by armed guards or police. In places like Rolling Hills Estates, California, the gates enclose an entire city. The whole town has limited access. Only those who work, live, or have legitimate business in the town may enter. I sometimes tease people, telling them we should make the city of Los Angeles a gated community. "I would sleep more restfully," I tell them, "if I knew that the ruffians and vagabonds from Malibu and Beverly Hills were turned away at the city limits."

All joking aside, gated communities are motivated by feelings of insecurity. The security guards at the gates comprise a form of border control. Real estate marketers imply—but never directly state—that the gates and guards provide homeowners exclusivity and protection that only just a bit more money can buy.

Another political analogy. A respondent to the 1990 U.S. Catholic magazine poll compared the problem of eucharistic sharing to the Berlin Wall. "The rules regarding eucharistic participation separate us from our brothers and sisters just as surely as the Berlin Wall separated the two Germanys. If we are to celebrate our common spirituality, let's tear down this and other unnecessary walls and become aware that this separation hurts 'us' as much as 'them.'"[22]

Prohibiting eucharistic sharing as border control. Do the Catholic norms for eucharistic sharing amount to anything more than border control? When we limit access to Holy Communion in our churches, have we not made the Church something like a gated community and the spiritual equivalent of a West Berlin?

By contrast, the enclosure we place around the Eucharist should be the result of the recognition and realization of a genuine relationship between the communicant and the Church. Communion in the Church is premised on an authentic and genuine relationship with the bishop, who offers communion through place and time with the apostles and the entire communion of Churches (the universal Church). Even in this analogy, bishops function as gate-keepers. One's relationship to the local bishop remains the key difference between baptized communicants and baptized noncommunicants.

Disobedient clergy. Bishop Tobin wondered aloud what motivates a presider to disobey the norms of the Catholic Church and "invite

---

[22] Richard T. Szafransky, "Let Everyone Come to Communion," *U.S. Catholic* (June 1990) 19.

everyone to Holy Communion?"[23] Some priests and other ministers, he thought, are motivated by a desire to be ecumenical or to be hospitable. They seek to create an atmosphere of inclusiveness and of kindness. A few priests are motivated also by a kind of self-regard. They may be acting to save face in their community as a nice guy or a good and kind man. These are only a few of the less honorable reasons why clergy may choose to be disobedient.

Clergy could be motivated by any number of questionable reasons to invite an assembly to share an open Communion. That alone does not make the invitation to open Communion wrong. The theological merits of open Communion must be evaluated without regard to the possible abuses that may or may not occur. Restrictions based on the fear of abuse are limited. For example, there are several good reasons for people to refrain at times from receiving Holy Communion. We do not say, because some people may abuse the reception of the sacrament, therefore no one may receive it.

"Tear down this wall!" In late June 2000, the Lutheran bishop of the Southeast Michigan Synod–Detroit, Rev. Robert A. Rimbo, addressed a gathering of Catholic liturgists at the Notre Dame Center for Pastoral Liturgy Conference, "Eucharist without Walls." In his address, Bishop Rimbo urged participants to commune and "face the consequences." He said, "It is time for us to begin communing together at the one table of the one Lord as the one Church, and consider the consequences of such when God reveals them to us."[24] Bishop Rimbo's speech was courageous. It was similar in tone to former U.S. President Ronald Reagan who stood at the Berlin Wall and said, "Mr. Gorbachev, tear down this wall!" The bishop was urging a kind of ecclesiastical disobedience when he said Christians should not wait for "the powers that be" to approve "what we consider sufficient for Eucharistic hospitality."[25]

Prophetic disobedience is different. Bishop Rimbo's speech called for ecclesial disobedience. How should we think about the people who took Rimbo's advice? Were they "prophetic" or "dissemblers"? What is the difference between them? From a simple perspective, one of the main differences is publicity and forthrightness. The prophet wears his or her disagreements on his sleeve; the dissembler buries them in the closet. "Communion on the sly" seems cowardly. By contrast, there is a kind of arrogance in the stance of the prophet. While the act of receiving "Communion on the sly" says, "You are wrong and I will lie to

[23] Thomas J. Tobin, "Receiving Holy Communion," *Priest* (June 1998) 29.
[24] Tara Dix, "Lutheran Bishop Endorses Intercommunion," *National Catholic Reporter* (July 14, 2000) 6.
[25] Ibid.

avoid having to tell you," the prophet says, "You are wrong and *I am here to tell you.*"

The result is that eucharistic sharing becomes another, more intense form of ecumenical dialogue because of the disobedience of some clergy and communicants. In their transgressions, they desire to witness to the Spirit of Truth to brothers and sisters. When questioned about the potential offense or hurt their actions may cause, these non-Catholic communicants could refer to the statements of more than several Catholic bishops, who aver that speaking the truth in love occasionally entails a modicum of pain and suffering.

How should Catholics respond to disobedience—of whatever sort? Sacramental sharing is not simply a local question. The practice cannot become the policy of a parish committee, the pastor, or even a local bishop. To admit a person to Communion in one local church is to admit a person to Communion in the whole Church. Admission to Communion in one place is the same as admission to Communion in every place.[26] Sacramental sharing affects the whole Church—not just the assembly gathered at a given place and time. This suggests that the practice of allowing dispensations for eucharistic sharing may (or may not) be helpful in different contexts.

Nonetheless, local authorities may occasionally dispense from the strict observance of the law. The need for mercy routinely dispenses the Christian from strict obligations to the law. Laws, we believe, do not exist for their own sake. They exist within the context of God's love for humankind.[27] For example, a Jesuit mission in Zimbabwe was given the dispensation to regularly offer the Eucharist to Protestant Christians from the same village. The nearest Protestant Church was hundreds of miles away.[28]

While this is an excellent, positive example, it has the unintended side effect of creating an uneven situation across Church jurisdictions. The relative laxity of some jurisdictions in light of the apparent strictness in others has the unwanted effect of exacerbating feelings of hurt, rather than relieving them.[29] Because dispensations are local and temporary, they have the potential to create more hurt, rather than less, particularly in mobile societies where men and women are willing to travel to parishes or dioceses where more hospitable conditions are the norm.

---

[26] OBOB, 97.
[27] Stuart Williams, "Sharing Communion: A Common Inheritance," *One in Christ* 31, no. 4 (1995) 359.
[28] Ibid., 363. Cf. *The Tablet* (Nov. 10, 1990) 1442.
[29] Ibid., 348.

Several authors have recommended the practice of a "eucharistic fast." They believe this offers a way to grow in awareness of the "suffering in not being able to take Communion from the table of another Church."[30] In the context of ecumenical gatherings, this may be appropriate. But, in the context of local church communities, the extended eucharistic fast would be positively harmful or it would be implemented unjustly—some would fast, while others would go on "feasting." Precisely the situation that St. Paul urged the Corinthian Christians to avoid.

We could guard the Eucharist more carefully. We could implement procedures for Communion registration, or more carefully limit people's access to the sacrament. There is no doubt that gates and guards enhance the apparent value of what we place behind them. Economists call this the law of scarcity. Yet, I would argue strongly against this inclination. Everywhere we turn, we find Jesus pointing out the inherent dignity of outsiders and riffraff. The Gospels point away from scarcity, to a law of abundance. There is always more than enough grace. There is always more than enough forgiveness. There is always more than enough mercy. Even when we are naked, poor, and hungry, we encounter enough of a gift from God to offer thanksgiving.

Ecclesial disobedience: a mixed response. At the end of the day, I remain mixed on the subject of disobedience. I can occasionally recognize its prophetic value. At the same time, I do not want to support the ecclesial disobedience of "bulls in china shops." There exist valuable reasons to respect the discipline of the different churches and Christian communities. For example, the Catholic bishops of the United Kingdom and Ireland appeal to non-Catholics to "respect our discipline."[31] Likewise, Paulist Father Thomas Ryan suggests that "being ecumenical" requires respect for each Church's self-understanding.[32]

In a pluralistic society—in a pluralistic Church—we do not advocate that people deliberately disregard the norms of holiness of different religious communities. Just as one would not enter a mosque or a Hindu temple without removing one's shoes, just as one would not enter a synagogue without a head covering, we dare not encourage fellow Christians to disregard the sanctity of the Eucharist or to receive "Communion on the sly." At the same time, it seems wrong to ask fellow Christians to acquiesce quietly to their own exclusion. Christians must

[30] Phillippe Larere, *The Lord's Supper: Towards an Ecumenical Understanding of the Eucharist*, trans. P. Madigan (Collegeville, Minn.: The Liturgical Press, 1993) 66.
[31] OBOB, 118.
[32] Thomas Ryan, "Eucharistic Sharing: Why the Churches Act Differently," *Ecumenism* 110 (1993) 33.

always act on the basis of conscience and their most faithful convictions. Catholic authorities should not seek to prevent non-Catholic churches from inviting Catholics to receive Holy Communion. And, whenever non-Catholics receive Holy Communion with me in the Catholic Church, I accept their actions as the conscientious indications of an intent to be one with Christ, with me, and with the Catholic Church.

The Opportunity to Embrace One Another

Within the Christian community we are called to grow in relationship to one another, and the Eucharist is the source of authentic growth in relationship. Award-winning theologian Miroslav Volf helps us understand the nature of relationship with his metaphor of the "embrace." To embrace another, he says, includes at least three separate acts.

1. There must be the intent to give one's self to others.
2. There must be the commitment to readjust one's self-identity to make space for the other.
3. There must be the recognition that, in this life, embraces must also be released and let go.[33]

Volf continues, at the heart of the Christian message is the idea that we must embrace others, even (especially) when they are evildoers. This imperative arises out of God's love itself. As Paul reminds us, "God loved us while we were still God's enemies" (Rom 5:10). This Easter troparion from the Byzantine liturgy expresses a similar theme:

> . . . Let us embrace each other joyously.
> O Pascha, ransom from affliction . . .
> Let us embrace each other.
> Let us call 'Brothers' even those that hate us,
> and forgive all by the resurrection.[34]

In other words, because of the death and resurrection of Jesus, we do not need to perceive other people as innocent in order to love them.

As Miroslav Volf states, "As I read it, the story of the cross is about God who desires to embrace precisely the 'sons and daughters of

---

[33] Miroslav Volf, *Exclusion and Embrace: A Theological Exploration of Identity, Otherness, and Reconciliation* (Nashville: Abingdon Press, 1996) 29.

[34] Troparion for Easter Matins, Orthodox liturgy. Cited in Volf, 130.

hell.'"[35] He says that, in authentic relationships with others—even among the children of hell—there must remain a balance between embrace and justice. Embracing another person cannot take place, he says, until the "truth has been said and justice has been done." The making of justice is the indispensable struggle against deception, injustice, and violence. According to Volf, the making of justice must always precede the making of an embrace.[36]

Exclusion as the root of all evil. Miroslav Volf observes that authentic righteousness is seeking purity in the cleansing of *one's self*. To remove the "beam from one's own eye" before worrying about the "speck in our neighbor's eye," therefore, forms the heart of Christian ethics. Redemption begins in the embrace of the other—however wounded he or she may be. By contrast, the original sinner is one who seeks purity as the cleansing of the world of others. The original sin is the denial of difference.[37] After all the ethnic cleansing, after all the occupations and genocides, after all the crusades, jihads, and wars (both hot and cold), the result of exclusion is "a world without the Other."[38] In the end, it is a world without the human.

Some types of exclusion. Volf identifies several forms of exclusion. Domination and caste systems are forms of exclusion. There is the exclusion of abandonment as when the wealthy withdraw to gated communities or herd the poor into ghettoes. Sometimes we translate exclusion into terms of moral imperatives. We define another person or group of people as though they were inevitably "immoral," "monstrous," or "impure": the exclusion of lepers and people with AIDS. There is the exclusion of indifference or contempt, when we act as though another person no longer exists. Through indifference, we become the priest or Levite from the parable of the Good Samaritan. We see, but choose not to see the person in need.

The will to exclude can express itself in the desire to annihilate the other. It can also express itself in the desire to assimilate the other. When people and groups are powerful, they express their will over the weak and offer them a contemptuous deal: "We will not exclude you, only if you become like us and a stranger to yourself."[39] Unfortunately, this contemptuous deal is no stranger to the life of the churches.

---

[35] Volf, 85.
[36] Ibid., 29.
[37] Ibid., 74.
[38] Ibid., 57.
[39] Ibid., 75. Volf cites the expression from the work of French anthropologist Claude Lévi-Strauss.

Volf helpfully shows how "exclusion" is not the same as "differentiation." *Exclusion* is "anti-creative," *differentiation* is creative. Exclusion means that we have denied a name to another person or thing; differentiation means we have created a name for them. To exclude is willfully to seek the elimination of another being from the community of beings; to name another is to give that one a rightful place within the community of beings, the world. According to Volf, exclusion amounts to the "un-naming" and the "voiding" of the existence of another. By contrast, differentiating is the creative gift given to us from the time of Adam. In the biblical sense of the word, to possess "naming rights" is to possess "human rights."[40]

Exclusion and inclusion in the life and ministry of Jesus. A true Church of Christ must be part of this extension of Jesus' loving embrace and cannot walk away from his mission to embrace all people. Whatever is true of Jesus must be no less true of his corporate and communal Body, the Church of Christ. Therefore, our unity in the Body of Christ depends, in fact, on our embracing one another with a love that we are neither capable of giving (on our own) nor of receiving (on our own).

In a sense, every baptized man and woman is called to love *impossible* people with an *impossible* love. Simply because a person or group is incapable of receiving the embrace of Jesus in its depths does not mean that Jesus has somehow walked away from that person or group. *To the extent that we, the baptized, our Churches and Christian communities, fail to love "impossible people impossibly," we have failed to be the Body of Christ.* If we fail to be who we are, if we have not discerned the Body of Christ, then we have no business celebrating the Eucharist.

The exclusion of exclusion. Christians often misunderstand the nature of heresy. My students often conceive of heresy as a mere going against Church teaching. Since the Council of Trent, Church authorities have conveniently defined heresy this way. However, the more traditional understanding of heresy sees it as the holding of certain beliefs that make salvation impossible. To recognize that there are heretics is to say that some of their positions marginalize points of faith that must remain central if there is to be any meaningful kind of salvation.[41]

Contemporary theologians, following the example of the very important twentieth-century theologians Henri de Lubac and Yves Congar, recognize that the "exclusion of exclusion" is the only kind of exclusion authorized in the conflicts that defined Christian orthodoxy. The ancient Christian writers condemned heresies and heretical authors for

---

[40] Ibid., 66.

[41] Dennis M. Doyle, *Communion Ecclesiology: Vision and Versions* (Maryknoll, N.Y.: Orbis Books, 2000) 21.

what they denied and excluded, not for what they affirmed and included. The ancient heretics—Marcion, Donatus, Arius, Pelagius, for example—proposed ideas and concepts that excluded the *possibility of salvation*.[42] By carefully reappraising the ancient heretical writers, we can see that, in many instances, they were right in what they affirmed but wrong in what they denied. In the view of Dennis Doyle, heresy lies not in being partial. It lies in being partial "in a way that excludes alternatives."[43]

Eucharistic sharing as a privileged place for inclusion and the exclusion of exclusion. Jesus was more than a prophet of inclusion. He *scandalously* included anyone in his table fellowship and he *excluded* only those who were particularly bent on excluding one another. Jesus not only renamed behaviors that had been falsely labeled "sinful"; he *recreated* the people who were thought to have been "sinners" and who suffered because of it.[44] The Gospel that includes us also transforms us. The Gospel that transforms us also excludes the "lions" that will not become "as peaceful as lambs," and the "serpents that would harm the infants." The "lion" has to become "lamb-like"; the "serpent" has to sheath its fangs—if they are going to sit down to the meal of peace.

According to classic Christian theologies, the death of Jesus creates a new covenant between God and humankind. The death of Jesus is the essential precondition for the existence and unity of the Church.[45] The religious identity of the Church—as a community—is linked intrinsically to this new covenant. The Eucharist manifests and extends this covenant with God. For Christians, it is the privileged place where covenant community is "taken, blessed, broken, poured, and shared."

Every Communion involves the communicant in a renewal of covenant with God and the community.[46] To say "Amen" to the Eucharist is to say, "I will persevere with you until death parts us." To say "Amen" to the Eucharist is to say, "I will work together with you in the saving mission of Christ." Holy Communion is an event of unconditional acceptance of all the participants.[47] Perhaps, one of the reasons Catholic authorities are most reticent to admit non-Catholics to receive Holy

---

[42] Ibid.

[43] Ibid., 71.

[44] Volf, 73.

[45] Matthias Klinghardt, *Gemeinschaftsmahl und Mahlgemeinschaft: Soziologie und Liturgie Frühchristlicher Mahlfeiern*, ed. K. Berger et al., *Texte und Arbeiten zum Neutestamentlichen Zeitalter* 13 (Tübingen: A. Francke Verlag, 1996) 317.

[46] Monika Hellwig, *The Eucharist and the Hunger of the World* (New York: Paulist Press, 1976) 72.

[47] Michael Welker, *What Happens in Holy Communion?*, trans. J. F. Hoffmeyer (Grand Rapids, Mich. / Cambridge, England: Eerdmans Publishing Co. / SPCK, 2000) 69.

Communion is because they are not prepared to offer these other Christians such an unconditional acceptance. Or perhaps they fear that these other Christians are not prepared to accept us unconditionally.

Catholic theologian James Dunn wrote, sharing the table "is the only mark of our mutual acceptance that really counts."[48] Besides kneeling down with us to receive the Eucharist together, what other marks of mutual acceptance may we expect from fellow Christians? What more could we reasonably ask? Even if Christians cannot agree that the Eucharist is the first place to express and to establish the embrace of Christian unity, let us be sure it is not the last place and that we are creating many alternative places. The Gospels proclaim it and the Spirit implants this desire in our hearts. How long may we delay the radical acceptance of one another to which God has called us?[49]

The Opportunity to Receive
Communion as a Gift of God

Unlike risks or challenges, opportunities offer new possibilities for growth and enrichment. An opportunity is a chance, a possibility that someone offers you. You can choose to accept the opportunity or you can choose to let the opportunity pass. Unfortunately, I have found myself—at times—fearing my opportunities as much as my challenges. Those opportunities would have unsettled my status quo, my equilibrium, in ways I could not envision—to my disappointment, I let them pass. In the life of the Church, we are no different. Some Church leaders fear opportunities because of the changes and uncertainties. There is always a tension between who we are and the opportunities God offers us to become something more.

David Power, a much admired sacramental theologian, recently offered the idea that a "theology of gift" may ease tensions between Churches. The idea of gift (the New Testament calls it *charism*) helps us appreciate the differences among ministers, among Christian communities, and among local churches with their great variety of expressions of Christian faith.[50] The idea of gift helps us understand that our opportunities come from God.

[48] Anne Primavesi and Jennifer Henderson, *Our God Has No Favourites: A Liberation Theology of the Eucharist* (Turnbridge Wells, England / San Jose, Calif.: Burns & Oates / Resource Publications, 1989) viii.

[49] Kondratha M. George, ed. "Eucharistic Hospitality," *The Ecumenical Review* 44 (1992) 81.

[50] David N. Power, "Roman Catholic Theologies of Eucharistic Communion: A Contribution to Ecumenical Conversation," *Theological Studies* 57, no. 4 (1996) 587f.

Anglican bishop of Cashel and Ossory (Ireland) John Neill says
something similar when he discusses the charismatic (gift) dimension
of the Eucharist. The Eucharist, he writes, is "a sign of something God
gives us." The Eucharist is an instrument by which God gives God's
self to us. It is a pledge of whatever God still shall give us in the future.[51] As I noted in earlier chapters, the Lord's Table belongs to the
Lord and not to ourselves.[52] Our altars are sacraments of the Lord's
Table. They are the table of the Passover feast, the Last Supper, and the
Lamb's High Feast, the messianic banquet, all at once. The sacrament is
always an opportunity to receive communion with God.

Communion by stages. While Communion is a gift of God and an opportunity we may choose to accept or reject, that does not mean that we
cannot *plan for full communion* and *prepare for unity.* Communion by
stages refers to the practice of some churches to move toward progressively deeper levels of communion in an orderly fashion. For many
Christian Churches interim sharing of the Eucharist has not delayed their
move toward full communion. When interim sharing is part of a determination to establish unity in stages, sharing the Eucharist has moved
these churches toward full recognition of the other's ministry and
toward shared decision-making in matters of faith and discipleship.[53]

The experience of the Anglican communion and of several other
Protestant Churches demonstrates that following a course of unity
by stages is particularly effective.[54] For example, Anglicans and Old
Catholics agreed to intercommunion already in 1931. Although this
agreement is not ideal from some perspectives, it nonetheless points to
several important elements of ecclesial union. First, the two churches
agreed to a mutual recognition of their catholicity and their independence. They concluded that autonomy in discipline and doctrine did not
destroy the possibility of their catholicity—understood here to refer
to their "wholeness" or "comprehensiveness in faith." Also, these
churches agreed that intercommunion (as they referred to it then) does
not require the acceptance of all doctrine, devotion, or liturgical practice. For them, intercommunion was premised on the mutual recognition of the essentials of faith in one another.[55]

[51] John Neill, "Christians' Desire to Unite in Communion is Quite Understandable," *The Irish Times* (December 18, 1997) 16.
[52] Martin Reardon, "Intercommunion and the Meissen and Porvoo Agreements,"
One in Christ 37, no. 1 (2002) 64.
[53] Ernest R. Falardeau, "Sharing the Eucharist and Christian Unity," *Ecumenical
Trends* 23 (1994) 11.
[54] Reardon, 58.
[55] J. Robert Wright, "Intercommunion and Full Communion: The Meanings of
These Terms for Anglicans and for Their Relations with Old Catholics," in *Christus*

Because of their experience with the Old Catholic Church and with other churches, the Anglican bishops (in England and elsewhere) have become strong advocates of the principle and practice of unity by stages. The typical approach identifies at least three stages along the way to full communion: (1) eucharistic hospitality, (2) mutual participation in liturgical ministries (short of concelebration), and (3) interchangeability of ministries (full, mutual recognition of ordination).

Catholics already practice unity by stages. Experience proves that the general principle of unity by stages is effective in creating strong human communities. Catholics promote a unity by stages when postulants and novices are considering life in religious communities. In the restored catechumenate, Catholics promote a unity by stages, when catechumens and the elect are distinguished from the baptized and the nonbaptized for a period of instruction and formation in the ways of discipleship.

Eminent Catholic theologians Karl Rahner and Heinrich Fries proposed a particularly subtle, Catholic adaptation of the model of unity by stages nearly twenty years ago. They allowed that, in the realm of doctrine, Catholic theology already provides for a hierarchy of truth, and it allows that conformity on less than essential matters is not required. However, as long as we maintain that all doctrine and the expression of all doctrine must be the same in all churches, Christian union will remain impossible.[56] We would have made conformity and silencing stand in for communion and difference.

For these reasons, it is exceptionally challenging to identify theological obstacles that prevent the adoption of this procedure. With modification, the Catholic Church may want to move toward unity by stages. Even if Catholic authorities will not permit us to adopt, in the short term, a more generous and less exclusionary practice of eucharistic sharing; other interim steps toward Christian unity—no less concrete, and no less generous—should now be identified and implemented. From a Catholic perspective unity by stages may need to include additional stages, such as a mutual recognition of teaching authority (magisterium). In any case, that would be for Church authorities to determine along the way.

More central to my point, Catholic authorities who now hold out for full communion sound like they are singing a tune similar to that quintessentially American turn-of-phrase, "My way, or the highway."

Spes: Liturgie und Glaube im Ökumenischen Kontext: Festschrift für Bischof Sigisbert Kraft, ed. A. Berlis (Frankfurt am Main: Peter Lang, 1994) 336.

[56] Jon Nilson, *Nothing Beyond the Necessary: Roman Catholicism and the Ecumenical Future* (New York: Paulist Press, 1995) 43.

Clearly, the Catholic Church can and must begin moving beyond the stage of bilateral dialogues and commissions.

Eucharistic Sharing and Our Salvation

For modern, Western Christians, it is important always to reckon with our innate instincts for individualism. We need always to be open to the modification of our personal faith with respect to input from revelation and from culture, from the theological and the ecclesial dimensions of faith. These dimensions of faith also remain open to input from the individual. Because they are much larger than one's self, given the economies of scale, the adjustment of theology and Church to one's own input will be much, much smaller than will be one's need to adjust to external factors. And adjust we do, even in ways we cannot suspect.

The communal dimension of Christian faith is among the most difficult aspects to describe, to teach, and to experience. When we say that faith is "communal," we do not mean to say that faith is not personal. We do not mean to say that faith is not in a very real sense, "one's own." We do not deny that a personal relationship with Jesus as the Lord and Savior of an individual life is a vital dimension of Christian faith and experience. Faith is always one's own. Faith always has a personal dimension. For every disciple, Christ is "uniquely mine," and "uniquely beloved." In emphasizing the personal dimension of faith, we easily overlook that faith exists in relation to the Church.[57]

An analogy may help. In college teaching, professors often use small groups to help students focus on tasks of critical thinking and interpretation. We find that peer-led teaching results in more effective learning. Still, students will complain if their grade is made to depend on the work of a group. They fear that a noncooperative group member could sink their grade average. Of course, that is the point. If a noncooperative group member can sink your grade, you will make every effort to get that group member to pull his or her weight within the group. Good teachers know that within small groups peers have far more leverage to move one another toward excellence than the teacher.

In the Church, we see a similar effect. Our success as a Church does not depend on individual outcomes, the salvation of one or two members. The apostle Paul said as much when he suggests that our salvation does not depend on our own work. Rather, it depends on how well we show forth Christ—as a group, as members of his body (Phil 1:27–2:5).

---

[57] Avery Dulles, "The Ecclesial Dimension of Faith," *Communio* 22 (1995) 419.

The Church always consists of a communion of saints, today and in the future kingdom of God.[58] To receive the Eucharist is to enter into this communion. It is to respond to the saints' call to action. When one says "Amen" to the Eucharist in Holy Communion, one is also accepting the invitation to join in the saving mission and ministry of Jesus Christ.[59]

This means that we are honor-bound to initiate and deepen every form of unity that we can, now and not later. Catholics can begin today to pray daily in common, to study the Scriptures in neighborhood cells, to share in the catechesis and education of youngsters, and to share in mission and service around the world. If we are truly unable to share the Eucharist because we are not yet united in all these other things, then we had better get down to the business of being united in all these other things so that the Lord will not return to find the Church a broken corpse instead of a risen and glorious body.

The Eucharist is not only a calling to mind of the past. It also has an anticipatory dimension. In the Eucharist, Christ connects us to God's absolute future. The saving event of Christ's passion, death, resurrection, and gift of the Spirit is sufficient for the salvation of absolutely everyone. Accordingly, the reign of God is a certainty. The only question is whether we choose to participate in God's salvation in the time and place that God gives us. The Eucharist thus discloses to us our past, our present, and our future. All of time is brought to bear on us in the present moment in and through the Eucharist.[60]

The Eucharist is a sacrament of hope. When we look at the Eucharist as the focus of Christian time, we see it immediately as a sacrament of hopeful confidence. Even if God's reign on earth is being thwarted, there is still a reason to receive and share in God's reign now. Even if God's Church on earth is being divided, there is still a reason to receive and share in God's undivided Church on Earth, as though it were united. The cynic would say that this turns the Eucharist into a child's exercise in make-believe. The less cynical will say that we have many opportunities "to encounter Church unity under the sign of hope."[61]

The ecumenical hope for Christian reunion is not utopian. This hope is premised on the knowledge that the sixteenth-century Protestant

[58] James Arne Nestingen and Wayne Zweck, "Communio, Inter-Communion with Non-Lutheran Churches, and the Lutheran Confessions / A Response," *Lutheran Theological Journal (Adelaide)* 33, no. 1 (1999).

[59] Hellwig, 81.

[60] Robert Sokolowski, *Eucharistic Presence: A Study in the Theology of Disclosure* (Washington, D.C.: The Catholic University of America Press, 1994) 213.

[61] John M. Russell, "Pannenberg on Eucharist and Unity," *Currents in Theology and Mission* 17 (1990) 120.

Reformation and the eleventh-century schism of East and West were historical events. They were not eschatological events. They were not sacramental events. *They have no heavenly power behind them.* It is simply not within the power of Church-dividing events to destroy or damage Christ's paschal mystery. Indeed, they were anti-eschatological and anti-sacramental events. They are anti-paschal events and Christians are hard-pressed to resist their negative effects. As merely historical and human acts, they are susceptible to being "superceded in the stream of history itself."[62]

The ecumenism of shared experience. In the public response to controversies over eucharistic sharing, some commentators have called upon Christians to move their ecumenical efforts in the direction of shared experience.[63] Ecumenist Jon Nilson points out that sharing life is the best basis for a quality ecumenism. Christians must multiply the opportunities to think, to act, and to pray together. Shared experience will mean one thing in a Catholic Worker House. It will mean a different thing in a Carthusian monastery. Shared experience in a storefront Pentecostal church in East Los Angeles will be quite differently expressed than it will at Riverside Church in Manhattan's upper West Side.

The challenge of shared experience as the basis for Christian ecumenism is that it functions so differently in the wide variety of contexts where we find ourselves attempting to live together in faith. The challenge of shared experience is first, not to become indifferent to the variety of gifts that God has given the Christian people. Another challenge is not to indulge in vaguely concealed contempt for "those people from that Church." The benefit of shared experience, as we have learned with intercultural and multicultural education, is that cultural, religious, and other differences between people are richly ambiguous and multidimensional. To make local ecumenism a reality means that one is committed to work in the spirit of pioneers for the unity of faith. It is to receive and embrace people just as they are, in the way they present themselves to us, trusting in God's ability to move them and shape them in faithful directions.

Communion-making is truth-making and vice-versa. Catholics are often fond of the expression, "We must speak the truth in love." Our desire to know and name the truth needs always to be tempered. We must combine it with the will to embrace the other person; no matter how

---

[62] Carl E. Braaten, *Mother Church: Ecclesiology and Ecumenism* (Minneapolis: Fortress Press, 1998) 24.

[63] Martin Pulbrook, "Wresting Authority from the Hardliners," *The Irish Times* (December 20, 1997) 12.

"erroneous" that person might be. Catholics sometimes know another expression, "Error has no rights." The expression, I understand, comes from Thomas Aquinas; but it needs serious correction. Thomas thought that error, like sin, is nothing. A nothing cannot possess rights. The problem is that errors do not exist apart from erroneous people. Erroneous people are not nothing, and they do have rights. Confuse erroneous people with their error, and you end up reducing people to nothing. We vilify them, silence them, dominate them. Eventually, kill them. But, because they were nothing, errors without rights, the killing was justified, and hardly murderous. To seek peace, therefore, means that we will need to change our theology—some of our deepest conceptions about God and God's relationship to humankind.

Miroslav Volf points out that, while true, the idea that peace in the world depends on peace between religions is not that significant. Peace between religions might simply mean peace between people who espouse different religions, but it tells us nothing about the source of their peace; their agreement to disagree. Moreover, peace between religious people would only do away with religious wars; it does nothing to halt economic, political, revolutionary, or maniacal warfare. Volf concludes, "If peace is what we are after, then a critique of the religious legitimation of violence—the critique of bellicose gods—is more urgent than reconciliation between religions."[64]

While we cannot have communion without truth, it is also true that we cannot have truth without the risk of personal and communal transformation. Only a community transformed by the paschal mystery can be the sort of communion we are discussing. At the heart of this transformation is the Eucharist. At the heart of this communion is the Eucharist. At least for Christians, human beings are not able to be peaceful and truthful people unless they have the Eucharist—rightly celebrated and generously shared.

Conclusions

Why do Christians share, give, and receive the Eucharist? Why do we seek to eat the bread and drink the wine? We receive the Eucharist to know Christ in and through our love for one another. We express our love for one another by sharing and giving one another the elements of the meal.[65] The Eucharist is a sign of encounter between the human and

[64] Volf, 285.
[65] Cf. Hellwig.

the divine. As a place of meeting, it is also a place of confrontation in the sense that the divine grace challenges us for our lack of wholeness and seeks to supplement our inability to manifest the entire image of Christ in ourselves and in our common life.[66] As a respondent to the *U.S. Catholic* magazine poll remarked, sinners were changed by their encounters with Jesus "not because of rules but because of love and acceptance."[67]

The current norms for eucharistic sharing in the Catholic Church jeopardize ecumenical relationships. They imply unsubstantiated, sweeping, and negative judgments on the worth of non-Catholics, their ministries, and their faith. In a word, Catholic authorities ought to help us recover the gracious immensity of Christian communion. It must be bigger than we can presently imagine, or else it would hardly be worth our time. Our efforts toward Christian unity, timid and fearful as they are, represent but a minuscule advance toward the communion God has prepared for us. God has given us the opportunity to heal the wounds of a millennium. *We must not let the opportunity pass.*

I am reminded of the "Indiana Jones" movie where Harrison Ford's character was made to find the Holy Grail hidden among a large selection of chalices. Select the wrong chalice, he was told, and he would die. Many of the chalices were made of precious metals: gold, silver, platinum. Most were encrusted with jewels: diamonds, emeralds, and rubies. These chalices would have made an emperor blush. Indiana is very wise and he selects the simplest, most humble cup among them all. This scrutiny of the Holy Grail tests whether the errant knight can see past his own avarice to the inestimable worth of the most simple and humble things.

The Eucharist discerns us . . . the humblest and the simplest . . . beyond our own fears and desires . . . *into the Body of Christ.* Without the Eucharist—shared widely and with deep integrity—we cannot become who we are. *To be and to become the Body of Christ on earth*: That is our risk. That is our challenge. That is our opportunity.

Questions for Reflection and Dialogue

1. *What should we do in the meantime?* Given the risks and challenges involved in eucharistic sharing, what should faithful Catholics do in the meantime—until our norms are changed or until full unity

---

[66] M. Robert Mulholland, "Discerning the Body," *Weavings* 8 (1993) 23.
[67] Szafransky, 19.

comes about? What actions can parish communities undertake—within the context of the present norms—to rise to the challenge of Christian unity? What opportunities is God giving you—right now—to welcome non-Catholics who worship among you?

2. *Blessing noncommunicants:* Is blessing noncommunicants a good idea? While many people see in the practice a helpful gesture of inclusion, others see in it a hurtful gesture of exclusion. What reasons would you give in favor of this new practice? What reasons would give you pause?

3. *Ecclesial disobedience:* Some people think that Christians should disobey norms they think are unjust and receive Communion against the norms. What are the risks in such an approach? Do you think such an approach would help or hurt the situation?

4. *Making communion:* In your own words, how would you describe what I have called the immensity of Christian communion? For you, how does the Eucharist create among us a truthful and peaceful place for living together with other people? For you, what is the connection between receiving Communion and the salvation that God wants to offer us?

For Further Reading

Halliday, R. T. "Visiting Each Other's Worship." *The Ecumenical Review* 45 (1993) 463–68.

Nilson, Jon. *Nothing Beyond the Necessary: Roman Catholicism and the Ecumenical Future.* New York: Paulist Press, 1995.

Volf, Miroslav. *Exclusion and Embrace: A Theological Exploration of Identity, Otherness, and Reconciliation.* Nashville: Abingdon Press, 1996.

Appendix 1:
Canon 844, Code of Canon Law 1983

844 §1 Catholic ministers may lawfully administer the sacraments only to catholic members of Christ's faithful, who equally may lawfully receive them only from catholic ministers, except as provided in §§2, 3 and 4 of this canon and in can. 861 §2.

§2 Whenever necessity requires or a genuine spiritual advantage commends it, and provided the danger of error or indifferentism is avoided, Christ's faithful for whom it is physically or morally impossible to approach a catholic minister, may lawfully receive the sacraments of penance, the Eucharist and anointing of the sick from non-catholic ministers in whose Churches these sacraments are valid.

§3 Catholic ministers may lawfully administer the sacraments of penance, the Eucharist and anointing of the sick to members of the eastern Churches not in full communion with the catholic Church, if they spontaneously ask for them and are properly disposed. The same applies to members of other Churches which the Apostolic See judges to be in the same position as the aforesaid eastern Churches so far as the sacraments are concerned.

§4 If there is a danger of death or if, in the judgment of the diocesan Bishop or of the Episcopal Conference, there is some other grave and pressing need, catholic ministers may lawfully administer these same sacraments to other Christians not in full communion with the catholic Church, who cannot approach a minister of their own community and who spontaneously ask for them, provided that they demonstrate the catholic faith in respect of these sacraments and are properly disposed.

§5 In respect of the cases dealt with in §§2, 3 and 4, the diocesan Bishop or the Episcopal Conference is not to issue general norms except after consultation with the competent authority, at least at the local level, of the non-catholic Church or community concerned.

Appendix 2:
Guidelines for Reception of
Communion in the United States, 1996

On November 14, 1996, the National Conference of Catholic Bishops approved the following guidelines on the reception of communion. These guidelines replace the guidelines approved by the Administrative Committee of the NCCB in November 1986. The guidelines, which are to be included in missalettes and other participation aids published in the United States, seek to remind all those who may attend Catholic liturgies of the present discipline of the Church with regard to the sharing of eucharistic communion.

For Catholics

As Catholics, we fully participate in the celebration of the Eucharist when we receive Holy Communion. We are encouraged to receive Communion devoutly and frequently. In order to be properly disposed to receive Communion, participants should not be conscious of grave sin and normally should have fasted for one hour. A person who is conscious of grave sin is not to receive the Body and Blood of the Lord without prior sacramental confession except for a grave reason where there is no opportunity for confession. In this case, the person is to be mindful of the obligation to make an act of perfect contrition, including the intention of confessing as soon as possible (canon 916). A frequent reception of the Sacrament of Penance is encouraged for all.

For our fellow Christians

We welcome our fellow Christians to this celebration of the Eucharist as our brothers and sisters. We pray that our common baptism and the action of the Holy Spirit in this Eucharist will draw us closer to one another and begin to dispel the sad divisions which separate us. We pray that these will lessen and finally disappear, in keeping with Christ's prayer for us "that they may all be one" (Jn 17:21).

Because Catholics believe that the celebration of the Eucharist is a sign of the reality of the oneness of faith, life, and worship, members of those churches with whom we are not yet fully united are ordinarily not admitted to Holy Communion. Eucharistic sharing in exceptional circumstances by other Christians requires permission according to the directives of the diocesan bishop and the provisions of canon law (canon 844 § 4). Members of the Orthodox Churches, the Assyrian Church of the East, and the Polish National Catholic Church are urged to respect the discipline of their own Churches. According to Roman Catholic discipline, the Code of Canon Law does not object to the reception of communion by Christians of these Churches (canon 844 § 3).

For those not receiving Holy Communion

All who are not receiving Holy Communion are encouraged to express in their hearts a prayerful desire for unity with the Lord Jesus and with one another.

For non-Christians

We also welcome to this celebration those who do not share our faith in Jesus Christ. While we cannot admit them to Holy Communion, we ask them to offer their prayers for the peace and the unity of the human family.

Committee on the Liturgy, United States Conference of Catholic Bishops, 211 4th Street, N.E., Washington, D.C. 20017-1194. (202) 541-3060.

Selected Links to Internet-Based Resources*

Conciliar Documents

Vatican II, Dogmatic Constitution on the Church, *Lumen gentium* (1964)

http://www.vatican.va/archive/hist_councils/ii_vatican_council/documents/vat-ii_const_19641121_lumen-gentium_en.html

Vatican II, Declaration on Ecumenism, *Unitatis redintegratio* (1964)

http://www.vatican.va/archive/hist_councils/ii_vatican_council/documents/vat-ii_decree_19641121_unitatis-redintegratio_en.html

Canon Law, Catechism of the Catholic Church

Code of Canon Law (1983)

http://www.intratext.com/X/ENG0017.htm

Catechism of the Catholic Church, Part Two: The Celebration of the Christian Mystery, Section 2: The Seven Sacraments of the Church, Chapter 1: The Sacraments of Christian Initiation, Article 3: The Sacrament of the Eucharist

http://www.vatican.va/archive/catechism/p2s2c1a3.htm

Papal Documents

John Paul II, Encyclical on Christian Ecumenism, *Ut unum sint* (1995)

http://www.vatican.va/holy_father/john_paul_ii/encyclicals/documents/hf_jp-ii_enc_25051995_ut-unum-sint_en.html

---

*This list of Internet-based resources was compiled on June 10, 2002. It does not claim to be exhaustive. Internet addresses change frequently. Please consult your preferred Internet search site for updated file locations.

John Paul II, Letter to the Bishops of the Church on the Mystery and Worship of the Eucharist, *Dominicae cenae* (1980)

http://www.vatican.va/holy_father/john_paul_ii/letters/documents/hf_jp-ii_let_24021980_dominicae-cenae_en.html

Vatican Congregations and Councils

Congregation for the Clergy, Letter on First Penance and First Communion (1977)

http://www.vatican.va/roman_curia/congregations/cclergy/documents/rc_con_cclergy_doc_19770331_penance-communion_en.html

Congregation for the Doctrine of the Faith, Letter to the Bishops of the Catholic Church on some aspects of the Church understood as Communion, *Communionis notio* (1992)

http://www.vatican.va/roman_curia/congregations/cfaith/documents/rc_con_cfaith_doc_28051992_communionis-notio_en.html

Congregation for the Doctrine of the Faith, Note on the Expression «Sister Churches», (2000)

http://www.vatican.va/roman_curia/congregations/cfaith/documents/rc_con_cfaith_doc_20000630_chiese-sorelle_en.html

Congregation for the Doctrine of the Faith, Declaration on the Unicity and Salvific Universality of Jesus Christ and the Church, *Dominus Iesus* (2000)

http://www.vatican.va/roman_curia/congregations/cfaith/documents/rc_con_cfaith_doc_20000806_dominus-iesus_en.html

Pontifical Council for Promoting Christian Unity, Directory for the Application of Principles and Norms on Ecumenism (1993)

http://www.vatican.va/roman_curia/pontifical_councils/chrstuni/documents/rc_pc_chrstuni_doc_25031993_principles-and-norms-on-ecumenism_en.html

Pontifical Council for Promoting Christian Unity, Guidelines for Admission to the Eucharist Between the Chaldean Church and the Assyrian Church of the East (2001)

http://www.vatican.va/roman_curia/pontifical_councils/chrstuni/documents/rc_pc_chrstuni_doc_20011025_chiesa-caldea-assira_en.html

Conferences of Catholic Bishops

Catholic Bishops' Conference of England and Wales, Ireland, and Scotland, *One Bread One Body: A teaching document on the Eucharist in the life of the Church, and the establishment of general norms on sacramental sharing* (1998)

http://217.19.224.165/resource/obob/obob03.htm

South African Conference of Catholic Bishops, Directory on Ecumenism for South Africa (no date provided)

http://www.sacbc.org.za/dir.html

U.S. Conference of Catholic Bishops, Guidelines for Reception of Communion (1996)

http://www.nccbuscc.org/liturgy/current/intercom.htm

World Council of Churches, Faith and Order Commission

Faith and Order Commission, World Council of Churches, *Baptism Eucharist and Ministry (BEM)* (1982)

http://www.wcc-coe.org/wcc/what/faith/bem1.html

Faith and Order Commission, World Council of Churches, "Towards Koinonia in Worship: Ditchingham Letter and Report" (1982)

http://www.wcc-coe.org/wcc/what/faith/ditch.html

Faith and Order Commission, World Council of Churches, "Becoming a Christian: The Ecumenical Implications of Our Common Baptism" (1982)

http://www.wcc-coe.org/wcc/what/faith/faverg.html

International Ecumenical Dialogues with the Roman Catholic Church

Anglican-Roman Catholic International Commission, Agreed Statement on Eucharistic Doctrine (1972)

http://www.pro.urbe.it/dia-int/arcic/doc/i_arcic_eucharist.html

Anglican Roman Catholic International Commission, Elucidation (1979)

http://www.pro.urbe.it/dia-int/arcic/doc/i_arcic_elucid_euch.html

International Reformed Catholic Dialogue, The Presence of Christ in the Church and the World: The Eucharist (1977)

http://www.pro.urbe.it/dia-int/r-rc/doc/i_r-rc_1-5.html

Joint Commission between the Roman Catholic Church and the World Methodist Council, "Common witness and salvation: Eucharist, ministry and spirituality": 6. The Eucharist (Dublin Report–1976: "Growth In Understanding") (1975)

http://www.pro.urbe.it/dia-int/m-rc/doc/i_m-rc_dublin6.html

Joint Commission between the Catholic Church and the Malankara Orthodox Syrian Church of India, Interim Report On Ecclesial Eucharistic Communion, (1990)

http://www.pro.urbe.it/dia-int/oo-rc_india/doc/i_oo-rc_india_1990 eec.html

Statements on Eucharistic Sharing by Individuals and Non-Catholic Churches

Owen Hardwicke, "One Bread, One Body"—A Response (1998)

http://www.bfpubs.demon.co.uk/hardwick.htm

House of Bishops (Church of England), *The Eucharist: Sacrament of Unity* (2001) (Adobe® Acrobat® required)

http://www.cofe.anglican.org/ccu/england/eucharist.pdf

Arthur Magida, Intercommunion Etiquette (2000)

http://www.beliefnet.com/features/intercommunion/index.html

Richard P. McBrien, The Eucharist As an Ecumenical Problem (2001)

http://www.the-tidings.com/2001/0511/essays.htm

Thomas Richstatter, Eucharist: Sign and Source of Christian Unity (2000)

http://www.americancatholic.org/Newsletters/CU/ac0500.asp

Robert A. Rimbo, "Eucharist Without Walls," speech, Notre Dame Pastoral Liturgy Conference (2000)

http://www.nd.edu/~ndcpl/education/rimbo.htm

Thomas J. Tobin, "Receiving Holy Communion" (1998)

http://www.petersnet.net/research/retrieve_full.cfm?RecNum=406

Index of References to Scripture

Index of References to Persons

Index of Subjects

abandonment, 202
absence, 64
abundance, 73, 182
acatholicae, 38
acceptance, 205
accountability, 96
adiaphora, 86
admirabile commercium, 138, 182
admission to Communion, 189, 199
adultery, 144
agreed statements, 17
anamnesis, 190
anointing, sacrament of, 214
antitheses, 87
apartheid, 106
apophatic ecclesiology, 67
apophaticism, 63
apostate, 15
apostolic letters, 27
apostolic succession, 7, 29, 41, 54, 70,
   81f., 90f., 93, 120f.
   continuity in, 94
   qualitative elements, 94
Apostolicae curae, 92f.
apostolicity, 95, 174
   transmission of, 95f.
Arians, 97f.
assent, 147f.
authoritarianism, 80, 97
authority, 97

Babel, 107
bans, 176

baptism, sacrament of, 12, 126, 130, 182
   shared, 191
   validity of, 130
berakah, 165 n. 135
Berlin Wall, 197
blessing catechumens, 193
blessing noncommunicants, 191–95,
   213
blessing penitents, 193
blessings, 140
blowback, 176
bodiliness, 152
Body of Christ, 126, 147, 149f., 183,
   190, 203, 212
burdens, 48, 174

Canon 844, 40f.
canon law, in general, 36
   purpose for, 37
catabatic, 63
catechumen, 129
catechumenate, 207
Catholic, 13
Catholic Church, 77
catholicity, 13, 76
challenges, 184
charism, 205f.
Chicago-Lambeth Quadrilateral, 93
Church, invisible, 120
Church, visible, 120
civil disobedience, 52
Code of Canon Law (1917), 38, 69, 159
Code of Canon Law (1983), 37, 40, 46
college of bishops, 96

paschal sacrifice, 62
Passover, 165 n. 135
Passover meal, 61
pastoral need, 7, 38, 40, 126, 136f., 141,
  183
peace, 211
Pelagianism, 17 n. 29, 101
penance, 214f.
penitence, 116
Pentecost, 80
philanthropy, 138
pilgrim Church, 79
placebo, 179
planned obsolescence, 69
pledge, 206
pluralism, 200
pneuma, 152
pneumatology, in ecclesiology, 84
polemical edge, 56, 59
polemicism, 22
Polish National Catholic Church, 43
Porvoo Statement, 86
positive theology, 63
presence, 65, 147
  enduring, 61
  total, 109
priestly power, 83
primacy, 88
primacy of the whole, 89
primus inter pares, 89
Prodigal Son, 178
profession of faith, 131f.
prohibitions, 142, 176f., 183, 188
properly disposed, 214f.
prophecy, 80
Protestantism, 34
provisionality, 69
purity, 202

Quam singulari, 133

Real Presence, 46, 55–57, 59–61, 153
  purpose for, 60
reconciliation, sacrament of, 15, 113f.,
  181, 194, 211
  first reception of, 135

reformation, 210
refusal, 140
relationship, 103
relativism, 105, 125
res sacramenti, 83
retrojection, 168
rights, 211
risks, 53f., 121
Rite of Christian Initiation of Adults,
  193f.
Roman Curia, 75
Romanization, 68

sacramentality, of the Church, 65, 74
sacraments, among Protestants, 91
sacrifice, 55f., 62, 65
Sacrosanctum concilium, 100
sacrum convivium, 182
salvation, 213
sarx, 152
saving effect, 78
scandal, 118, 171
scarcity, 200
schism, 210
schismatics, 13, 33, 38, 85, 97
sectarianism, 119
sects, 38
self-examination, 154
self-giving, 65, 155
self-offering, 62
self-righteousness, 118
separated brethren, 13
service, 83
sham, 51f.
shared experience, 210
sign of peace, 114
Sister Churches, 92
Smyrnaeans, Letters to the, 85
solidarity, 168
solummodo, 72, 74
soma, 150
source, 100
Spirit, 152
status reversal, 150
subject, 14, 30
subsistence, 71, 73f.
subsists in, 71f.